Environment, Media and Communcation

Anders Hansen

Routledge
Taylor & Francis Group

LONDON AND NEW YORK

First published 2010
by Routledge
2 Park Square, Milton Park, Abingdon, Oxon, OX14 4RN

Simultaneously published in the USA and Canada
by Routledge
270 Madison Avenue, New York, NY 10016

Routledge is an imprint of the Taylor & Francis Group, an informa business

© 2010 Anders Hansen

Typeset in Times New Roman by
Keystroke, Tettenhall, Wolverhampton
Printed and bound in Great Britain by
TJ International, Padstow, Cornwall

British Library Cataloguing in Publication Data
A catalogue record for this book is available from the British Library

Library of Congress Cataloguing in Publication Data
Hansen, Anders, 1957–
    Environment, media and communication / Anders Hansen.
        p. cm. — (Routledge introductions to environment series)
    Includes bibliographical references and index.
    1. Mass media and the environment. I. Title.
P96.E57H36 2009
070.4′493337—dc22   2009030556

ISBN10: 0–415–42575–1 (hbk)
ISBN10: 0–415–42576–X (pbk)
ISBN10: 0–203–86001–2 (ebk)

ISBN13: 978–0–415–42575–9 (hbk)
ISBN13: 978–0–415–42576–6 (pbk)
ISBN13: 978–0–203–86001–4 (ebk)

Environment, Media and Communication

'This book is a valuable contribution to the study of environmental communication because the author has conducted extensive research to inform readers about the construction of environmental messages in various communication channels including news, advertising, and cultural formats. An in-depth discussion of environmental campaigns makes this a practical guide for working professionals as well as an educational book for college students.'

Lea Jane Parker *Northern Arizona University, USA*

'Hansen has been following the environment-media-communication story with a sharp eye for nearly two decades. He gathers all that experience into this comprehensive but readable volume that is a great starting point for environment students wanting to get their heads around media and vice versa.'

Joe Smith *Open University, UK*

Media and communication processes are central to how we come to know and understand the environment as well as how environmental problems are defined, contested, addressed and responded to. *Environment, Media and Communication* examines the central role played by media and communication processes in shaping public debate and understanding concerning the environment.

The first part of the book introduces a general framework for studying and understanding the role of media and communication in relation to environmental issues. It proceeds with an examination of the main players and forums in public communication about the environment. First, this focuses on the strategies and influence of key stakeholders in environmental debate and controversy. Second, it examines how news values, organisational arrangements and objectives of the media, and the practices of journalists and other media professionals impinge on the framing and communication of environmental issues. The next section introduces research on popular culture images of science, nature and the environment and their history and inflection across a range of media forms, including those of film and advertising. This section discusses how deep-seated cultural narratives have reflected, and in turn shaped, particular ideological interpretations of nature and the environment. The final part of the book discusses the major frameworks which have been used for examining media influence on public understanding, public opinion and political decision-making, and it concludes by pointing to the communication models which have most to offer in terms of explaining media and communication roles in relation to the environment.

This book offers a comprehensive introduction to theoretical approaches and models for the study of media and communication roles regarding the environment, drawing on empirical research evidence and examples from Europe, America, Australia and Asia. The book will be of interest to students in media/communication studies, geography, environmental studies, political science and sociology as well as to environmental professionals and activists.

Anders Hansen is Senior Lecturer in the Department of Media and Communication, University of Leicester, UK. He is Chair of the IAMCR Working Group on Environment, Science and Risk Communication. His books include *Mass Communication Research Methods* (edited four-volume set, Sage, 2009), *Media and Communication Research* (with D. Machin, Palgrave/Macmillan, 2010), and *The Mass Media and Environmental Issue*s (Leicester University Press, 1993).

Routledge Introductions to Environment Series
Published and Forthcoming Titles

Environmental Science texts

Atmospheric Processes and Systems
Natural Environmental Change
Environmental Biology
Using Statistics to Understand
  the Environment
Environmental Physics
Environmental Chemistry
Biodiversity and Conservation,
  2nd Edition
Ecosystems, 2nd Edition
Coastal Systems, 2nd Edition

Titles under Series Editor:
David Pepper

Environment and Society texts

Environment and Philosophy
Energy, Society and Environment,
  2nd edition
Gender and Environment
Environment and Business
Environment and Law
Environment and Society
Environmental Policy
Representing the Environment
Sustainable Development
Environment and Social Theory,
  2nd edition
Environmental Values
Environment and Politics, 3rd Edition
Environment and Tourism, 2nd Edition
Environment and the City
Environment, Media and
Communication

Forthcoming

Environment and Food
Environment and Economy
Environmental Policy, 2nd Edition
Environmental Governance

Contents

Figures

Tables

Exercises

Boxes

Series editor's preface

The modern environmentalist movement grew hugely in the last third of the twentieth century. It reflected popular and academic concerns about the local and global degradation of the physical environment which was increasingly being documented by scientists (and which is the subject of the companion series to this, Environmental Science). However it soon became clear that reversing such degradation was not merely a technical and managerial matter: merely knowing about environmental problems did not of itself guarantee that governments, businesses or individuals would do anything about them. It is now acknowledged that a critical understanding of socio-economic, political and cultural processes and structures is central in understanding environmental problems and establishing environmentally sustainable development. Hence the maturing of environmentalism has been marked by prolific scholarship in the social sciences and humanities, exploring the complexity of society–environment relationships.

Such scholarship has been reflected in a proliferation of associated courses at undergraduate level. Many are taught within the 'modular' or equivalent organisational frameworks which have been widely adopted in higher education. These frameworks offer the advantages of flexible undergraduate programmes, but they also mean that knowledge may become segmented, and student learning pathways may arrange knowledge segments in a variety of sequences – often reflecting the individual requirements and backgrounds of each student rather than more traditional discipline-bound ways of arranging learning. The volumes in this Environment and Society series of textbooks mirror this higher educational context, increasingly encountered in the early twenty-first century. They provide short, topic-centred texts on social science and humanities subjects relevant to contemporary society–environment relations. Their content and approach reflect the fact that each will be read by students from various disciplinary backgrounds, taking in not only social sciences and humanities but others such as physical and natural sciences. Such a readership is not always familiar with the disciplinary background to a topic, neither are readers necessarily going on to further develop their interest in the topic. Additionally, they cannot all automatically be thought of as having reached a similar stage in their studies – they may be first- , second- or third-year students.

The authors and editors of this series are mainly established teachers in higher education. Finding that more traditional integrated environmental studies and specialised texts do not always meet their own students' requirements, they have often had to write course materials more appropriate to the needs of the flexible undergraduate programme. Many of the volumes in this series represent in modified form the fruits of such labours, which all students can now share.

Much of the integrity and distinctiveness of the Environment and Society titles derives from their characteristic approach. To achieve the right mix of flexibility, breadth and depth, each volume is designed to create maximum accessibility to readers from a variety of backgrounds and attainment. Each leads into its topic by giving some necessary basic grounding, and leaves it usually by pointing towards areas for further potential development and study. There is introduction to the real-world context of the text's main topic, and to the basic concepts and questions in social sciences/humanities which are most relevant. At the core of the text is some exploration of the main issues. Although limitations are imposed here by the need to retain a book length and format affordable to students, some care is taken to indicate how the themes and issues presented may become more complicated, and to refer to the cognate issues and concepts that would need to be explored to gain deeper understanding. Annotated reading lists, case studies, overview diagrams, summary charts and self-check questions and exercises are among the pedagogic devices which we try to encourage our authors to use, to maximise the 'student friendliness' of these books.

Hence we hope that these concise volumes provide sufficient depth to maintain the interest of students with relevant backgrounds. At the same time, we try to ensure that they sketch out basic concepts and map their territory in a stimulating and approachable way for students to whom the whole area is new. Hopefully, the list of Environment and Society titles will provide modular and other students with an unparalleled range of perspectives on society-environment problems: one which should also be useful to students at both postgraduate and pre-higher education levels.

David Pepper
May 2000

Series International Advisory Board

Australasia: Dr P. Curson and Dr P. Mitchell, Macquarie University

North America: Professor L. Lewis, Clark University; Professor L. Rubinoff, Trent University

Europe: Professor P. Glasbergen, University of Utrecht; Professor van Dam-Mieras, Open University, The Netherlands

Acknowledgements

The author and publishers would like to thank the following for granting permission to reproduce material in this work:

Figure 1.1, www.BigStockPhoto.com; Figures 2.1 and 3.1, Sage Publications Ltd; Figure 6.1, PZ Cussons (UK) Ltd; Figure 6.2, The Jordans & Ryvita Company Ltd; Figure 6.3, Jack Daniel's Properties, Inc.: The trademark Jack Daniel's appears courtesy of Jack Daniel's Properties, Inc. Jack Daniel's & the Old No. 7 Logo are registered trademarks of Jack Daniel's Properties, Inc.

I am very grateful to David Pepper for inviting me to contribute to this series, and for his encouragement and support throughout. To Andrew Mould and his colleagues at Routledge for their help and patience. To anonymous reviewers for their helpful comments, and to Joe Smith for his insightful and constructive feedback on an earlier draft.

Many more people than can be listed here have provided important inspiration, ideas, feedback, support and/or friendship during my 'journey' with the subject of media and the environment in the last couple of decades, including, in the case of some, as contributors to the IAMCR Working Group on Environmental Issues, Science and Risk Communication or as fellow participants in the PCST network. Allow me to mention just a few, some of whom are recent fellow travellers, others whose journeys started before mine: Stuart Allan, Alison Anderson, Paul Brown (former *Guardian* environment correspondent), Jacquie Burgess, Anabela Carvalho, John Corner, Simon Cottle, Suzanne de Cheveigné, Vladimir de Semir, John Durant, Julie Doyle, Barrie Gunter, Cees Hamelink, Miki Kawabata, Alex Kirby (former BBC environment correspondent), Olga Linné, David Machin, Shunji Mikami, David Morrison, the late Roger Silverstone, Annika Egan Sjölander, Brian Trench and Esa Väliverronen.

Thanks are also due to Andrew Dunn, Media and Communications subject librarian at the University of Leicester, for always being instantly available with helpful advice and guidance on tracking down relevant information.

For responding enthusiastically and critically to the research, arguments and theories put before them, and for contributing to a sharpened sense of media and communication roles, I thank my national and international students on the *Science, Environment and Risk Communication* module and the *News Management, Communication and Social Problems* module in the Department of Media and Communication at the University of Leicester.

At home, thank you as always to Debbie, Thomas and Charlotte for being the outstanding and wonderful people that you are and for – 'like' – everything.

1 Introduction

The environment, environmental, climate change, global warming, greenhouse effect, acid rain, ozone depletion, species extinction, carbon footprint, carbon offsetting, Greenpeace, deforestation, soil erosion, flooding, desertification, pollution, ecology, organic foods, GM crops, GMOs, nuclear winter, pesticides, toxic waste, landfill, deep storage, sustainable development, sustainability, eco-[anything] and green-[anything]. . .these are terms, which are – or have become – familiar parts of the vocabulary of public life.[1] And like the term 'the environment' itself, they have come to be associated with a particular public 'conversation' about 'problems' to do with our relationship with our natural environment. They have come to be associated with what we might call an environmental discourse, which, in its particular form and with its particular view of the world, is itself of relatively recent origin, dating back only some fifty years to the early 1960s. Indeed, many see as an important symbolic starting point of a new environmental perspective – distinct from, for example, earlier conservation perspectives – the publication in 1962 of American biologist Rachel Carson's evocatively titled book *Silent Spring*.

There are a couple of significant things to note about the public vocabulary on the environment and environmental change: first, it is a vocabulary which is strangely familiar and recognisable, but probably, for most, only in a superficial kind of way; that is, behind most of these terms lurk some immensely complex issues that require a great deal of scientific, philosophical, ethical, moral, economic, etc., engagement well beyond what most of us have the time, or perhaps inclination, to delve into. Second, it is very much a time-/history-bound vocabulary in the sense that it fades in and out of public focus *and* in the sense that parts of it, including the meanings and connotations associated with particular terms, change and evolve over time.

Furthermore, it is of course not merely – or even perhaps predominantly – a linguistic or word-based vocabulary, but very much a *visual* vocabulary.[2]

Exercise 1.1

Visualising the environment

What visual images spring to mind when you see or hear the term 'the environment'? Make a little descriptive list of the images that first come to mind, or better still, do a rough sketch of one or two images.

Now ask a few friends, classmates, family members or others who might be amenable to do the same little exercise.

Compare your lists/images. Explore the similarities and differences, and discuss why, in your view, these images were the ones that most instantly came to mind.

Comment: when I have done this exercise with my students, we have often found considerable similarities that seem to transcend any diversity of geographical origin or cultural background. To be sure, some images will have a 'personal experience' dimension to them – for example, a treasured geographical location – but most images tend to be 'stock' images from a wider public vocabulary, and in many cases the principal manifestation and source of such stock images would appear to be 'the media'. Of course, tracing the images in our heads back to a particular source is well nigh impossible, as there are often multiple sources and as images in our heads are possibly generally composites, built up over extended periods of time. One aim of this exercise then is to start thinking about where our understandings of what 'the environment' is or what it looks like come from, and about how they are constructed through public communication and through the media.

Thus, as with the words/terms listed above at the start, the following images would be familiar to most and would probably in most cases be instantly recognisable as 'belonging' to the (present) visual vocabulary of the environmental discourse, rather than, for example, to the discourses of travel brochures, history textbooks, geography or other science textbooks, etc.

But images such as these do not acquire their 'meaning' by themselves, nor indeed – despite their seeming photographic 'window-on-reality' quality – do they inherently or intrinsically carry a particular meaning or merely 'represent' what they ostensibly show. The elevation to iconic or representative status, and the public identification of these images as belonging to a particular discourse, requires visual signification 'work' in much the same way as terms such as 'climate change' and 'carbon footprint' only become meaningful to us through repeated explanation and association.

Like word-meaning, the meaning of pictures or images is anything but static; the elevation of particular images to 'iconic' – in the sense of 'representative' – status as images *representing* a particular meaning, such as 'climate change' or 'environmental devastation' or, perhaps more obliquely, 'threatened environments' is an ongoing process drawing on, what Linder (2006: 129–30) aptly refers to as 'an extensive collection of semiotic resources' and involving 'a substantial amount of appropriation and pastiche between them, as they exploit newly established signs in novel variations'.

A key characteristic of the building of a public (visual) vocabulary of the environment and environmental issues is the *abstraction* or *de-contextualisation* of images *from* specific identifiable geographic or cultural environments *to* generic, iconic or 'representative' global environments (Hansen and Machin, 2008). The main point of relevance to the discussions in this book is the point that the meanings and significance which we come to associate with the key terms of the public word and image vocabularies on the environment are the result of a great deal of active – and in many cases highly deliberate – signification and communicative 'work'. Images of melting ice, ice-floes, Arctic/Antarctic landscapes, glaciers, etc. become synonymous with – come to mean or signify – 'threatened environments' and ultimately 'global warming' or 'climate change', where in the past they would have signified something quite different such as 'challenge' or a test of human endeavour and perseverance or indeed simply 'pristine' and aesthetically pleasing environments, as yet untouched and unspoilt by man.

While the roles of formal education in acquainting us with the public word and image vocabulary of the environment should not be overlooked, much, maybe most, of what we learn and know about 'the environment', we know from the media, broadly defined. Indeed, this applies not only to our beliefs and knowledge about those aspects of the environment, which are regarded as problems or issues for public and political concern, but extends much deeper to the ways in which we, as individuals, citizens, cultures and societies view, perceive and value nature and the natural environment.

Figure 1.1 *Images of
. . . ? – Visual
vocabularies of the
environment.*
*(a) The last polar bear.
Available from:
www.bigstockphoto.com
[bigstockphoto_The_Last
_Polar_Bear_2136446;
accessed 2 July 2009].*

*(b) Melting glacier.
Available from:
www.bigstockphoto.com
[bigstockphoto_Melting_Glacier_
3495643; accessed 2 July 2009].*

(c) Melting glacier. Available from: www.bigstockphoto.com [bigstockphoto_Melting_ Glacier_3852141; accessed 2 July 2009].

(d) Coal-burning power plant. Available from: www.bigstockphoto.com [bigstockphoto_Coal_Burning_Power_Plant_1366970; accessed 2 July 2009].

Historically, such views have oscillated between the two extremes of, on the one hand, a utilitarian perspective which sees the natural environment as a hostile domain to be controlled and exploited in the name of progress, and, on the other hand, a more romantic view of the natural environment as fragile, pure, pristine beauty in need of protection. Our views of the environment have been, and are being, articulated and shaped through multiple media and forms of communication: paintings, architecture, poetry, literature, film, music, posters, the press, broadcast and other electronic media, including, of course, most recently the internet.

What particularly distinguishes the history of the recent half-century or so is the crucial role played by the mass media and communication in not only helping to define 'the environment' as a concept and domain, but more particularly in bringing environmental issues and problems to public and political attention. Thus, since the emergence and rise of the modern environmental movement in the 1960s, the mass media have been a central public arena for publicising environmental issues and for contesting claims, arguments and opinions about our use and/or protection of the environment. Indeed, a defining feature of many of the most well-known and most politically effective environmental pressure groups has been and continues to be their view of the mass media as an integral and essential part of their campaigning strategy.

Where in earlier eras much political decision-making with regard to the environment may have been based largely on expert and scientific evidence/testimony, with a keen eye on economic development and 'progress', such decision-making has increasingly been influenced and governed by how environmental and related issues are presented to and perceived by the public. Communicating about the environment may have been seen in the not-so-distant past as mainly a matter of making the public understand the science and scientific evidence behind controversial environmental issues. Some of the most controversial environmental issues and debates of the recent period show a very different picture. Whether looking at the ozone layer, climate change, whaling, hunting, animal experimentation or the multiple issues relating to rapid advances in genetic modification and the bio-genetic sciences, it is clear that the battles over these issues are now much more to do with persuasive communication, with 'winning hearts and minds' than they are to do with understanding the 'science' behind these issues.

Communication then is a central aspect of how we come to know, and to know about, the environment and environmental issues, and the major media are a central public arena through which we become aware of environmental issues and the way in which they are addressed, contested and, perhaps, resolved.

This book is about how we study and understand the role of communication and media in relation to the environment and environmental issues. It examines the ways in which communication research has contributed, and can contribute, to our understanding of the role played by the mass media and associated communication processes in making the environment and environmental problems issues for public and political concern. A key objective of the book is to draw attention to the highly 'constructed' nature of public communication, conversation and debate about the environment and nature, to show that there is little or nothing that is 'natural' or accidental about the processes by which we as publics come to learn about and understand environmental issues or problems – indeed, that the mere notion that the environment is an 'issue' or a 'problem' is itself the product of active rhetorical 'work' and construction in the public sphere.

The chapters which follow thus aim to show some of the complexity of the processes of communicating the environment, to draw attention to the central significance of language/discourse, imagery and cultural values in these processes, and to indicate that communicating about the environment and environmental issues is about a great deal more than just imparting information: it is crucially about power in society, the power to define our relationship with nature and the environment and the power to define (to paraphrase Ryan, 1991) what the 'problem' with the environment is, who is responsible and what course of action needs to be taken.

The book thus addresses questions such as: how far has the rise of the environment on the political agenda been brought about by the mass media? How is the political process influenced by media coverage of environmental issues? To what extent is media coverage itself influenced or structured by economic pressures, by the professional norms and practices of journalists, by news values and/or by the publicity and news management practices of the major stakeholders in environmental debate (including business, industry, government, environmental pressure groups, scientists, etc.)? Who gets to define what environmental issues are about or how they should be addressed and resolved? How do the mass media contribute to policing the boundaries of 'acceptable' public debate about the environment? How do mediated images contribute to the formation of public opinion? In what ways do different publics draw on media representations for making sense of environmental issues? How are nature and references to what is regarded as 'natural' used in media and public debate about controversial issues? How are nature and the natural used in advertising to sell everything from cosmetics and cars to corporate identity?

The book's discussion of these and associated key questions is used to demonstrate the centrality of media and communication in environmental debate. This is illustrated with examples from the growing body of research on media and environmental issues, science and risk communication, drawing on work encompassing not just the conventional focus on news reporting, but a wider range of media and media genres.

The book is thus organised as follows: **Chapter 2**, *Communication and the construction of environmental issues*, outlines and discusses a general theoretical framework for understanding and analysing the role of media and communication in relation to environmental issues. It introduces the notion that the environment generally does not 'speak for itself' but that environmental problems only become problems or issues for public concern and political decision-making through claims-making and communication. The chapter introduces and discusses the application of a constructionist perspective to environmental issues as well as to the sociology of news and other media. It demonstrates how the constructionist focus on competing definitions offers an analytically more productive approach to understanding media roles than more traditional concerns about bias and objectivity in media reporting, and it points to some of the key analytical tools and foci furnished by this approach, including its focus on claims-makers and claims-making, on discourse, on issue careers, on issue resonance, on issue ownership and competition, etc. The construction of the environment as a social problem is seen as essentially a rhetorical achievement, and the chapter thus points to the centrality in communication analysis of studying the rhetorical idioms, motifs, claims-making styles, frames, settings or public arenas deployed in public discourse about the environment.

Chapter 3, *Making claims and managing news about the environment*, applies the previous chapter's introduction to the constructionist perspective to news and shows that there is little that is 'natural' about environmental news; even 'natural disaster news' can best be understood in terms of something which has to be actively constructed. The chapter focuses on the communication strategies and influence of key stakeholders or interested parties in environmental debate and controversy. How do environmental pressure groups, government departments, scientific establishments, individual scientists/experts, business and industry seek to use, manage or influence the communication about controversial environmental issues through the mass media? How dependent are they on media coverage, and how successful are they, or have they been, in 'spinning' environmental stories to their advantage? How successful have they been in influencing public opinion and political decision-making through carefully planned communication and publicity practices? What are the key ingredients of successful claims-making about environmental issues?

Relevant criteria of success are discussed, and comparisons/examples of both successful and unsuccessful communication strategies and media campaigns are given. A particular focus in this chapter is on the emerging research evidence on how key claims-makers (including corporate business as well as environmental pressure groups) seek to exploit the internet and other newer forms of communication for information and campaigning purposes. While much attention in the communications literature has been on the communication and campaigning strategies of environmental pressure groups, the chapter concludes with a focus on the increasingly powerful influence and role of corporate communication and image-management strategies in the public sphere.

Chapter 4, *The environment as news: news values, news media and journalistic practices*, turns from the previous chapter's emphasis on media-external *sources* and *claims-makers* to the main mass media themselves. It focuses on the roles, organisational arrangements, practices and 'communicative work' of the media and media professionals. The chapter discusses how research on news values, on organisational structures and arrangements in media organisations, on the professional values and working practices of journalists and other media professionals can help explain why some environmental issues become news, while others do not; why some environmental issues become issues for media and public/political concern, while others fall by the wayside.

The development of an 'environment beat' and of specialist environmental correspondents is examined, and the chapter discusses whether environmental correspondents are fundamentally different from other types of reporters or take a different approach to their subject and to their sources than general reporters. How do journalists reporting on the environment and environmental controversy deal with the scientific uncertainty which characterises much of environmental debate, how do they secure credibility in their reporting, and how do they deploy traditional journalistic criteria such as objectivity and balance? The impact of new information and communication technologies on journalistic practices is discussed: do new technologies and economic pressures on news organisations combine to shift the balance of power between journalists and their sources in the direction of the sources? The chapter ends with a discussion of the limitations of the sociology-of-news framework, and the ways in which some of these limitations have been addressed through perspectives focusing on cultural resonances in the discursive construction of environmental issues.

Chapter 5, *Popular culture, nature and environmental issues,* picks up the suggestion at the end of the previous chapter, that in addition to the traditional sociology-of-news emphasis on economic pressures, organisational arrangements and professional values/practices, it is necessary – if we wish to understand media coverage of the environment – to take wider cultural resonances and narratives into consideration as well. Chapter 5 thus starts with a focus on the notions of scripts, cultural packages, interpretive packages and cultural resonance, and considers their significance for understanding the nature and potential 'power' of popular media representations of nature and the environment.

The chapter surveys research on the kind and origins of images – particularly of science and nature – which have been influential in media and popular constructions of nature and the environment generally and in media and popular culture constructions of nuclear power, the new genetics and biotechnology particularly. The discussion in this chapter moves beyond the focus on news coverage of the environment, and considers how nature and the environment are constructed ideologically in other media genres, including television entertainment programming and more particularly in wildlife film and television nature programmes. The persistence of key cultural narratives and stories – for example, the Frankenstein story – and the ideological clusters, packages or scripts which are evoked by – often single – trigger-words are explored.

The chapter explores the significance of lexis or word choice in media constructions of environmental issues, and the similarly significant contribution of narrative analysis to uncovering the deeper ideological values communicated through wildlife film and nature programming. Drawing on historical studies of selected film genres (e.g. 'science fiction' and 'wildlife/nature films') the chapter discusses how deep-seated cultural narratives have reflected, and in turn shaped, particular ideological interpretations of nature and the environment, including changing dominant interpretations of the environment as either an object of control and exploitation or as something to be protected.

Chapter 6, *Selling 'nature/the natural': Advertising, nature, national identity, nostalgia and the environmental image*, explores the promotional use of nature and the environment in advertising, and continues the previous chapter's examination of how constructions of nature and the environment change over time. It shows how advertising has been used for promoting environmental messages and awareness, for selling 'green' or 'environment-friendly' products and for improving or promoting the image of large corporations or industries. While explicit environmental appeals and green marketing come and go in advertising, nature imagery and appeals to the natural have been a prominent and relatively consistent feature of commercial advertising for a very long time. The chapter explores how nature/the natural and the environment are constructed and deployed for selling products, and it explores how the uses of nature contribute important boundaries and definitions of appropriate consumption and 'uses' of the natural environment. The uses of nature and environmental images in advertising are examined in relation to the concepts of nostalgia and national/cultural identity, and the chapter investigates variations in images across different cultures and the extent to which such images are either culturally specific or increasingly global/universal.

Chapter 7, *Media, publics, politics and environmental issues*, considers how communication researchers have tackled the perennial 'holy grail' question of how media representations and media coverage of the environment influence public and political perceptions and action. Ultimately, the assumption, whether explicit or implicit, behind most research into media representations of environmental issues is that these play a role in shaping and influencing public understanding/opinion and political decision-making in society. This chapter discusses some of the major frameworks and approaches – for example, agenda-setting research, public opinion research, framing analysis and cultivation analysis – which have been used for examining media influence on public understanding, public opinion and political decision-making. It explores the evidence, from these different research approaches and frameworks, for how media representations of environmental issues influence political processes or are interpreted and used by different publics. What evidence, for example, is there from communication research that the media form a significant part in shaping the agenda and nature of public opinion? Do the dynamics of public opinion and media representation in turn influence political decision-making?

We look at the referencing and use of 'media coverage' for rhetorical and political purposes in public environmental controversy, and I argue that this can be seen as an important type of 'effect' or influence, albeit one much less commonly thought of in general discourse on media influence.

I conclude, via a brief discussion of alternative approaches to studying media roles in relation to public understanding(s) of environmental issues, by emphasising the 'circulation of claims' perspective over a linear perspective on media roles and by emphasising the complex and multiple ways in which media coverage interacts with other 'forums of meaning-creation' (Gamson, 1988) in society.

2 **Communication and the construction of environmental issues**

This chapter:

- Introduces the constructionist perspective on social problems as a framework for analysing and understanding the role of media and communication in relation to environmental issues.
- Highlights the centrality of claims, claims-makers and the claims-making process in analysis of the emergence, elaboration and contestation of environmental issues.
- Discusses the construction of social problems as essentially a rhetorical achievement, and points to the analysis of rhetorical idioms, motifs, claims-making styles and settings or public arenas as core components.
- Examines how/whether the constructionist perspective extends to the analysis of natural disasters/accidents.
- Introduces the idea of issue careers and the notion that social problems move through a series of stages in an 'issue-attention' cycle.
- Introduces the concept of framing and discusses how it helps in analysing and understanding media roles in the construction of environmental issues.

Constructing social problems/constructing environmental issues

Why and how should we study media and communication in relation to environmental issues? Perhaps the answer to this emerges from the simple observation that not all environmental problems are publicly recognised as such – as problems requiring some kind of social/political/legislative attention and action – and from the equally puzzling observation that environmental issues or problems – over time – fade in and out of public focus in cycles that often seem to have little to do with whether they have been addressed, resolved, averted or ameliorated. Both observations suggest that communication – what is being said about environmental phenomena – is important, and they suggest that a public forum or arena, for example, the media, is necessary for environmental phenomena to be recognised as issues for public or political concern.

Environmental issues or problems do not simply emerge and announce themselves as issues requiring a social/political response in the form of legislation, research or a change in public practices and social arrangements. This is not something that is peculiar to environmental problems – similar points have frequently been made in relation to crime, delinquency, poverty, gender and social inequality, racial discrimination, etc. – although, as we shall see in subsequent chapters, there may be some unique aspects of environmental issues that have particular implications for the way in which they come to public attention and become problems for public and political concern.

A key breakthrough in sociology, and one which points directly to the centrality of 'media and communication', was the emergence in the late 1960s and early 1970s of what became known as the constructionist perspective on social problems. The fundamental argument of this perspective was that 'social problems' are not some objective condition in society that can be identified and studied independently of what is being 'said' about it. Problems and issues of various kinds only become recognised as such – as 'problems' or 'issues' – through talk, communication, discourse which defines or 'constructs' them as problems or issues for public and political concern.

One of the first to articulate this perspective was American sociologist Herbert Blumer, who took issue with the way that sociologists had traditionally identified social problems on the basis of public concern. Blumer argued that this was problematic, as many 'ostensibly harmful conditions are not recognised as such by the public, and thus are ignored by sociologists'. Instead, Blumer called for a definition of social problems which recognises these as 'products of a process of collective definition' rather than 'objective conditions and social arrangements' (1971: 298). The key task for research then, according to Blumer, is 'to study the process by which a society comes to recognize its social problems' (1971: 300).

The focus on process and communication evident in the early work of Blumer and fellow American sociologists Malcolm Spector and John Kitsuse received its full articulation in an early article by Spector and

Kitsuse (1973) and again in what can appropriately be regarded as the founding book of social constructionism, namely their 1977 book *Constructing Social Problems* (reprinted 1987 and 2000). In this, Spector and Kitsuse define social problems as:

> *the activities of individuals or groups making assertions of grievances and claims with respect to some putative conditions.* [. . .] *The central problem for a theory of social problems is to account for the emergence, nature, and maintenance of claims-making and responding activities.*

(2000: 75–76; emphasis in original)

This approach/framework then suggests (a) that problems/issues only become 'social problems/issues' when someone communicates, starts shouting about them, makes claims (in public) about them, and (b) that the important dimension to study and understand is the *process* through which claims emerge, are publicised, elaborated and contested.

Exercise 2.1

Are natural disasters socially constructed?

Using the online versions of a selection of newspapers, take a look at their coverage of the major earthquake in China's Sichuan province in May 2008. Look at a selection of coverage as the coverage developed in the two weeks immediately after the earthquake on 12 May 2008.

Try and identify some of the key components of the coverage: what does the news coverage focus on – initially, and after the first few days?

Where are the main sources of information about the earthquake? In other words, 'who' defines the nature of the event/disaster for us? Where do they get their information from? What is the balance of 'informed speculation' versus 'first-hand' accounts?

Note how the event/disaster – terrible, obtrusive and highly visual though it is – does not simply convey its own 'meaning'. Rather, the meaning of the earthquake is 'constructed' verbally through quotes from experts, victims, rescue-personnel, etc. and through commentary from the media themselves.

Now take a look at some of the explanations, questions raised and assessments presented in the coverage. At what point does the coverage move from reporting the extent of devastation, loss of life, suffering, rescue effort, etc. to raising questions about the extent of preparedness for this kind of disaster, including questions not just about emergency planning but also about investment in earthquake-resistant buildings, etc.?

Box 2.1

Are natural disasters socially constructed?

The key argument for the constructionist approach to social problems is the simple recognition that (most) problems do not simply exist by themselves in some objective universe, but that they only become 'social' problems when someone draws public attention to them, makes claims in public about them. While this may seem a straightforward explanation for most social issues or problems, the obvious counter-argument in relation to environmental issues is that there are clearly some environmental issues or problems that very much *do* announce themselves by way of their sheer magnitude, visibility and the destruction wrought by them. Thus, earthquakes, hurricanes, tsunamis, flooding, volcanic eruptions, etc. would all seem to be relatively unpredictable and unforeseeable 'acts of nature', beyond human control and hence beyond any kind of *construction*. Stallings (1990, 1995), Smith (1992, 1996) and others have, however, persuasively shown that even where we are dealing with major natural disasters, we need to call on the constructionist approach to understand the processes by which such disasters come to be defined socially.

Conspicuous, intrusive and devastating as they may be, natural disasters – or for that matter, major unexpected or unforeseen accidents related to man-made structures or processes – do not automatically 'mean' anything, that is, meaning has to be assigned to them or constructed around them. The 'meaning' of devastating floods may be 'divine intervention/retribution', 'nature's revenge' or 'the inevitable results of climate change', but the process of assigning meaning to an event essentially requires the discursive 'work' of claims-makers. Likewise, as Stallings (1995) demonstrates in his analysis of the construction of the 'earthquake threat', the promotion (the choice of word of course is telling) of a natural threat, which is beyond human control, to the status of *social problem* requires much claims-making work through multiple societal forums including: scientific (expert panels and committees), political (Congressional hearings), legal, and media (national news) forums.

While natural disasters per se are indeed for the most part relatively 'pure' acts of nature, they nevertheless then fit the constructionist mould in terms of – before the disaster strikes – society's policies and preparation for dealing with expected disasters, and – in the aftermath of disaster – the immediately ensuing public arguments about what could/should have been done in terms of social preparedness, how to be better prepared 'next time', how to ensure that new housing estates are not built on flood-plains, or how to ensure that buildings in an earthquake-prone area are built on appropriate foundations and designed to withstand earthquakes.

Objectivity/balance/bias

There is a highly significant and important further dimension to the social constructionist perspective, and one which has particular relevance to media and communications. If social problems are identified as such as a result of processes of claims-making rather than as objective conditions, then the key question for research is not to establish whether a claim is right or wrong, or a true or false representation of a social issue. Rather, the task for research is to establish why and by which means some claims gain prominence and acceptance, while others – which may be equally valid – do not.

> [. . .] we must be willing to refrain from tacitly privileging the status of, say, scientists' versions of the condition in question and instead treat those accounts, and the sensibility they express, as items in our explications of the social problems language game (cf. Aronson 1984). Similarly, instead of incorporating interest- and value-based 'explanations' in our theorizing, we should, after Mills (1940), recognize them as vernacular displays and thereby study them in their own right – for the ways in which the associations drawn by counterclaimants regarding claimants' motives can contribute to the shifting trajectories of social problems discourse.
>
> (Ibarra and Kitsuse, 1993: 29–30)

This is relevant to media and communication research because it directly counters problematic traditional realist notions of the news-media as a 'window on the world' or as a 'mirror-representation of reality', and it speaks directly to the classic concerns in news and journalism about accuracy, objectivity, bias/balance, and fairness in news reporting. The constructionist perspective enables news research to bypass the futile measurement of accuracy and objectivity in news, futile essentially because one person's accuracy is another person's bias. Accuracy/bias/ objectivity/balance, etc. are of course not some objective or measurable inherent characteristic of news reporting, but depend rather on the perspective/stance/norms/views which those 'consuming' the news bring to bear.

A key problem with the core journalistic value of objectivity, particularly where this is translated as being synonymous with giving equal prominence to opposing arguments in a public controversy, is that it may often in itself lead to a distortion or misrepresentation of the balance of opinion on a given subject. Prominent examples include media reporting in the 1980s on scientific opinion about the safety/risk of nuclear power

(Rothman and Lichter, 1987) and, more recently, analyses of media coverage of the climate-change debate (Boykoff and Boykoff, 2004; Boykoff, 2008) showing that the elite media's concern with providing 'balanced reporting' results in giving the impression that scientific opinion on the causes and consequences of climate change is split down the middle, when indications from, for example, reviews of scientific publications about climate change (Oreskes, 2004) indicate a near-total consensus among climate scientists (this is discussed in more detail in Chapter 7).

Constructionism and media/communication

If we accept the constructionist argument that environmental problems – and social problems generally – do not 'objectively' announce themselves, but only become recognised as such through the process of public claims-making, then it is also immediately clear that media, communication and discourse have a central role and should be a central focus for study. In light of this, it is perhaps surprising that the early formulations of the social constructionist perspective offered relatively little comment on media and communications. The development of a social constructionist perspective in mass media and communications research was left to sociologists with a particular interest in communications, notably such prominent American sociologists as Harvey Molotch, Herbert Gans and Gaye Tuchman.

The constructionist argument has implications for understanding media roles both in relation to how claims are promoted/produced through the public arena of the media and for understanding how the media are a central, possibly *the* central, forum through which we, as audiences and publics, make sense of our environment, society and politics. This boils down to the argument that most of what we as individuals know, we know, not from direct experience (experiential knowledge), but from the symbolic reality constructed for us through what we have been told (by friends, family, teachers and other 'officials' of a host of social institutions: schools, churches, government departments or agencies) or have read about or have heard/seen *re*-presented to us through media of various kinds (Adoni and Mane, 1984; Surette, 2007). The centrality of the media in this context is further emphasised by the fact that much of the symbolic construction of reality by a host of social institutions is now itself principally encountered through their representation in and through the media.

Public agendas and power

The social constructionist perspective's emphasis on 'claims-making' in public arenas as the constitutive component in the creation of 'social problems' usefully draws our attention to the importance and centrality of getting issues of concern onto the public, and more significantly, the political agenda.

In this respect it thus has interesting similarities to the traditions of research in political science and in communication research known as 'agenda-building' and 'agenda-setting', which in turn link with key traditions in the study of 'power' in society. An early and often-quoted formulation from political science which inspired the agenda-setting tradition in media and communication research was Bernard Cohen's statement that 'The press may not be successful much of the time in telling people what to think, but it is stunningly successful in telling its readers what to think *about*' (Cohen, 1963: 13). In other words, the 'power' of the media to influence public and political processes resides principally in signalling what society and the polity should be concerned about and in setting the framework for definition and discussion of such issues.

In their work on agenda-building, political scientists Roger Cobb and Charles Elder (1971) in their discussion of the political process likewise pointed to the centrality of *agendas* recognised by the polity and as forums for the public/political definition of *issues* of conflict 'between two or more identifiable groups over procedural or substantive matters relating to the distribution of positions or resources' (p. 32). In contrast to earlier pluralist perspectives on 'power' in society, which had focused on 'decision-making' as a central component of the exercise of power, these perspectives recognised that the ability to control or influence what issues get onto the public/political agenda in the first place was itself a core part of exercising power in society (Lukes, 1974).

But while the tendency in media research has very predominantly been to focus on the issues that *do* make it onto the media and public agenda – perhaps not least because these are conspicuous and lend themselves most easily to being studied – media research has contributed rather less and had significantly less to say about the type of claims-making or publicity management that is aimed principally at keeping issues off or away from the public and/or media agenda. As sociologists critical of power perspectives focused on 'decision-making' were pointing out around the same time as the social constructionist perspective emerged, the ability to keep issues from appearing on the political agenda and thus to ensure that they don't become issues for decision-making, that they remain 'non-decisions' in other words, is as much an exercise of power as making decisions about issues that *are* on the agenda is. Edelman (1988) takes this argument a step further by hinting that the placing of certain issues on the public agenda simultaneously achieves the granting of 'immunity' to those issues that are not on the public agenda:

> Perhaps the most powerful influence of news, talk, and writing about problems is the immunity from notice and criticism they grant to damaging conditions that are not on the list.
>
> (Edelman, 1988: 14)

While the constructionist perspective then generally focuses our attention on the importance of propelling *claims* into/onto the public arena, it is also clear that an important aspect of the claims-making process may be to keep issues from emerging in particular (public) forums, and thereby influencing the degree to which issues become recognised, or not as the case may be, as candidates for public concern, discussion or political decision-making.

Issue careers

The emphasis on the *process* of claims-making also led early constructionists to identify the distinctive stages/phases that social problems pass through as they emerge, are elaborated, addressed, contested and perhaps resolved, in other words the 'career' path of social problems. Spector and Kitsuse (acknowledging the work of Blumer and the much earlier work of Fuller and Myers, 1941) thus suggest a four-stage natural history model to describe the career of social issues. Downs (1972), in a much quoted article (not least in studies of environmental, science and risk issues), similarly proposed what he called an 'issue-attention cycle' to explain the cyclical manner in which various social problems suddenly emerge on the public stage, remain there for a time, and 'then – though still largely unresolved – gradually [fade] from the centre of public attention' (Downs, 1972: 38). Downs suggests – and he happens to use 'ecology' or environmental issues as his example, which may in part account for the frequency with which his article has been cited in research on media and the environment – that the career of public issues takes the shape of five distinctive stages: (1) a pre-problem stage; (2) alarmed discovery and euphoric enthusiasm; (3) realising the cost of significant progress and the sacrifices required to solve the problem; (4) gradual decline of intense public interest; and (5) the post-problem stage, where the issue has been replaced at the centre of public concern and 'moves into a prolonged limbo – a twilight realm of lesser attention or spasmodic recurrences of interest' (Downs, 1972).

Criticism of natural history models has focused on the notion that they offer a much too simplistic and linear model of the evolution and progression of social problems. As Schneider (1985) points out, Wiener (1981) for example 'argues that the sequential aspect of natural history models probably misleads us about the definitional process. She believes a more accurate view is one of "overlapping", simultaneous, "continuously ricocheting interaction" (Wiener 1981: 7)' (Schneider, 1985: 225). Wiener's evocative metaphor of 'continuously ricocheting interaction' is a particularly prescient and apt formulation relevant to communication research, as it directly counters the long-dominant – in communication research – linear view of communication, and begins to capture – as I shall argue more fully in Chapter 7 – the highly dynamic and interactive nature of social communication processes.

Hilgartner and Bosk (1988) similarly criticise natural history models for their 'crude' suggestion of 'an orderly succession of stages' and for inadequate recognition that 'Many problems exist simultaneously in several "stages" of development, and patterns of progression from one stage to the next vary sufficiently to question the claim that a typical career exists' (p. 54). While these are valid points, they may not in fact be entirely fair criticisms of what was actually proposed by Spector and Kitsuse and others. Spector and Kitsuse thus never suggested a simple linear progression, but indeed emphasised the *heuristic* nature of the model and, more importantly, the open-ended nature of the processes described. Downs similarly, particularly with his description of the fifth stage of issue careers and of course through the deliberate use of the word 'cycle', implied a recursive, cyclical process replete with loops.

I suggest that where some media and communication researchers have gone wrong in applying the issue-attention cycle model is most likely in confusing the *media*-career of a social issue with the social/political (or public opinion) career of issues.[3] It is perhaps symptomatic of this that a recent study by Brossard et al. (2004), which makes excellent use of Downs's framework for a novel cross-national analysis, refers (whether deliberately or due to a slip of the pen is unclear) to Downs's issue-attention cycle as the 'media-attention cycle'. Spector and Kitsuse, and indeed Downs, were of course looking at the general social career of issues (part of which may relate to the media) but they never proposed that the media career was synonymous with the social career or indeed that – as some communication researchers seem to have assumed – the social career can be 'read off' or deduced from the mapping/charting of the media career.

That the latter is particularly problematic is also clear from numerous agenda-setting studies (discussed more fully in Chapter 7) which have indicated that media coverage is *not*, in Schoenfeld et al.'s (1979) words, a good 'thermometer' or indicator of public sentiment or concern about the environment, for example, a drop in media attention does not necessarily imply that the public has lost interest in an issue or has ceased to be committed to dealing with a social problem.

While heeding then the advice from Wiener, Hilgartner and Bosk and others, that the career of social problems rarely follows a simple linear trajectory, the natural history models remain useful as heuristic models for the simple reason that they focus our attention on the notion of a *career*, the idea that issues evolve over time, and the idea that there are distinctive phases or stages in this process. They further alert us to the notion – and this is perhaps the most significant dimension – that issues don't simply evolve in some vague general or abstract location called 'society', but rather that they develop and evolve in particular social arenas (Hilgartner and Bosk, 1988) or forums, including political forums and the media, which: (a) interact with each other in important ways that determine how issues evolve; (b) *host* the stages of problem definition; and (c) themselves influence or frame these stages in important ways.

The ups and downs of media coverage of the environment

As indicated above, Downs (1972), in his aptly titled article 'Up and down with ecology – the issue-attention cycle', used the case of environmental issues to illustrate the stages in the 'career' of social problems. Numerous studies since have provided ample evidence that media coverage of environmental issues certainly goes up and down in seemingly cyclical patterns, which bear some resemblance to Downs's model, while also confirming that there are many more aspects to what drives this process than can be accounted for within Downs's model.

In very general terms, longitudinal studies of media coverage of environmental issues (e.g. Brookes et al., 1976; O'Meara, 1978;

Strodthoff et al., 1985; Bowman and Fuchs, 1981; McGeachy, 1989; Hansen, 1994b; Einsiedel and Coughlan, 1993; Ader, 1995; Brossard et al., 2004; Boykoff, 2007, 2008) show that media interest in environmental issues began in the mid-1960s, increasing to an initial peak in the early 1970s, then declining through the 1970s and early 1980s, followed by another dramatic increase in the latter half of the 1980s, peaking around 1990, then receding again through the 1990s, only to experience a considerable new resurgence in the first decade of the 2000s. This broad-brush characterisation inevitably obscures the very significant variations from issue to issue as well as the much more frequent ups and downs which can be observed within each of these broad periods. The purpose of painting this highly abstracted general trend is to make three key points about general media coverage of environmental issues:

One, that the concept of 'environmental issues' or of the 'environment' as a social problem only emerged on the public agenda in the 1960s. This is not to say that the media had not covered such issues as pollution or man-made erosion before, but it is to say that the new perspective or 'framework' of ecology and its associated more holistic view of the environment only emerged on the public arena in the 1960s. Longitudinal studies have also confirmed that the 'environmental/ecological' perspective which emerged in the 1960s, gradually but steadily consolidated in media coverage over the next couple of decades (Bowman and Fuchs, 1981), to the extent that Einsiedel and Coughlan were able to conclude in 1993 that 'What seems to differentiate the more recent period of the late 1970s through the early 1990s is that "the environment" has been vested with a more global character, encompassing attributes that include holism and interdependence, and the finiteness of resources' (p. 141).

The second point of this broad generalisation is to emphasise that society seems to go through broad phases of varying receptiveness to issues such as 'the environment'. When trying to map and explain the more detailed level of media coverage (and news-worthiness) of specific issues, media researchers need to take into consideration the wider 'climate of opinion' characteristic of the particular historical period under scrutiny; in other words, it is instructive to consider whether we are, broadly speaking, within a generally 'receptive' period or whether we are going through a period where society is, if not directly hostile to, then perhaps bored with 'the environment' or obsessed with the pursuit of objectives and values which run counter to environmental concerns.

Exercise 2.2

Interacting issue agendas

The late 1980s witnessed a considerable surge in social, political and media interest in the environment. Media analyses have shown how the amount of coverage of environmental issues increased dramatically in the latter half of the 1980s towards a peak in the very early 1990s. Then, rather abruptly, the intensity of interest dropped away again during the first half of the 1990s. Numerous factors, as we shall see in more detail in the following chapters, influence these 'ups' and 'downs', but it has been suggested that the global economic downturn of the early 1990s contributed significantly to the decline in media – and perhaps public – interest in the environment and environmental protection. Bluntly put, tough economic pressures meant that people had other more pressing things to worry about than 'saving the environment'.

Consider the parallels with the emerging global economic crisis that began to show in 2008. As in the early 1990s, the current economic crisis emerged during a time when the environment, or at least any part of the environment seen as potentially affected by climate change, was high on public, political and media agendas. Consider the extent to which and how – unlike in the early 1990s – political and media discourse about 'rescuing the economy' has frequently gone hand in hand with discourse on how to rescue us and the environment from climate change and its likely effects. Is it possible that economic crisis and environmental crisis can be construed as part of the same problem – demanding concerted action and solutions? Will media coverage of environmental matters remain prominent on the media agenda as we exit the first decade and move into the second decade of the new millennium, or will 'the environment' once again – as in the early 1990s – slip considerably down the media's list of prominent public issues/problems?

The third and final purpose is to make the point that what we might, equally broadly, call the environmental/ecological paradigm, once introduced in the 1960s, has remained firmly on the media and public agenda ever since, and while it's had distinctly more wind in the sails during some periods than others, and while its history has been characterised by all the conventional hallmarks of cycles of claims and counter-claims, we have not as yet seen any hints that a wholesale paradigm shift is likely to occur any time soon. In fact, it could be argued that the environmental paradigm – far from showing signs of increasing fragmentation – has become increasingly holistic through the rise of global concerns about climate change.

The apparent cyclical trends and the apparent poor fit between amount of media coverage and claims-making (e.g. by scientists), which studies have

Box 2.2

Claims-making and trigger-events

The social constructionist perspective helpfully draws our attention to the central and all important role of 'claims-making', that is, that issues only become issues for public and political concern if someone draws attention to them and makes claims about them. A cursory look at the ups and downs of media coverage of environmental issues, however, also tells us that claims-making may not in and of itself be sufficient to ensure widespread publicity and media coverage for an issue. Crucially, claims need (to be made) to resonate with wider public interests/concerns/fears to be successful. As Ungar (1992: 484) puts it: 'Recognition in public arenas, which is a *sine qua non* of successful social problems, cannot be reduced to claims-making activities, but depends on a conjunction of these *and* audience receptiveness. Claims-making, after all, can fall on deaf ears or meet with bad timing'.

In this context, much media research has pointed to the significance of 'trigger events'. Thus despite warnings from scientists, ecologists, energy experts and others about the depletion of energy reserves, it took the trigger event of the Arab oil embargo of 1973–74 to propel this issue into a position of media prominence (Schoenfeld et al., 1979; Mazur, 1984). Mazur (1984) likewise demonstrates how serious nuclear power plant accidents in the 1970s went entirely unreported, while some minor (by industry and scientific standards) incidents which occurred subsequent to the Three Mile Island accident in 1979 received considerable media coverage. A major trigger event such as the Three Mile Island accident thus greatly sensitises the media to similar and related events, and helps increase the sheer volume of coverage and attention devoted to – in this case – nuclear events and issues. It also, perhaps more importantly, helps establish a dominant frame or perspective for subsequent coverage of similar and related issues.

More recently, the most celebrated example of an issue that only gained prominence in the media when a range of important factors began to coalesce is global warming/climate change. In two early analyses, Ungar (1992) and Mazur and Lee (1993) thus show how sustained claims-making by scientists about the damage to the ozone layer and indications of a process of increased global warming took place for a considerable time without these issues receiving much media attention. This changed dramatically when the seemingly exceptionally dry summer of 1988 (in Northern America and Northern Europe) furnished the media – and public concern – with a direct and immediate reference point. It was not that climatologists and other scientists believed that the dry summer of 1988 was anything other than a 'normal' occurrence in cyclical weather patterns, but it provided a fertile context for the promotion of claims about global warming/climate change as caused by harmful human practices.

found in analyses of media coverage of selected environmental issues then tell us: (1) that sustained claims-making about an environmental issue may not in itself be sufficient to secure its prominence on the media agenda; and (2) the ups and downs of issues on the media agenda cannot be taken as evidence of the seriousness of the issue or of whether the issue has been resolved or appropriately addressed through legislation, allocation of resources, research, etc.

Trumbo (1996), McComas and Shanahan (1999), Mikami et al. (2002) and Brossard et al. (2004) have all usefully drawn on Downs's 'issue attention' cycle for explaining the cyclical phases of media coverage of global warming/climate change, as have Nisbet and Huge (2006) in their comprehensive study of a different environmental issue, plant bio-technology. Trumbo's (1996) analysis provides a particularly clear exposition:

Box 2.3

Climate-change coverage and the issue-attention cycle

Excerpts from Trumbo (1996: 276, 277 and 280)

Figure 2.1 presents the distribution of the sample through time. Inspection of this distribution supported the idea that the attention paid to this issue might be divided into distinct phases for analysis.

Using the ideas of Downs, three distinct phases were identified. The overall distribution shown in Figure 2.1 fits Downs's five-stage model fairly well. Downs proposes that attention to an issue will remain low until a dramatic discovery brings a sudden increase in salience. While the issue–attention cycle does not offer specific predictions about changing salience during the middle three stages it does suggest general aspects of the content of these stages and also suggests that salience during these stages should be at its highest before feathering into a decline. Finally, Downs directly predicts that the final stage will involve a lowering of the salience of the issue, but not a lowering to the levels seen in the first stage.

An examination of the time distribution of stories clearly suggests two important points in the series: mid-1988 when Hansen testifies before Congress and mid-1992 when the Earth Summit concludes. A fifth-order polynomial was found to fit the time series so that these important points in the issue's life fell near the curve's inflections. The curve clearly suggests Downs's overall propositions as they would be applied to the volume of media attention. Dividing the series into these three segments and fitting

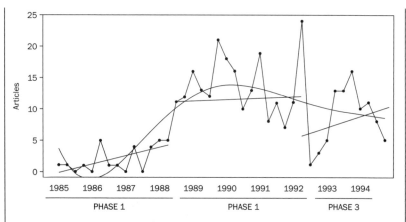

Figure 2.1 *Items in five newspapers, by quarters 1985–1995. Based on a 50 per cent sample, divided into three phases with linear fits compared. The full curve fit is fifth-order polynomial. The linear components are: phase 1: y = –0.14 + 0.29x, μ = 2; phase 2: y = 13.7 + 0.01x, μ = 14; phase 3: y = –9.9 + 0.5x, μ = 8.*

linear functions to each segment shows that the means and the slopes vary between the phases (analysis of variance significant at p<0.001). Stories were thus coded as being in phase 1, 2 or 3. Because of the content of the news, the three phases are being labelled as pre-controversy, controversy, and post-controversy. [. . .]

[. . .]

Conclusion

This project does not hold as an express purpose the operationalisation of Downs's issue-attention cycle. But the model can be used as a more general basis for a division of the decade's media coverage of climate change into three distinct phases. It must also be emphasised that the issue-attention cycle is a social process model and is not specifically designed to evaluate news media attention to an issue. Nonetheless, elements of the issue-attention cycle do seem to fit a reading of the news coverage of climate change. This, combined with the good fit between the observed quantity of news attention and the expectations of the Downs model, suggests that it might be reasonable to interpret the three phases used in this study as a partial expression of the issue-attention cycle.

Overall, these results suggest that the most appropriate way to relate Downs's model to the changes observed in media coverage of climate change is to argue that what has been observed across this decade is just the first three stages of the cycle. [. . .]

While comparison of studies of media coverage of climate change in different countries[4] gives a clear indication that a range of factors (including media organisational arrangements, political 'leanings' of particular media organisations, journalistic practices and values, and perhaps wider culturally determined agendas – discussed in more detail in the next two chapters) impinge on the precise ups and downs of media coverage, such comparisons have also provided tantalising evidence of broader cyclical patterns that resonate well with stages in Downs's issue-attention cycle. Where Downs's model is particularly helpful is in providing a framework for identifying and making sense of the different stages in the cycle of media coverage – that is, it enables us, when looking at the ups and downs of media coverage, to begin to answer the question 'what drives the coverage at this particular stage, and what is going on during this particular period of coverage?'. It is of course crucial, as Trumbo notes, to bear in mind that Downs's model concerns the general social career of issues – it was not designed specifically for explaining the *media* career of an issue, and we should not lose sight of the fact that the media are just one – albeit a central one – of the public arenas in which social problems are articulated.

Claims-making and framing

The key achievement of the constructionist perspective on social problems lies in the recognition that problems do not become recognised or defined by society as problems by some simple objective existence, but only when someone makes claims in public about them. The construction of a problem as a 'social problem' is then largely a rhetorical or discursive achievement, the enactment of which is perpetrated by claims-makers, takes place in certain settings or public arenas, and proceeds through a number of phases.

American sociologist Joel Best (1995) suggests that analysis of the construction of social problems needs to focus on (1) the claims themselves; (2) the claims-makers; and (3) the claims-making process. To these we might add the public arenas (Hilgartner and Bosk, 1988) or settings (Ibarra and Kitsuse, 1993); as arenas or settings (including the media, the courts, parliamentary politics, the scientific community) set their own boundaries for or impose their own constraints on what can and cannot be said. I shall discuss the constraints of the media in more detail in the next chapter, as well as the actors involved in the claims-making process. Here, however, I will focus on the rhetorical/

discursive aspect of the claims-making process by drawing on Ibarra and Kitsuse's (1993) notion of 'vernacular resources' and on the concept of framing.

In an exceptionally clear exposition, Ibarra and Kitsuse (1993) restate the emphasis in Spector and Kitsuse's original statement about social problems as claims-making, that language or discourse is at the heart of the construction of social problems ('As parts of a classification system, condition-categories [referred to in the original statement as "putative conditions"] are first and foremost units of language' 1993: 30). The object of study is therefore, as Ibarra and Kitsuse put it – borrowing from Mills (1940) – the 'vernacular displays' (p. 29) of those involved in the claims-making process:

> If pressed for a summary description of the phenomena in need of identification and theoretical reconstruction, we would name those 'vernacular resources' drawn upon in claims-making activities. Vernacular resources are the conventional means by which members can realize the signifying processes called claims. Thus, they can refer to forms of talk, frames of interpretation, and contexts for articulation inasmuch as these effectively organize and circumscribe members' social problems discourse. To state the matter in still another way, vernacular resources include those rhetorical idioms, interpretive practices, and features of settings that distinguish claims-making activities as a class of phenomena while also differentiating instances of claims-making from one another.
>
> (1993: 32–33)

Ibarra and Kitsuse proceed to outline the core foci of constructionist analysis as follows:

> [. . .] constructionist studies of social problems discourse can profitably proceed by distinguishing four overlapping but analytically distinct rhetorical dimensions: rhetorical idioms, counterrhetorics, motifs, and claims-making styles. The last of these leads us into the study of settings.
>
> (1993: 34)

As we shall see below there is considerable overlap and compatibility between these rhetorical dimensions and the framework proposed by Gamson, who talks about 'packages' and refers to many of the same linguistic features and rhetorical devices as Ibarra and Kitsuse. Where Ibarra and Kitsuse's scheme is particularly useful is in its inclusion of 'claims-making styles' and 'settings' as key factors influencing what can be said, how and with what implications.

Ibarra and Kitsuse suggest the following five foci:

- *Rhetorical idioms* are definitional complexes, utilising language that situates condition-categories in moral universes. (. . .) Each rhetorical idiom calls forth or draws upon a cluster of images (p. 34). Examples:
  - The rhetoric of loss
  - The rhetoric of unreason
  - The rhetoric of calamity
- The *counterrhetorics* are discursive strategies for countering characterisations made by claimants. They tend to be less synoptic or thematic: For example, instead of arguing for ozone layer destruction, it is the claimant's description, proposed remedies, or something other than the candidate problem that is rebutted. These counterrhetorics tend not to counter the 'values' conveyed in the rhetorical idioms so much as they address their current application and relevance. (1993: 34–35). Counterrhetorics divide into:
  - Sympathetic counterrhetorics, including such rhetorical strategies as *naturalising, costs involved, declaring impotence, perspectivising, tactical criticism.*
  - Unsympathetic counterrhetorics, including such rhetorical strategies as *antipatterning, the telling anecdote, and the counterrhetorics of insincerity and hysteria.*
- *Motifs* are recurrent thematic elements, metaphors and figures of speech that encapsulate, highlight or offer a shorthand to some aspect of a social problem. Examples: *epidemic, menace, scourge, crisis, blight, casualties, tip of the iceberg, the war on* (drugs, poverty, crime, gangs, etc.), *abuse, hidden costs, scandal, ticking time bomb* (p. 47). Ibarra and Kitsuse point to the particularly pertinent 'need for understanding their *symbolic currency,* that is, why some motifs are prized while others are considered best avoided' (p. 48).
- *Claims-making styles* shift attention from the language in which claims are cast to the bearing and tone with which the claims are made. For example, claimants (and counterclaimants) may deliver their claims in *legalistic* fashion or *comic* fashion, in a *scientific* way or a *theatrical* way, in a *journalistic* ('objective') manner or an 'involved citizen' (or '*civic*') manner. (1993: 35).
- *Setting*: How do the formal qualities of particular settings structure the ways in which claims can be formulated, delivered, and received? What kinds of rhetorical forms can be employed because of the imperatives or conventional features constituting the various locations? What are the various categories of persons populating these settings, and how do

their characteristics entail accountably interacting with claims and claims-makers? (pp. 53–54).

The last question is particularly relevant to media and communications researchers as it points directly to core concerns about media organisational arrangements and journalistic practices/values, which structure the relationship with sources (claims-makers) and impact on the articulation and framing of claims.

Although Ibarra and Kitsuse (1993) do not explicitly position themselves within the context of 'framing', much of what they say resonates very well with the concept of framing as it has grown to be used in media and communication research. Reese (2001), for example, defines frames as '*organizing principles* that are socially *shared* and *persistent* over time, that work *symbolically* to meaningfully *structure* the social world', while Gitlin (1980) sees frames as 'principles of selection, emphasis, and presentation composed of little tacit theories about what exists, what happens, and what matters'. Frames, in other words, draw attention – like a frame around a painting or photograph – to particular dimensions or perspectives and they set the boundaries for how we should interpret or perceive what is presented to us (i.e. is the glass described as 'half full' or 'half empty'?). Gamson (1985), with particular reference to the media, suggests that 'news frames are almost entirely implicit and taken for granted. [. . .] News frames make the world look natural. They determine what is selected, what is excluded, what is emphasised. In short, news presents a packaged world' (Gamson, 1985: 618).

Miller and Riechert (2000: 46) make an important further addition to the definition of framing by suggesting whose interests are served. They thus suggest that framing is usually thought of as 'driven by unifying ideologies that shape all content on a topic into a specific, dominant interpretation consistent with the interests of social elites'. While this recovers an important Marxian/Gramscian element by suggesting that frames generally work in the interest of powerful classes or elites in society, we should also recognise that framing can, in principle, be made to work for any social group or interest. However, the framing task is clearly much more challenging and difficult for those who are working 'against the grain' by trying to un-seat a dominant, culturally deep-seated, interpretive package or frame, than for those who are able to anchor their arguments firmly within a dominant interpretative framework and thus able to work 'with the flow' rather than against it.

In a synoptic – and much quoted – overview of the 'framing' concept and its various disciplinary origins, Entman (1993) defines framing as follows:

> To frame is to *select some aspects of a perceived reality and make them more salient in a communicating text, in such a way as to promote a particular problem definition, causal interpretation, moral evaluation, and/or treatment recommendation* for the item described.
>
> (Entman, 1993: 56)

Claims-makers, like news professionals, then draw attention to particular interpretations through *selection* (e.g. our attention is drawn to some aspects while others, not selected, are kept out of view) and *salience or emphasis*, which promotes particular definitions/interpretations/understandings rather than others. Perhaps the most significant point about how a problem is defined, is that the definition invariably carries with it the allocation of responsibility or blame as well as – implicitly or explicitly – directions for the problem's solution. As Entman argues in a more recent article:

> All four of these framing functions [problem definition, causal interpretation, moral evaluation, treatment recommendation] hold together in a kind of cultural logic, serving each other, with the connections cemented more by custom and convention than by the principles of valid reasoning or syllogistic logic. The two most important of these functions are the problem definition, since defining the problem often virtually predetermines the rest of the frame, and the remedy, because it promotes support of (or opposition to) actual government action.
>
> (Entman, 2003: 417–18)

As succinctly put by Charlotte Ryan (1991: 57), the notion of framing directs the analysis of claims-making and the construction of social problems to ask three core questions: (1) What is the issue? (definition), (2) Who is responsible? (identification of actors/stakeholders), (3) What is the solution? (suggested action/remedies). And to answer these questions we can usefully draw on the analytical framework offered by Gamson and Modigliani (1989) which helpfully sets out the notion of a 'signature matrix' to indicate the constituent parts of frames – in other words, enables us to answer the question: by which rhetorical/linguistic and other devices is a frame constituted and sustained?

Gamson and Modigliani's (1989) discussion of framing is particularly useful because it draws attention to the two core meanings of 'framing' in media research: on the one hand, framing as a term for the stories/ discourses/ideologies/packages available to us for making sense of our environment, and, on the other hand, framing as the workings or operation of the constituent parts that together contribute to a particular frame. Gamson and Modigliani thus suggest 'that media discourse can be conceived of as a set of interpretive packages that give meaning to an issue. A package has an internal structure. At its core is a central organizing idea, or frame, for making sense of relevant events, suggesting what is at issue' and 'a package offers a number of different condensing symbols that suggest the core frame and positions in shorthand, making it possible to display the package as a whole with a deft metaphor, catchphrase, or other symbolic devices' (p. 3).

The constituent parts, which together contribute to or build the 'frame', can, according to Gamson and Modigliani (1989), be identified as five *framing devices* that suggest how to think about the issue (metaphors; exemplars (i.e. historical examples from which lessons are drawn); catchphrases; depictions; and visual images (e.g. icons)) and three *reasoning devices* that justify what should be done about it (roots (i.e. a causal analysis); consequences (i.e. a particular type of effect); and appeals to principle (i.e. a set of moral claims)).

What is offered then is an analytical framework for characterising and unpacking the interpretive packages in 'a signature matrix that states the frame, the range of positions, and the eight different types of signature elements that suggest this core in a condensed manner' (Gamson and Modigliani, 1989: 4).

While a number of studies (e.g. Beckett, 1997; Menashe and Siegel, 1998) have made exceptionally good and faithful use of Gamson's 'signature matrix' in its entirety, other studies have used it more eclectically. Both Ibarra and Kitsuse's discussion, and perhaps more so Gamson and Modigliani's analytical model, should, I suggest, be seen as essentially suggestive lists of key questions/tools for identifying and analysing the devices and frames that come into play in the claims-making process and for identifying and analysing the rhetorical means by which some claims-making is more successful than other types of claims-making.

Exercise 2.3

Claims-makers, rhetorical devices, settings and frames

Using the online version of a major national newspaper, identify a recent news item about any environmental issue (try, for example, to look for items written by the newspaper's environment or science correspondent/editor).

Why is this story in the news on this particular day? What or whose action, in what forum or setting, has caused the topic/subject of this story to be 'news'?

Who are the key claims-makers quoted or referred to in the story? Are they scientists, experts, politicians, business/pressure group/agency representatives, 'ordinary' people?

What kind of forum or 'setting' do they represent? How – if at all – do the conventions of the forum/setting seem to impinge on or shape what is being said about the topic/subject of the news story?

Are there any words/terms in the report that 'stand out' either as characteristic of a particular discourse (e.g. a science discourse or a legal discourse), or as examples of what Ibarra and Kitsuse refer to as motifs, for example, 'epidemic', 'war on. . .', 'tip of the iceberg', 'ticking time bomb', etc.?

How does the way that the news is constructed, including the particular terms/words used, shape the answer to the three framing questions: (1) What is the issue/problem? (2) Who/what is to blame? (3) What is the (implied) solution?

Conclusion

The constructionist perspective provides a framework for analysing and understanding why some environmental issues come to be recognised as issues for public and political concern, while others – potentially equally important issues – never make it into the public eye, and thus fail to command the political attention and resources required for their resolution. The constructionist perspective focuses our attention on the role of claims-makers and on the public definition of social problems as essentially a rhetorical/discursive achievement. Drawing on the notion of 'vernacular resources' and on the concept of framing, the chapter outlined a number of key analytical foci and tools for examining the construction and contestation of environmental issues: these included Ibarra and Kitsuse's rhetorical idioms, counter-rhetorics, motifs, claims-making styles and settings; Gamson and Modigliani's focus on media or meaning 'packages' and their constitution through a 'signature matrix' of framing and reasoning devices; and the concept of framing understood as selection and salience, communicating a particular problem definition, which in turn carries with it implied causes, moral evaluations and solutions.

The constructionist perspective further shows that social problems do not simply appear in some vague location called society, but that they are actively constructed, defined and contested in identifiable public arenas – notably the media – and that the careers of social problems are characterised by distinctive stages or phases. While claims-making and definition takes place in a number of arenas, the mass media are a particularly important arena or hub, because it is through the media that we as publics predominantly learn about what goes on in other key arenas (such as parliament, science, or the courts). But the media are not simply an open stage; as a public arena they are governed by their own organisational and professional constraints and practices, some of which have been signalled in this chapter (e.g. the journalistic value of 'objectivity' and 'balance'; the role of 'trigger events'), while others will be discussed in more detail in the following two chapters.

Further reading

Best, J. (2002). Constructing the sociology of social problems: Spector and Kitsuse twenty-five years later. *Sociological Forum, 17*(4), 699–706.

Cox, R. (2006). *Environmental Communication and the Public Sphere*. London: Sage. See, in particular, Chapter 2: Rhetorically Shaping the Environment.

Hannigan, J. A. (2006). *Environmental Sociology* (2nd ed.). London: Routledge. See, in particular, Chapter 5: Social Construction of Environmental Issues and Problems.

Schneider, J. W. (1985). Social problems theory: the constructionist view. *Annual Review of Sociology, 11*, 209–29.

3 Making claims and managing news about the environment

This chapter:

- Applies the previous chapter's introduction to the constructionist perspective to news and shows that there is little that is 'natural' about environmental news; even 'natural disaster news' can best be understood in terms of something which has to be actively constructed.
- While recognising the importance of news values and of the political, economic and cultural factors which circumscribe the production of news, the chapter focuses on the activities and communication strategies of claims-makers.
- Examines claims-makers in the broadest sense of the term, including environmental pressure groups, government and business/industry.
- Discusses the distinction between 'insider' and 'outsider' groups and the extent to which different types of claims-maker seek or depend on media coverage.
- Introduces the key claims-making tasks as (1) commanding attention; (2) claiming legitimacy; and (3) invoking action.
- Examines how claims-makers (environmental pressure groups as well as corporate business) have sought to exploit the internet and other newer forms of communication for information, news management and campaigning purposes.
- Discusses corporate image-management strategies.

Introduction – the 'constructed-ness' of news

Considering the masses of news coverage of natural events, disasters and emergencies associated, as we are told, with climate change and related environmental damage during much of the first decade of the twenty-first century, one could be forgiven for assuming that the 'environment' is by nature and by definition 'newsworthy'. Even – and contrary to what was argued in the previous chapter – that it, the environment, becomes news almost by itself, and that there is little or nothing 'constructed' about either the prominence of environmental coverage or the nature of environmental topics that receive coverage. This would perhaps particularly seem to be the case with major natural disasters as well as with smaller-scale regional emergencies, such as recurrent flooding and associated damage.

Major natural disasters from the most recent decade that stand out as singularly 'news-worthy' in and of themselves include one of the deadliest natural disasters in history, the Indian Ocean earthquake of 26 December 2004, which triggered a series of tsunamis wreaking havoc and devastation in countries bordering the Indian Ocean – most catastrophically Indonesia, Thailand, India and Sri Lanka; Hurricane Katrina in August 2005, the costliest and one of the deadliest in the history of the United States; the Pakistan/Kashmir earthquake of October 2005; widespread flood damage in many European countries in 2007; the Burma cyclone and subsequent flood damage in May 2008; and the earthquake of 12 May 2008 in Sichuan Province in China.

It only takes, however, a slightly closer – and a slightly longer-term – look at such coverage to realise that there is little or nothing that is automatic or natural about news coverage of the environment or environmental events. The first anomalies begin to appear when observing how some major disasters, having received masses of news coverage for a while, then suddenly all but disappear from the media agenda, not because they have been alleviated or resolved, but perhaps because other events, disasters, or issues have literally pushed them off the news agenda in what Hilgartner and Bosk (1988) aptly have described as the intense competition for space on a media agenda with limited 'carrying capacity'. Occasionally, the competition for news space is even between disaster stories of a similar type, for example, massive coverage of the China earthquake of May 2008 to some extent squeezed out media attention to the ongoing problems in the wake of the cyclone devastation earlier in May 2008 in Burma. But a comparison of the nature and extent of news coverage of these two events must also take into consideration the very different geo-political 'news status' of these two countries as well as practical factors such as severe restrictions on journalistic/news access imposed by the Burmese government.

Another key indication of the complex and 'un-natural' processes behind news coverage emerges when our attention is suddenly drawn to major environmental disasters or problems which have existed and been developing for a considerable length of time, but only now show up on the news radar: numerous instances of coverage of drought, famine and related socio-political upheaval in Sub-Saharan Africa over the last twenty years fall into this category; so too do some instances of flood devastation, which, although seemingly sudden and unexpected, may have been caused or exacerbated by years of human damage (e.g. logging) to natural flood defences (recent coverage in the summer of 2008 of widespread flooding in the Indian state of Andra Pradesh would appear to fit this category). Wide variations in both the amount and nature of news coverage of environmental disasters/emergencies depending on *where* geographically they happen and *who* is affected further alert us to the continued significance of Galtung and Ruge's (1965) classic study of news values, particularly the importance of geo-political and 'cultural proximity' as a key determinant of what gets covered, how and for how long.

If further indication were needed of the complex processes governing news coverage of the environment, consider the evidence from numerous studies of long-term trends in environmental news coverage. Invariably, such studies have shown what Downs in his prescient article published in 1972 aptly referred to as the 'ups' and 'downs' of coverage: the quantity and nature of coverage given to the environment and environmental issues has gone up and down in phases that bear little resemblance to the (scientific) discovery, material existence (as, for example, measured through scientific, economic or social indicators), persistence or resolution of environmental problems.

In order to understand the ups and downs in media coverage, as well as to understand why some issues receive much more coverage than others, we need then to look closer at the complex processes which influence the production of news. Environmental news, in other words, is not just something that happens and automatically gets recorded and reported by the media. News, as numerous key news studies (Tumber, 1999) from the last seventy years or so have amply demonstrated, is made, created, and selectively reported. The making of news is a complex process of interaction between, on the one hand, institutions and individuals in society who act as sources or subjects of news, and on the other hand, the news media whose own organisation and professional practices influence what institutions, events and individuals get reported. Further layers of influence circumscribing the production of news include *political, economic* and – not least (see also Chapter 4) – *cultural* factors.

In this chapter, we focus on media-external influences on the communication process, on the communication strategies and influence of key claims-makers and stakeholders in environmental debate and controversy. The type of claims-maker that perhaps most easily comes to mind in relation to environmental debate and controversy is probably environmental pressure groups, but there are clearly many others – government departments, scientists, economists and not least the businesses and industries whose operational practices are often the subject of environmental debate and controversy.

Claims-making, social construction and key tasks

If, as argued in the previous chapter, the construction of the environment as a social problem depends on successful public claims-making, then the mass media constitute a key public arena, in which the voices, definitions, and claims of claims-makers (notably representatives of government, public authorities, formal political institutions, professional communities and associations, pressure groups, etc.) are put on public display and compete with each other for legitimacy. But the media are not merely a convenient public arena or window; they play – through the organisational and professional arrangements of news-making – an active role in the construction, inflection, and framing of both issues and claims-makers. Gaining media coverage may often seem the most immediate task for claims-makers, but as Ryan states in her book on media strategies for grassroots:

> [. . .] gaining attention alone is not what a social movement wants; the real battle is over whose interpretation, whose framing of reality, gets the floor.
>
> (Ryan, 1991: 53)

'Framing' in media coverage hinges on two dimensions: (1) selection/ accessing of sources/claims-makers; and (2) presentation/evaluation of arguments/actors:

> Framing essentially involves selection and salience. To frame is to select some aspects of a perceived reality and make them more salient in a communicating text, in such a way as to promote a particular problem definition, causal interpretation, moral evaluation and/or treatment recommendation for the item described.
>
> (Entman, 1993: 52)

It is reasonable to expect a fair degree of 'fit' between *who* is quoted in media coverage and *how* issues are framed or defined. Indeed, in a study of US news coverage of climate change, Trumbo (1996), for example, found a strong association between the types of claims-makers (scientists, politicians and interest groups) accessed by the media and the types and prominence of different frames, leading him to conclude that '[. . .] changes occurring in the life-course of this issue [climate change] apparently involved shifts linked to who was getting their message into the media rather than how the media was choosing to present the information' (Trumbo, 1996: 281).

But while analysis may confirm an association between the types of claims-makers accessed and the relative prominence of general thematic clusters or frames in media coverage, such an analysis does not go far enough. Crucially, it does not show us how different sources and their testimonies or claims are framed by the media, or how, through the framing and definitional work engaged in by the media themselves, sources and their claims may achieve legitimacy and credibility through media coverage, or alternatively, may be systematically undermined by such coverage.

In a seminal article, published in 1976, Solesbury makes the crucial distinction (often overlooked by media analysts, pressure groups and others keen to equate amount of media coverage with successful claims-making) between, on the one hand, gaining media coverage for a particular cause or issue, and on the other, ensuring that the tone or framing of the coverage is such that the 'message' conveyed to the larger public is one of legitimacy and support for the claims being made. To these two tasks, Solesbury adds a further crucial task or stage in the claims-making process, namely that of 'invoking action'. The three key tasks for claims-makers making claims about a putative problem then are: (1) commanding attention; (2) claiming legitimacy; and (3) invoking action.

Resonant of Downs's (1972) issue career stages, Solesbury's three stages critically disentangle – what is often ignored or confused in the hyped-up rhetoric of claims-makers themselves and indeed in some media analyses – these three separate achievements to emphasise that media coverage cannot be assumed to be 'the right kind of media coverage'. Coverage may be positive and be conferring legitimacy, lending credibility to the claims being made, *or* it may be critical, negative, undermining the legitimacy of both claims and claims-makers, or worse still marginalising and branding the claims-makers as insincere or 'extremist'. Nor does media coverage itself guarantee social or political action, that is, that something is actually done to address or resolve the problem about which claims are being made. As well as providing a sobering yardstick for claims-makers themselves for the planning and evaluation of claims-making strategies, Solesbury's three-tasks list serves as a useful reminder and tool for media-analysts seeking to assess media and communication roles in claims-making and campaigning processes.

Box 3.1

Commanding attention and claiming legitimacy (or perhaps not)

The much studied – and celebrated – case of Greenpeace's action against the Anglo-Dutch oil company Shell over its plans to dump a redundant North Sea oil-storage installation, the Brent Spar, in the Atlantic Ocean in 1995 provides perhaps one of the clearest illustrations available of the complex mix of actors/agents, claims, claims-making processes, issue careers, news processes, etc. which combine to produce a social/political outcome or change. The full findings of several comprehensive analyses of the Brent Spar controversy (see, for example, Bennie, 1998; Jordan, 1998a; Hansen, 2000; de Jong, 2005; Bakir, 2006) will not be reiterated here. Instead, I shall focus on one particular aspect: the difficulties for claims-makers in managing or even influencing the media framing of their claims and actions. The following is an excerpt from an analysis (Hansen, 2000: 62–66) of the reporting in four British newspapers (two broadsheet/quality newspapers and two tabloid/popular newspapers) of the 1995 controversy between Greenpeace and Shell over the proposed deep-sea dumping of the Brent Spar.

Framing Greenpeace

Greenpeace and its campaigners were generally referred to as 'Greenpeace', 'protesters', 'campaigners' and 'activists'. However, the *Telegraph*, in keeping with the anti-Greenpeace tone already indicated, and consistent with what linguists have described as the phenomenon of overlexicalisation,[5] deployed a rather wider and clearly more negative set of descriptors.

Greenpeace and its actions were described variously in terms such as 'nuisance', the formulaic[6] phrase 'single-issue + politics/campaigners/ group/pressure group', 'self-righteous', 'rebels', 'bearded', 'doleful', 'extreme eco-warriors', 'eco-sentimentalists', 'emotional', 'misguided', 'militant group', 'undemocratic', 'irresponsible', 'propagandists', 'arrogant', 'more fervent than competent' (DTL 7 September), 'bullyboys'. A Greenpeace spokesman 'gibbers', rather than speaks, in a *Sunday Telegraph* quote (25 June). Where the *Mail* and the *Mirror* tended to portray the battle between Greenpeace and Shell in terms of a battle between daring, heroic, homely, idealistic protesters and a 'huge', 'large', 'multinational', greedy 'giant', the *Telegraph*, particularly conscious of the potential representation of the battle over Brent Spar as a David (Greenpeace) versus Goliath (Shell) battle, endeavoured to expose this as a fallacious and mythical representation by focusing repeatedly on the size (business), value and power of Greenpeace as itself a multinational organisation:

> THE BRAINS BEHIND GREENPEACE VICTORY: OIL RIG SUCCESS PROVES POWER OF £9M GROUP
>
> (DTL 21 June)
>
> NOTEBOOK: GIANTS FIGHT AND THE NATION LOSES
> (DTL 24 June)

The framing of Greenpeace as a powerful threatening (to business, democracy and the public) organisation was further emphasised by the metaphoric labelling of its politics as 'environmental jihad' (DTL 24 June), 'harassment' (DTL 21 June), a 'black art . . . seducing or bullying public opinion by media manipulation ranging from hype and distortion to public demonstrations and criminal disobedience' (DTL 5 October).

Previous research on media coverage of social movements and pressure groups has noted that one of the key problems is to keep media coverage focused on campaign issues, as opposed to personality clashes among movement leaders, movement organisation, internal schisms and break-away groups (Gitlin, 1980; Kielbowicz and Scherer, 1986). While analyses of other newspapers (Hansen, 1993) have indicated Greenpeace's past success in keeping media attention focused on its campaign causes and issues, the *Telegraph* in particular focused much of its coverage on Greenpeace as an organisation. Much of this coverage, as already indicated, centred on demonstrating that Greenpeace was not the idealistic grassroots 'David' of the moral high ground, but a powerful, undemocratic, multinational and multi-million-pound (e.g. DTL 21 June) organisation:

> SUNDAY COMMENT: WHY WE SHOULD BACK THE FRENCH ATOMIC TESTS – GREENPEACE IS NOT ABOUT THE ENVIRONMENT BUT THE EXERCISE OF POWER, ARGUES WILLIAM ODDIE
>
> [. . .] It [the battle] is between democratic politics – with all its faults – and a well-funded, undemocratic, unaccountable and irresponsible internationalist politics, which is growing disconcertingly in its power. I refer to the ecological movement, here epitomised principally by the rich and powerful transnational lobbyist Greenpeace.
>
> (STL 13 August)

In contrast to the *Telegraph*'s negative framing of Greenpeace, the *Mail*, although by no means uncritical or uniformly positive, generally framed Greenpeace protesters in a way which showed them as devoted, daring (only the *Mail* and the *Mirror* ever referred to Greenpeace's occupation of the Brent Spar as 'daring'), committed and ingenious.

DAWN MISSION PAYS OFF FOR THE LADY FROM MONTANA: FIASCO OVER BRENT SPAR

The woman pilot who landed the last two Greenpeace activists on the Brent Spar was the toast of the crew on the Solo yesterday.

Paula Huckleberry, a former US Army pilot, had caught Shell's minders off guard with her dawn raid.

Her daring mission took just 40 minutes and, by the time the oil company's water cannons were trained back on the platform, she was on her way back to the vessel.

(DML 21 June)

THE BAR-ROOM BATTLE PLAN SCRIBBLED OUT ON BEER MATS

[. . .] He and his fellow activists talked through their various options time and again and Captain Jurgens jotted down the main points on the back of a couple of beer mats.

He could not have known then that those scribbles would be the blueprint for a battle that would herald the environmentalists' finest hour.

[. . .] We basically prepared the general outline of the campaign and as we didn't have anything but a ballpoint and beer mats, that's what we used.

[. . .] The campaign was masterminded from the Greenpeace UK office in London

(DML 21 June)

The portrayal of Greenpeace as the potentially 'threatened' 'peaceful demonstrators', rather than a threatening powerful organisation was further underlined by the *Mail*'s revelation in several articles that the Government had authorised Royal Marine Commandos to be on stand-by to help Shell evict the Greenpeace protesters from the Brent Spar platform:

MYSTERY OF 'SBS MISSION TO BRENT SPAR'

A commando force of around eight men from the Special Boat Squadron may have been on stand by to storm the Brent Spar oil platform shortly before Shell abandoned plans to sink her in the Atlantic, according to an MP last night.

(DML 22 June)

ANNE'S HUSBAND WANTED PROTEST RIG STORMED: SECRET MEMO REVEALS MARINES POISED TO EVICT GREENPEACE BY FORCE

(MOS 25 June)

> GOVERNMENT ADMITS MARINE TASK FORCE TARGETED
> GREENPEACE
>
> > (DML 15 July)

The incompatibility of this particular news angle with the *Telegraph*'s framing of Greenpeace as a powerful and manipulative organisation may help explain why it received no mention in the *Telegraph*.

In sharp contrast to the wide range of negative terms/labels used by the *Telegraph*, glorifying battle-terms such as 'hero/heroes/heroic', 'army of green warriors', 'Greenpeace commandos', 'fighters' and 'daredevils' were unique to the *Mirror*. The *Mirror* from the outset painted the controversy as a fight between the brave and heroic Greenpeace ('HEROES DID GREAT JOB: FISHERMEN PAY TRIBUTE TO GREENPEACE OVER BRENT SPAR', DMR 23 June 1995; 'OIL RIG HERO GETS SHELL DISCOUNT CARD', DMR 24 June 1995; 'DEMO MAN WANTS HUG FROM LOVE: BRENT SPAR HERO AL BAKER ARRIVES BACK IN THE SHETLANDS', DMR 24 June) fighting on behalf of us (the readers) and nature against a greedy, powerful, inflexible and irresponsible multinational company.

> Greed That's Poisoning Our Seas: Shell's Sinking Of The Brent Spar
> Oil Rig
>
> > (DMR 20 June)

> WE SHELL NOT BE MOVED: DUMPING OF BRENT SPAR
> COULD BE THE FIRST OF MANY – THERE ARE 350 RIGS IN
> THE NORTH SEA
>
> > (DMR 20 June)

> MR GREEN TARGETS BRITAIN: AS BRITAIN IS TAGGED THE
> DIRTY MAN OF EUROPE, GREEN HEROES TALK OF NORTH
> SEA ORDEAL: EUROPEAN GREENS TARGET BRITAIN'S
> POLLUTING COMPANIES.
>
> > (DMR 22 June)

The *Mirror* went further than simply legitimating Greenpeace's actions. In a manner typical of the particular mode of readership address often adopted by tabloid papers (see Hall et al., 1978) the *Mirror* cast itself in the role of representing, speaking on behalf of, and campaigning on behalf of its readers. The *Mirror* thus not only claimed to be the first to have reported on the scandal and problems of dumping, but also portrayed itself as having been largely instrumental in bringing about the Shell U-turn on dumping of the Brent Spar.

> GLAD OIL OVER: DAILY MIRROR VICTORY AS PETROL
> GIANT HALTS RIG SINKING: GREENPEACE WERE JUBILANT
> WHEN SHELL DROPPED THE PLANS TO DUMP BRENT SPA
> [*sic*].
>
> > (DMR 21 June)

HOW WE DID IT: BRENT SPA [*sic*] SCANDAL WAS FIRST
REVEALED BY DAILY MIRROR WHICH HIGHLIGHTED
POTENTIAL DISASTER

JUNE 20: A day of drama ends in Shell's climbdown.

10am: The Mirror contacted Shell to find if they meant to continue with
the dump plans. Shell confirmed that explosive charges were set.

[. . .]

4pm: The Mirror quizzed Shell over claims that a Dutch company
offered to dispose of the rig 'on shore for £19 million' – not Shell's
£46 million-plus. Sea disposal was costing around £11 million.

6pm: Shell announced its U-turn and revealed they will bow to pressure
from Greenpeace, the Mirror and the public.

(DMR 21 June)

VICTORY FOR THE PEOPLE: MIRROR COMMENT ON SHELL
DECISION NOT TO SINK BRENT SPA [*sic*]

(DMR 21 June)

Unlike the other papers, the *Mirror* rhetorically constructed an active role for
its readers, a sense of participation, by characterising Shell's change of mind
as a result of 'people power' (DMR 22 June and 27 June), by inscribing its
readers into the same general 'battle' language used for describing the
conflict between Shell and Greenpeace,[7] by referencing its readers with the
active battle metaphor 'the Mirror's army of readers', by constructing
relationships between Greenpeace and its readers (Greenpeace was quoted as
thanking the *Mirror*'s readers for their support – DMR 22 June), and by
addressing its readers directly using the personal pronoun 'you' (e.g. '£700M:
YOU SHELL OUT TO CLEAN UP 200 RIGS: YOU'LL PAY £700M FOR
OIL FIASCO' DMR 22 June).

Public arenas and source power

While many sources and voices contribute to the claims-making process
which helps give some environmental issues visibility and prominence in
public arenas like the mass media, it is also clear from a long tradition of
studies in the sociology of news, that access to the media is highly
selective, unequal and hierarchical. In an early formulation, Hall (1975)
thus argued that the mass media and other key institutions 'contribute to
the development and maintenance of hegemonic domination [. . .] They
"connect" the centres of power with the dispersed publics: they mediate
the public discourse between elites and the governed. Thus they become,

pivotally, the site and terrain on which the making and shaping of consent is exercised, and, to some degree, contested' (Hall, 1975: 142). Like numerous news studies demonstrating the distinctive 'authority orientation' (Ericson et al., 1989) of news media and the privileged and 'habitual access' (Molotch and Lester, 1974) given to powerful institutions, Hall and his colleagues argued that the practical pressures of news work combined with the key journalistic professional demands of 'impartiality and objectivity' to 'produce a systematically structured over-accessing to the media of those in powerful and privileged institutional positions' (Hall et al., 1978: 58).

While early and now classic studies of news coverage of demonstrations, movements and protest largely confirmed the marginalisation in media coverage of dissenting 'voices' as well as of resource-poor groups and interests (Halloran et al., 1970; Goldenberg, 1975; Gitlin, 1980), the 'hegemonic domination' argument and its particular notion of powerful 'primary definers' has been subjected to considerable criticism and revision in the last two decades. The relatively monolithic notion of hegemonic power articulated by Hall et al. (although itself a vast step forward in relation to earlier more simplistic Marxian notions of power and dominant ideology) has been challenged by empirical studies of sources and 'voices' in a range of types of news coverage, including environmental issues (Cottle, 1993), science and medicine/health (Hansen, 1994; Miller, 1999), crime (Schlesinger and Tumber, 1994), the voluntary sector (Deacon and Golding, 1993) and trade unions (Davis, 2002). In a seminal book published in 1990, Schlesinger (1990: 66–67) criticised the oversimplification, inherent in the primary definer thesis, of the relationship between media/media professionals and their sources for inadequately accounting for:

1. contention between official sources in trying to influence the construction of a story;
2. the well-established fact that official sources often attempt to influence the construction of a story by using 'off-the-record' briefings – in which case the primary definers do not appear directly as such, in unveiled and attributable form;
3. inequalities of access among the privileged themselves;
4. longer-term shifts in the structure of access. [. . .] The structuralist model is *atemporal*, for it tacitly assumes the permanent presence of certain forces in the power structure;
5. the model of reproduction of Hall et al. deals with the question of the media's relative autonomy from the political system in a purely

uni-directional way. The movement of definitions is *uniformly* from power centre to media.

Essentially, then, as cogently argued by Schlesinger and shown empirically by numerous studies of source–communicator relationships across a range of news categories, media access and definitional power, while certainly highly selective and indeed circumscribed by available economic and cultural resources, cannot be reduced to a simple classification into powerful elites/institutions with privileged access versus resource-poor individuals and groups marginalised by or excluded from the public arena of the mass media. In terms of the construction of environmental news and environmental issues as social problems, perhaps the main insight derived from Schlesinger's critique and from studies of environmental news is the highly dynamic and fluid nature of the claims-making process, and of the media's position therein.

We are thus far removed from Hall's notion of powerful institutions and elites acting in relative unison, and instead much closer to notions of a complex – and most of all fluid and constantly changing – system where claims, in Hegelian dialectical fashion, inevitably generate counter-claims, which then synthesise into new claims, provoking new counter-claims and so on and so forth. In this dialectical process, new fissures constantly open up within the powerful elites and new alliances are continuously formed, just as new and innovative ways of framing claims – making them resonate with cultural climates of opinion – and adjustments to ideological and rhetorical shifts are made. However, it remains important not to equate a more dynamic and complex view of the source–media relations or of the claims-making process with a pluralist view that loses sight of the significant structural constraints – including economic and cultural resources – by which they are circumscribed.

Exercise 3.1

Contested claims-making/competing claims-makers

There is considerable research evidence to suggest that the news media tend predominantly to turn to and to give privileged access to 'authoritative' and powerful sources in society. Likewise, there is much research evidence (see also further on in this chapter) to show that pressure groups have mixed success when it comes to 'being heard' by the news media. However, even at the relatively simple level of analysing *who* is quoted or referred to and *how often* the picture may vary considerably from issue to issue, and as always, such patterns may change over time.

Consider the following abstract summarising a study of news sources in debate about genetic modification in agriculture:

> Biotechnology research and application has become a controversial social issue; social movement organisations and leaders emerge as the primary voice for public support or protest. However, news theories suggest that the news is primarily presented through established routine agencies, primarily government sources. As such, these theories would suggest that social movement organisations opposing genetic engineering in agriculture would have limited success in presenting their claims through established mainstream media. Through content analysis of 250 randomly selected Illinois newspapers, whose circulation is 40,000 or more, and television sources, the authors found that social movement organisations had considerable success in having their claims presented. Ideological position of the organisation appears to be less important than the bureaucratic credentials of the main spokesperson in terms of success of gaining coverage.
>
> (Reisner and Soult, 2007)

Identify – for example, by searching the online news archives of selected newspapers or broadcast organisations – a selection of news items about genetically modified crops or genetic modification in agriculture and food production.

Who are the key claims-makers/sources quoted or referred to?

Do environmental pressure groups, individual farmers, 'ordinary' consumers, etc. 'get heard'? And if so, are their statements or accounts given similar prominence to more authoritative sources, such as politicians, representatives of biotechnology companies, independent scientists, etc.?

Finally, are there any examples of news media highlighting disagreement or clashes within different categories of sources (e.g. different pressure groups disagreeing with each other, scientists disagreeing with each other, major biotechnology businesses disagreeing with each other)?

While the claims-makers who often on the surface appear to be most directly and visibly engaged in attempts at managing and influencing media coverage of environmental issues are perhaps environmental pressure groups, there is a growing body of evidence showing that government, industry, business, research institutions, and professional associations all increasingly engage in the provision, packaging and management of news. Two areas which have been particularly well documented in the last two decades are those of government news management and political spin generally, and the increasing use of public relations (PR) by a wide range of not just traditionally powerful and resource-rich elites but also by 'outsider' and resource-poor campaigning groups (Davis, 2003). Davis (2003) points to the significant growth in the use of professional PR practices across the board in what he refers to as 'the new public relations democracy' (p. 40) while also drawing attention to the seemingly contradictory trends which have characterised this development:

> Certain powerful sources are using PR to secure their long-term favourable media relations in sections of the national media. At the same time, however, 'resource-poor' and 'outsider' sources have also used public relations to gain more frequent and favourable coverage.
>
> (Davis, 2003: 40)

In his survey of PR and its implications for source–media relations, Davis (2003) argues, resonant with the 'primary definer' criticism delineated above,

> [t]hat there is not a simple balance sheet that links media access (or appearances) with favourable media coverage. One cannot simply tally up government, corporate and other source levels of access in order to ascertain who is being more favoured by the media. For example, non-appearance and little obvious media access may be the intention of the source. Frequent appearances in the media are equally likely to be instigated by rival sources and journalists, and can often result in poor media relations and unfavourable coverage. Media access by certain sources is often utilised for the benefit of others. Research on public relations therefore reveals that media-source relations are rather more complex than previous work on sources and news production has assumed. Just as those relations are more complex, so too are the benefits brought by PR to sources. (p. 40).

In the following we shall examine in more detail how various sources/claims-makers seek to influence and use the media in their 'construction' of environmental issues as issues for political and social concern. But first it is necessary to emphasise that while the term 'pressure group' appropriately alludes to a deliberate and active approach to influencing and managing public and media discourse, it would be mistaken to assume that all other sources/claims-makers are either simply passive targets for enquiring journalists or indeed necessarily any less calculating, scheming or potentially manipulative in their approach to news media and public discourse.

Claims-making and media visibility

It is tempting to assume that attaining public visibility through media coverage and publicity is the single most important objective for claims-makers in general, and for pressure groups or issue advocates in particular. After all, much media and public opinion research has echoed the notion that 'if you don't exist in the media, you don't exist' (a reference attributed to American journalist Daniel Schorr in Wallack et al., 1999: ix). And it does not merely apply to news coverage and news media. Prominent American communications researcher George Gerbner poignantly refers to absence from media coverage as a form of 'symbolic annihilation', a notion which has also been widely used in the prominent strand of communication research known as cultivation analysis (Gerbner et al., 1986). Cultivation analysis is based around the notion that the media are the important 'story-tellers', fictional and factual, of our time, continuously supplying us with a wealth of morality tales about who exists, who is important, who wields power over whom, what is right and wrong, what is acceptable, etc.

While these arguments are indeed persuasive and 'fit' very well with a constructionist perspective's emphasis on the crucial importance of claims-making – including not least claims-making in public arenas such as the media – it is, however, also necessary to remind ourselves (as discussed in Chapter 2 with reference to Edelman, 1988), that the careful *management* of publicity – including outright suppression of certain arguments, claims, issues – may be strategically more effective than an all-out endeavour to achieve media and wider publicity for publicity's sake. Wallack et al. (1999) tellingly refer to this in a book, *News for a Change*, otherwise devoted to strategies for influencing and managing media publicity:

> A while ago, I was completing a presentation on media advocacy when someone from the audience asked, "But if we get a lot of attention in the media, won't it just mobilize the opposition?" I was very surprised. The question seemed to suggest that remaining invisible was a desirable strategy. I realized that it wasn't the first time I had heard this question, although this was the clearest that it had ever been stated. It seems that for some advocates, being invisible and not drawing attention to their issue is seen as a kind of strategy; they avoid controversy and make only tentative requests for change.
>
> Many others, however, know that power and visibility are important to amplify concerns and advance effective approaches. They know that reticence and invisibility are the problem, not the solution.
>
> (Wallack et al., 1999: ix)

Widespread publicity may, in other words, have a negative influence on a group's or claims-maker's objectives, particularly if the main effect is to galvanize opposition. As Ibarra and Kitsuse (1993) (discussed in the previous chapter) indicate, every claim generates a counter-rhetoric or counter-claim. It is, however, the 'power-framework' delineated by Lukes (1974), Edelman (1988) and others which provides the main corrective or qualification to the constructionist perspective's unfettered emphasis on claims-making, namely by stressing that the ability to keep claims and issues *off* the public agenda is just as significant, if not more, an exercise of power as the ability to successfully place claims and issues on the public agenda or in public view.

A related 'side effect' of pressure group claims-making is the extent to which (again in the fashion of Ibarra and Kitsuse's argument that every claim generates a counter-claim) it prompts a sharpening of opponents' publicity practices. As Signitzer and Prexl (2007), in their analysis of *greenwashing*, point out, activism pressure often tends to stimulate in corporate organisations what PR theorists call 'an excellent public relations function' (Grunig et al., 2002), a redoubling of corporate PR efforts to pre-empt, counter, engage with, accommodate, undermine, frame, etc. the arguments and claims of pressure groups. Again, Greenpeace's Brent Spar campaign against Shell illustrates this point, in the sense that it prompted Shell into re-thinking its PR strategy.

In terms of understanding how different claims-makers and pressure groups adopt different approaches to media, government and publicity, Grant (2000), in his useful analysis of pressure groups, offers a helpful distinction between *insider* groups and *outsider* groups:

> Insider groups are regarded as legitimate by government and are consulted on a regular basis. Outsider groups either do not wish to become enmeshed in a consultative relationship with officials, or are unable to gain recognition. Another way of looking at them is to see them as protest groups which have objectives that are outside the mainstream of political opinion. They then have to adopt campaigning methods designed to demonstrate that they have a solid basis of popular support, although some of the methods used by the more extreme groups may alienate potential supporters.
>
> (Grant, 2000: 19)

This distinction is useful, not so much for a categorical taxonomy of pressure groups, but for understanding how pressure groups – even within the same general domain or issue area, such as 'the environment' – may adopt widely different approaches to government, the institutions of formal politics, and the media. It is perhaps most useful to see the insider/outsider distinction as not so much a categorical either/or classification, but rather as a continuum, where different pressure groups position themselves at various points, changing over time, between the insider and outsider extremes. Some groups, recognised as legitimate and credible by government, may work most efficiently and effectively behind closed doors, that is, away from the gaze of the media and other public arenas, through the mechanisms of formal political lobbying and institutional processes. Others, like Friends of the Earth for example, may be formally involved in government consultation processes – and be publicly 'seen' to be involved – on some issues, while, on others, it may be crucial to their publicity strategy to be, and to be seen to be, completely separate from and outside of any process of consultation with government. And others still, most notably Greenpeace, will staunchly maintain an outsider position and strategy, based crucially on a critical (of government and formal institutional politics in particular) and independent stance, 'unsoiled' by any hint of collaboration with or co-option by the powers that be.

In terms of media and publicity strategies then, and simply put, insider groups are distinctly publicity-shy, seek to avoid media coverage and publicity, and indeed depend largely for their effectiveness on staying out of the public limelight, on remaining as publicly invisible as possible. Outsider groups, on the other hand, depend – in the absence of formal or direct channels of communication with government and political decision-making processes – entirely on the mass media, on their ability to gain and maintain in the media and other public arenas, a high profile both for themselves and for the issues on which they campaign. Outsider groups depend on media and related public publicity principally for two reasons: (1) public visibility – and crucially, legitimacy – to help recruit members and financial support for the group's campaigning activities; and (2) as the main channel for achieving public and political attention and action regarding the issues on which pressure groups campaign (e.g. Cracknell, 1993; Deegan, 2001; Smith and Ferguson, 2001).

It is the strategies of these outsider claims-makers or groups – particularly vis-à-vis the media – that we shall examine in more detail in the following.

Outsider environmental pressure groups and the media

Environmental pressure groups are possibly best known for their ability to make news through spectacular stunts or demonstrations, the most visible aspect of their activities. Indeed, prominent groups such as Greenpeace have traditionally been seen as masters of the art of creating visually appealing news events backed by dramatic film footage made readily available to interested media. But the newsworthiness of environmental pressure groups would soon wear off if they had to rely solely on their creation of spectacular protest 'performances'. Actions such as sailing in small dinghies in front of the harpoons of industrial whaling ships, or sailing underneath the barrels of toxic waste being dropped from large cargo ships, or blocking waste pipes discharging noxious chemicals into the sea are of course eminently newsworthy and visually striking, but they are not sufficient for remaining on the media agenda or for maintaining media visibility in the long term.

One of the main reasons why 'successful' pressure groups have been able to sustain their media coverage is to do with the fact that the major part of their work consists of gathering intelligence about – and drawing the media's attention to – environmental issues which are already being discussed in the forums which the media regularly report on. The most notable and newsworthy of these forums is of course the political forum – the forum of parliamentary and governmental activity.

Theatrical stunts and visually daring protest action of course have inherent newsworthiness, but such actions cannot in themselves explain the long-lasting and sustained accessing of successful pressure groups in media coverage. Nor can such access be explained by additional arguments concerning the skills of such groups in catering to the needs of media organisations in terms of news cycles, provision of sources, provision of visual material, exploitation of deadlines, etc. These aspects are important, but sustained success as a claims-maker and in terms of getting media coverage requires more. Particularly important is the ability to link to or latch onto developments, events and (important) people in existing established and legitimate news forums.

Most of the issues on which successful pressure groups campaign and successfully gain media coverage are issues which already have an institutional forum rather than completely new issues which have not been problematised in some form or other before. Success as a claims-maker is thus partly explained by the careful timing of press releases and publication of reports to coincide with (or often, slightly precede): political events (e.g. debates in Parliament; the publication of government papers/reports); international meetings and conferences (e.g. the World Trade Organization (WTO) talks; World Monetary Fund meetings; the annual meetings of the most powerful economic powers); treaty renewals (e.g. the Antarctic Treaty Nations; the treaty on whaling through the International Whaling Commission; the nuclear test-ban treaty); industry or public authority announcements (e.g. announcements of nuclear industry decisions concerning suitable sites for storage of low-level radioactive waste); the publication of independent scientific reports (Hansen, 1993).

In this respect, effectiveness as a claims-maker arises from the exposure of agenda items which are part of the routine and legitimate forums of politics, government, public authorities, international politics, etc.; but while they are routine forums for media attention, it is the claims-making activity of pressure groups which helps direct the attention of the mass media to aspects and interpretations which might otherwise have gone unnoticed or might have been deliberately glossed over. Pressure group claims-making activity then is often at its most effective, not so much in terms of constructing entirely new problems for social and political attention, but in terms of framing and elaborating environmental dimensions which are already in the public domain as issues or problems.

At one level this is a simple process of gaining coverage by attacking or making claims about people, institutions and forums which are already by themselves newsworthy and the focus of routine interest. At a more complex level, it points to the importance of pressure group 'work' as intelligence gathering and surveillance of developments in environmental policy-making and decision-making. Eyerman and Jamison (1989: 113) aptly refer to this important component of pressure group work as the 'transformation of knowledge into an organisational weapon'. Continuous monitoring (surveillance) of developments in key political decision-making forums and strategic information gathering, followed by strategic framing and dissemination of information are among the core tasks for 'successful' claims-making, without which spectacular protest actions and demonstrations would soon cease to command the attention of the public media. Although not referring to this as 'framing', Eyerman and Jamison's formulation expresses essentially exactly that:

> [i]t is the selective gathering of campaign-related facts, the selective dissemination of arguments to the media and other public fora, the

> selective testimony at hearings and conferences and international
> meetings that gives Greenpeace its enormous influence.
>
> (Eyerman and Jamison, 1989: 113)

Journalists, even specialist journalists (science, environment, health, medical, consumer affairs, agriculture journalists), could not hope to even begin to monitor systematically the wide range of institutions, industries, bodies, political forums, etc. involved in decision-making about environmental issues. This requires an organisation or organisations with expertise and resources for precisely such a task. Seen from this perspective, it is perhaps not surprising that successful pressure groups often enjoy a great deal of rapport with journalists. In many respects, they help make the journalists' task easier by offering 'information subsidies' (Gandy, 1982) and perhaps easily digestible interpretations or commentaries on what are often highly complex political processes involving complex scientific, economic or other research and data.

Kielbowicz and Scherer (1986: 87) note the importance to media coverage of 'having identifiable leaders authorised to speak for a large following; they seem authoritative, like the head of a large business or government agency'. However, a focus on high-profile, charismatic or celebrity-type leaders or personalities within a pressure group can also backfire. Gitlin (1980), in his analysis of the American student movement of the 1960s, for example, observed how media coverage increasingly centred on personality clashes and internal schisms within the movement, while losing sight of the key issues promoted by the movement. Greenpeace is particularly interesting for its general and comparative success in deflecting media attention away from itself as a pressure group and away from personalities within the group, while succeeding (generally – but, as we saw above under Box 3.1 in relation to the *Telegraph's* coverage of Greenpeace during the Brent Spar controversy, not always) in focusing the media's attention on the issues at hand. This is partly achieved through a highly de-centralised structure, where local/regional issues are generally campaigned upon and addressed by local/regional campaigners and spokespersons, which in turn contributes to the organisation's credibility within the local/regional communities immediately affected by the issues campaigned upon (see also Hansen, 1993).

An interesting variant type of claims-making is the form where a pressure group is actively *used* by other forums or institutions (or individuals within such institutions) for leaking information and bringing it to the attention of the media. In such instances, the pressure group becomes a conduit or a vehicle for disseminating information, a role which in itself confers legitimacy and prestige on the pressure group.

The more common practice, however, is for a pressure group to attach itself to – and, more importantly, to *frame* – developments in other institutional forums by producing 'evidence' or 'information' which carefully targets a particular aspect of such developments. The evidence generally takes the form of opinion polls, surveys, scientific analyses or studies commissioned by the pressure group, but as Eyerman and Jamison (1989) have pointed out, this is not principally a question of educating the public or producing knowledge or science for the people; rather, it is a question of producing knowledge and information which can be used strategically in public arena debates.

Like advertisers and PR professionals, successful pressure groups are knowledgeable about the different organisational values, editorial policies, news requirements, political orientation, and – perhaps most importantly – target audiences of different media. Instead of a blunderbuss or shotgun approach to the media, successful groups normally adopt a highly targeted approach, carefully 'packaging' their information and campaigning to suit the particular needs of selected media (Lacey and Longman, 1993). In this respect, they may also seek to cultivate good relationships with selected journalists, who in return for good and fair reporting may be given privileged access to and insights into upcoming campaigns. The careful differentiation of course also caters to the very different visual and textual requirements of television versus radio/print media.

Environmental pressure groups are generally more successful in drawing media attention to particular environmental issues, than in gaining coverage for their own definitions of such issues. The mass media are notoriously authority oriented. Thus studies of environmental media coverage have virtually without exception shown that the sources who get to be quoted in media coverage and who get to define environmental issues are – as in most other types of news – predominantly those of public authorities, government representatives, industry and business, and independent scientists. Environmental pressure groups are far less prominent as quoted sources in media coverage (Greenberg et al., 1989; McGeachy, 1989; Hansen, 1990; Hornig et al., 1991; Trumbo, 1996).

Studies of actors and primary definers appearing in actual media coverage indicate that while environmental groups may be important as initiators or catalysts of public debate or controversy, and subsequent media coverage, they do not, on the whole, command a prominent role in terms of the definitions which are elaborated and contested in the media arena.

While an environmental pressure group such as Greenpeace has generally demonstrated an impressive capacity for securing media coverage for its claims, its capacity to control the way its claims have been framed and inflected by individual media is more doubtful.

Individual media thus exercise a considerable amount of 'ideological work', not merely in terms of the differential accessing of sources and selective prominence (e.g. through headlining) given to particular sources, but perhaps more significantly, through their differential choice and promotion of particular lexical terms (e.g. Greenpeace as 'terrorists', 'a nuisance', 'undemocratic'), particular discourses (e.g. law and order, democracy, science), and, consequently, particular frames.

It is perhaps particularly telling of the limits to pressure group influence on media coverage that the above analysis (Hansen, 2000) of media coverage of Greenpeace's campaign against Shell over the Brent Spar – a campaign that has generally been celebrated as prime example of successful pressure group action – found the basic 'framing' of Greenpeace's action (in terms of its 'legitimacy' and 'credibility') to have changed little, if at all, during the course of the campaign:

> [T]he core frames, characteristic of each individual newspaper's coverage, did not emerge gradually over the period of coverage or as a particular response to developments in the controversy [. . .], but were in place from the outset, indicating the limits to claims-maker influence. While successfully 'commanding attention', Greenpeace had much less uniform success with the second key task (Solesbury 1976) in the claims-making process, that of claiming or securing legitimacy.
>
> (Hansen, 2000: 71)

Box 3.2

Claims-maker tasks and news management strategies

Three key tasks for claims-makers in the construction of social problems (Solesbury, 1976):

1. Commanding attention
2. Claiming legitimacy
3. Invoking action

News management strategies of pressure groups and other claims-makers:

- Newsworthiness of publicity stunts and demonstrations; but much more is needed for sustaining coverage in the longer term: for example, intelligence gathering and surveillance.
- Exploiting knowledge of media routines, news values, news cycles, journalistic and editorial preferences, economic pressures on media.
- Selective targeting of media outlets, exploiting news competition between media, knowledge of audience profiles for different media, and enhancing control over framing of coverage.
- Organisational and spokesperson arrangements designed to deflect media interest away from personalities and personality clashes within pressure groups, and to keep media attention focused on the campaign or issue at hand.
- Most pressure/campaign issues are already part of newsworthy institutional forums.
- Careful *timing* of press releases and commissioned reports in relation to:
  - Planned or scheduled political events.
  - International meetings and negotiations.
  - Treaty renewals (and similar 'diary items').
  - Industry, business and public authority announcements.
- *Framing* of items which might otherwise have gone unnoticed:
  - Attacking newsworthy people, organisations or institutions.
  - Surveillance of policy-making.
- Helping or '*information subsidising*' the under-resourced journalist and media:
  - Selective spot-lighting of policy or negotiations.
  - Provision of 'ready-made', visually attractive, news footage and commentary.
  - *Framing* through commissioned research which targets developments in other institutional forums.
  - *Alliance* with research/science/academia.
- Issue campaigners and pressure groups are often more successful in drawing attention to broad issues than in promoting their own definitions.

Globalisation, activism and old/new media

Environmental activists and claims-makers have a long and distinguished history of making innovative use of public arenas and associated media technologies. Necessity – limited resources, limited access to mainstream news media, limited access to political decision-makers, etc. – has to a large extent been the mother of invention in this respect. Pressure groups like Greenpeace and Friends of the Earth understood from a very early stage the essential role of visuals (including in the form of the age-old tradition of 'bearing witness') and spectacle (public protest taking the form of symbolic performances) as keys to gaining mainstream media visibility and coverage (see also Rose, 2005 and Doyle, 2007, on the centrality of visualisation in pressure group campaigning). Like their much more powerful counterparts in government and public organisations/institutions, successful environmental pressure groups have been skilled in providing, what Gandy (1982) refers to as 'information subsidies' to media news professionals and organisations short of both time and resources.

As new media technologies have become available to wider publics, environmental pressure groups have been quick to adopt and adapt them for their campaigning strategies, including for both external and internal (within pressure group organisations) communication purposes. Fax machines, video recorders and video cameras were quickly pressed into service as long ago as the 1980s. VNRs or Video-News-Releases became an important way to provide resource-strapped media organisations, hungry for visual material to fill the rapidly expanding number of news programmes and news channels in the late 1980s, with news material. It is, however, also important to note the limitations of VNRs for campaigning purposes, as they are often met with a natural professional resistance and scepticism on the part of journalists, editors and other media professionals, who are wary of being seen to be manipulated or being seen to be merely conduits for pressure group 'propaganda' (Hansen, 1994; Hansen and Linne, 1994; Rose, 1998; Manning, 2001).

Email, portable satellite communication equipment capable of virtually instantaneous transmission of evolving 'news events' (including pressure group protest 'performances') and, more recently within the last 10–15 years, the exponential growth of the internet and mobile phone technology have likewise been highly enabling technologies quickly adopted by and incorporated into the communication strategies of environmental pressure groups.

Perhaps one of the main attractions of the internet for environmental pressure groups and claims-makers is the prospect of altogether by-passing traditional news organisations and news media, instantly overcoming all the associated difficulties of gaining access and of controlling/managing the framing of campaign messages. Combined with developments in visual recording technology, the World Wide Web facilitated an unbroken chain of control – by activists themselves – over the orchestration of protest and public performance, the recording and 'packaging' or framing of protest, and the communication to potential 'masses' or wider publics of such news/campaign messages.

Exercise 3.2

Measuring pressure group influence on mainstream news media

Identify a recent pressure group campaign, demonstration or similar protest event, that received some coverage in a selection of mainstream news media (e.g. in major newspapers available in either electronic full-text data archives or through their own online webpages, or major online news of broadcast organisations such as the BBC (http://news.bbc.co.uk). Compare this coverage with the pressure group's own publicity and accounts of the action on its own website or through material placed by the pressure group on You Tube (http://www.youtube.com) or other websites.

Is the overall 'message' of the mainstream media coverage similar to or significantly different from the 'message' conveyed by the pressure group's own communications?

In order to address this question, focus, for example, on some or all of the following questions:

Are there recognisable visual or verbal sequences in the mainstream news coverage that clearly originate from the pressure group's own communications?

What particular aspects do the mainstream news media select and focus on in their coverage? – Are these emphases different from those of the pressure group's own communications?

Who (e.g. scientists) or what (e.g. published research) is quoted or referred to as 'authoritative' sources in the mainstream news and in the pressure group's communications?

What is the balance in media coverage and in pressure group communications between a focus on events (e.g. clashes with the police or other authorities, damage to property) and a focus on issues (e.g. pollution, energy policy, climate change)?

Are there marked similarities or differences in the types of words (e.g. adjectives, metaphors, etc.) that are used?

Are there marked similarities or differences in the visuals that are used (e.g. photographic angles and frames)?

Your answers will give some idea of the extent to which pressure groups can manipulate or influence mainstream news media coverage, and they will give an indication of whether the pressure group can be said to have successfully communicated its message to/through the mainstream news media.

The innovative use of the internet by the Mexican separatist movement the Zapatistas in the province of Chiapas for waging 'symbolic guerrilla warfare' has become a celebrated case among activists and academics alike (see e.g. Castells, 2004). Likewise, the convergence of disparate protest groups around anti-globalisation notably in Seattle in November 1999, has prompted both research and reflections on the role played by new communications technologies, and the internet in particular, for rapid information exchange and news framing detached from the central control of mainstream media and political authority, and for organising and orchestrating disparate protest groups into coordinated action (DeLuca and Peeples, 2002; Wall, 2002; Cottle, 2006).

Away from the glare of rousing enthusiasm about the vast (democratic) possibilities of the internet and related new communication technologies – much of which is little more than a repetition of the enthusiastic fanfare of hopes for a democratisation of communication with which every new communications technology has historically always been greeted – a growing body of research on the use of new media by social movement organisations, pressure groups and indeed claims-makers in general has shown a rather more nuanced – and indeed much less sweepingly enthusiastic – picture of the potential or actual role of new information and communication technologies (ICTs).

Euphoric notions about the implications of the internet's collapsing of 'space' and 'time' (i.e. virtually unhindered instantaneous communications access across geographical, national, cultural and political boundaries and divides) for movement and pressure group mobilisation have been tempered by the persistence of a 'digital divide' – that is, imbalances and inequalities in access to new ICTs – along traditional demographic and geo-political lines, and by research evidence showing a less-than-wholesale change in movement strategies related to new ICTs. Movement and pressure group adaptation of new ICTs, circumscribed by traditional geographical and cultural parameters, has been gradual and seen generally as an add-on rather than a replacement in relation to older media and communication strategies. Thus, Gillan and Pickerill (2008), in a detailed comparative analysis of anti-war activism in Australia, Britain and the United States after 9/11, find confirmation for Tarrow's (2005) notion of 'rooted cosmopolitanism' – a primary commitment to locally contextualised action combined with a desire for transnational support (Gillan and Pickerill, 2008: 59). Their analysis shows that the use of ICTs is less about practical coordination, organisation, mobilisation and consolidation of protest action or of coalitions across borders, and much more about information exchange and about 'symbolic expressions of solidarity' (p. 75):

> 'Being global' is less about building formal connections between international groups and far more about re-scaling the meaning of local actions to a global audience. This is achieved primarily by articulating a form of imagined solidarity, while simultaneously maintaining the importance of domestic issues.
>
> [. . .] although concrete action remains predominantly affixed to place and to the political context of the nation, Internet connections help activists locate their action within much broader movements. In so far as anti-war web sites link to a wide range of world-views they enable the construction of imagined solidarity. The value of informational linkages does not, therefore, lie in their potential for enabling more formal alliances between organisations (pace Diani 2001). Rather, we find that because the sharing of information across borders allows activists to gain a sense of solidarity, Internet networks help the rooted cosmopolitan to feel global.
>
> (Gillan and Pickerill, 2008: 76)

In more general terms, studies of new ICTs, political action and pressure groups have found that new media have been incorporated as additional and complementary means of communication, rather than replacing more traditional forms (Pickerill, 2003; Lax, 2004; Kavada, 2005). Kavada (2005) in a comprehensive analysis of internet use by Oxfam, Amnesty International and the World Development Movement thus concludes that 'the internet is used more as an extension of the offline media rather than as an autonomous medium with its own strategy and techniques. This is the case for all the examined websites and is particularly obvious in the functions of participation and campaigning' (p. 218). Findings such as these help put initial euphoric statements and hopes regarding the implications of the internet for pressure groups into perspective. At the same time they provide a window on the exciting opportunities afforded. More significantly perhaps studies such as those just mentioned point to the imperative of exploiting new ICTs, particularly when considering that pressure groups of course are far from being the only claims-makers to incorporate new ICTs in their campaigning strategies (see the discussion below about corporate image strategies).

Stephen Lax similarly summarises some of the evidence relating to campaigning groups, such as Greenpeace and Amnesty International, as follows:

Established campaigning groups can use ICTs to great benefit for their internal organisational functions, in the same way that the intranets are used by most businesses and public organisations – including political parties (Gibson and Ward, 1999). The promotion of ICTs by groups like GreenNet and trades unionists for campaigning organisations is testimony to the importance of these technologies as a relatively low-cost means of information exchange (Herman and Holly, 2001). There is less evidence, however, to suggest that new ICTs offer unique qualitative advantages for campaigning purposes over other methods and technologies, or that they are spawning mass protest movements. Traditional campaigning techniques such as gaining media coverage (Jordan, 1998[b]), sending mailshots, and political lobbying continue, and 'old' technologies such as telephones and fax machines are equally more important than ever before to the running of an effective campaign.

(Lax, 2004: 223–24)

Box 3.3

Hyper-linking, framing and debate management on the internet

In an interesting early study of how government organisations, business and campaign organisations use the internet, Rogers and Marres (2000) focus on what can be learnt from how these various claims-makers in the climate-change debate hyper-link and how hyper-linking is used strategically as part of the construction and management of public debate. With a series of linking maps showing the connections/links between .GOVs, .COMs and .ORGs involved in the climate-change debate, Rogers and Marres demonstrate that (1) the organisations analysed have distinctive linking styles; (2) 'organisations take care in making hyperlinks, leading to the premise that the hyperlinks (and the "missing links") reveal which issue and debate framings organisations acknowledge, and find acceptable and unacceptable' (p. 141); and (3) as well as using websites to set out their own stance and argument on climate change, they engage – including via linking – with the positions/arguments of (carefully selected) other organisations. The latter of course is central to the appearance of 'reasoned' and rational debate (as opposed to total exclusion of other organisations' arguments, which would give the impression of propaganda or censorship).

Figure 3.1 (from Rogers and Marres, 2000: 156) thus focuses on linking between major companies and environmental organisations involved in the climate-change debate. Of particular interest here is the finding that key oil companies like Shell and BP link to the World Wide Fund for Nature (WWF)

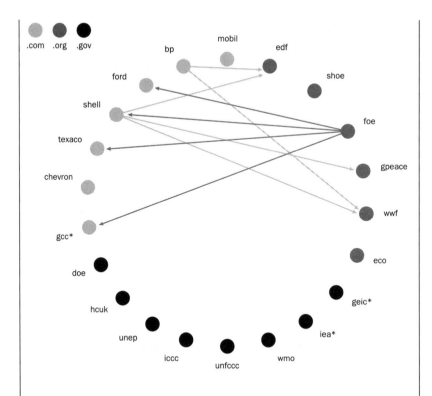

Figure 3.1 *Rogers and Marres's (2000) hyperlink map of actors in the climate-change debate.*

and, in the case of Shell, to Greenpeace, while neither Greenpeace nor WWF link to any of the companies. Friends of the Earth (FoE), by contrast, links to no less than four companies, including key 'adversaries' – in the climate-change debate – like Ford and Shell.

Rogers and Marres (2000: 156–57) conclude as follows:

> Broadly speaking, hyperlinking by one organisation to another, and reciprocal hyperlinking, may be said to represent a single or common acknowledgement of meaningful participation in the debate. To link is to recognise; linking by a leading participant brings the other party into the (interlinked) circle of the debate on the web. It even makes the party into a participant, from its point of view, and subsequently the surfer's. Similarly, non-linking is a sign of non-recognition, or, more radically, is an act of silencing through inaction. (Greenpeace does not link to Shell, but Shell links to Greenpeace.) Using the debate-scaping technique as a 'tool for thought', one notes the seeming eagerness with which the ostensibly less powerful parties link, while more powerful

largely do not. The more powerful don't feel the need to acknowledge further discursive activity and participation.

A hyperlink debate map may be said to reveal the extent to which organisations recognise others as meaningful participants, and is generally useful for participants, journalists and debate rapporteurs.

The use of new ICTs, including the internet perhaps in particular, then opens up a wide range of new possibilities at a variety of levels, all of which are characterised by the key new ICT features of time/space compression and comparatively low cost: (a) internal organisation, management and communication; (b) protest and action planning and coordination; (c) communication with members as well as recruitment of new members; (d) campaigning and discursive/rhetorical 'sparring' in the public sphere of the internet; (e) campaigning and identity building, including the framing and boundary drawing that is associated with website design, messaging, linking practices (see Box 3.3).

Box 3.4

Using the internet for countering media and public claims: example: Monsanto

The agricultural company Monsanto website (www.monsanto.com/default.asp) has an 'Issues: for the record' rubric, that appears – as the heading implies – to be aimed at engaging with or countering public claims made about Monsanto and its products. The text and links of one of the items listed under the 'Issues: for the record' rubric are reproduced in full below to illustrate both the engagement with claims-making on the internet ('If you search the internet for Monsanto, you will likely come across claims. . .') and the rhetorical and linking strategy ('Don't take our word for it; click on the links below. . .') deployed to counter the claims made against Monsanto. Notice in particular the combination of social science research evidence, testimonies from Indian farmers and linking to news media reports (i.e. the *Guardian* newspaper):

'Farmer Suicides in India – Is There a Connection with Bt Cotton?'

If you search the internet for Monsanto, you will likely come across claims that failure of our Bollgard cotton seed products has caused many farmers in

India to take their own lives. Not everything you see or read on the internet is fact and this is a good example.

The reality is that the tragic phenomena of farmer suicides in India began long before the introduction of Bollgard in 2002. Farmer suicide has numerous causes with most experts agreeing that indebtedness is one of the main factors. Farmers unable to repay loans and facing spiralling interest often see suicide as the only solution.

In fact, a 2004 survey of cotton farmers in India by Indian Market Research Bureau International (www.thehindubusinessline.com/bline/2005/04/07/stories/2005040701600700.htm) showed a 118 per cent increase in profit for farmers planting Bollgard over traditional cotton. The same survey showed a 64 per cent increase in yield and a 25 per cent reduction in pesticide costs.

Farmers are Monsanto's customers, and we are successful only if our customers are successful. Farmers in India have found success with Bollgard. We have many repeat customers and many new ones there every year.

Don't take our word for it; visit the links below to hear farmers in India talk about Bollgard and their success.

Conversations about biotechnology – Indian farmers (www.monsanto. com/biotech-gmo/asp/country.asp?cname=India)

More information on these topics

- International Food Policy Research Institute discussion paper: Bt Cotton and Farmer Suicides in India – Reviewing the Evidence (October 2008). (www.ifpri.org/)
- The Guardian (UK): Indian Farmer Suicides not GM Related, Says Study (5 November 2008). (www.guardian.co.uk/environment/2008/nov/05/gmcrops-india)
- Indira Gandhi Institute of Development Research Study: Suicide of Farmers in Maharashtra. (www.igidr.ac.in/suicide/ExecutiveSummary_SFM_IGIDR_26Jan06.pdf)
- Indian Institute of Management – The Adoption and Economics of Bt Cotton in India: Preliminary Results from a Study. (www.iimahd.ernet. in/publications/data/2006-09-04_vgandhi.pdf)

> (from: www.monsanto.com/monsanto_today/for_the_record/
> india_farmer_suicides.asp; accessed 1 May 2009).

From a traditional media and communications perspective, perhaps the single major implication of new ICTs for the public construction of the environment as a social problem is the twin emergence and mass proliferation of sources of information about the environment combined with the concomitant erosion, if not disintegration, of control over news and information about the environment, environmental problems, environmental damage – and the associated public assignment of responsibility – and environmental protest. Cox (2006) points to the growth since the early 1990s in 'online environmental news services' offering a vast and rapidly growing amount of 'independent' environmental news from across the globe. Cox goes on to conclude that:

> In many ways, alternative media – Internet services such as the Environmental News Service, other Web sites, and blogs – are challenging conventional media theory about such topics as political economy and the gatekeeper function. With the unlimited availability and interconnectivity of Internet sites, scholars will need to rethink who – if anyone – controls access to news and information and what determines newsworthiness.
>
> (Cox, 2006: 195)

As argued above, much of the evidence so far on the implications of the internet for environmental and comparable movements points perhaps to less sweeping changes than implied by Cox in the above quote. It remains, however, that we need to know a great deal more about how the proliferation and diversification of information, the ease of finding/accessing information, and the concomitant erosion of control over news, images and information about environmental issues and environmental controversy affect the public sphere construction of the environment as a social problem.

As shown earlier in this chapter, one of the hallmarks of successful environmental pressure groups is their ability to combine newsworthy eye-catching publicity stunts with careful intelligence gathering and packaging, and the ability to serve up carefully researched intelligence/information in a form that exploits the news values, journalistic routines and organisational arrangements of mainstream news organisations. In a news-gathering environment characterised by ever-tightening economic pressures, the increasing ability to gather news via the internet without ever leaving the newsroom, must clearly have major implications for how environmental correspondents and other media professionals covering the environment go about their work. We shall examine this further in the next chapter.

Another important dimension, but one that has received comparatively less attention so far, concerns the credibility implications of news and news-source proliferation on the internet. If mainstream media/news organisations, who have traditionally been seen as credible and reliable conveyors of news and have commanded a relatively high degree of trust from their audiences, are increasingly by-passed by or in direct competition with a wealth of other sources offering different accounts of events, arguments and debates, then how does this affect the way in which news is consumed and assessed by various audiences/publics? If in cyberspace every account or opinion is traded equally, then how do audiences go about determining what is credible and reliable and what isn't? But perhaps the slightly alarmist tone implicit in this question needs to be tempered by the simple observation that publics (although considerable variations across age and other demographics need to be taken into account) continue to turn to the major news media for authoritative, trustworthy and 'trusted' information and continue to exercise a healthy degree of scepticism as well as a discerning and in many cases increasingly media-literate critical approach to information, whether provided by government, pressure groups or big business.

Corporate image strategies

As indicated several times in the above discussion of environmental pressure groups and their media management and publicity strategies, such groups are of course not alone in using communication strategies as a means of influencing, framing and manipulating public awareness, opinion, discourse and action with regard to environmental matters. Far from it. Nor indeed are they necessarily the most effective, and rarely can they call on the kind of economic and political resources available to their key opponents or competitors in the sphere of public claims-making, notably big business and industrial corporations and governments. Business, industry, government and their associated institutions and representatives make use of many of the same PR and media management strategies deployed by environmental pressure groups. In doing so they are advantaged by the ability to bring far greater economic and political resources to bear in terms of campaigning and lobbying, than environmental 'outsider' groups.

While much of the most effective 'campaigning' and 'advocacy' work of governments and industry/business takes place through formal political channels, institutions and lobbying processes, PR and public 'image management' more generally have increasingly become central and crucial dimensions, not least as a response/reaction to the claims-making activities of environmental pressure groups. Many of the major environmental, scientific and health-related controversies of the past decades can thus be characterised to a large extent as discursive or rhetorical public contests/battles fought in terms – not of right or wrong, or on the grounds of scientific evidence, although science plays an important and prominent role in the construction of claims – but in terms of 'image', culturally resonant arguments, fear-tactics, 'spin', style and 'slick' campaigning.

The Anglo-Dutch oil giant Shell was taken by surprise at the impact of Greenpeace's Brent Spar campaign in 1995, surprise perhaps mainly that Greenpeace's campaign succeeded in stirring up public and political unease, and in some countries public protest actions against a company that had very carefully 'played by the book'. Shell had thus carefully gone through all the necessary scientific research and arguments, and through all the legally required processes to arrive at the course of action subsequently vehemently resisted by Greenpeace and seemingly by large sections of the public. Shell, by its own admission, recognised that it had perhaps been too focused on the science and the formal legal process, and had failed to adequately consider 'the hearts and minds' of the public (Head of Shell UK, Dr Chris Fay, interviewed in a 1995 BBC2 documentary about the Brent Spar controversy). Shell very quickly remedied its brief and intermittent lapse of concentration on the public image battle through a combination of traditional image management strategies, including PR, clever website usage (more on this in the final section of this chapter) and image advertising.

While press releases continue to be an important part of the media and public sphere strategies of business and industry, corporations are also acutely aware that mainstream news organisations – or more specifically the journalists and media professionals working in these organisations – are weary of what they tend to regard as a tiresome flood of thinly veiled promotional propaganda. Most of all, deep-seated professional criteria of objectivity and impartiality dictate that major media organisations and professional journalists have to be seen to be above giving a platform to the promotion of particular interests. But then press releases are just one of the many weapons in the arsenal of corporate image management strategies. Given their often abundant economic resources, large corporations often use image or issue advertising as a key strategy for influencing public/political opinion. Pressure groups of course do so too, but the key difference is one of available economic resources for this highly expensive strategy.

Cox (2006) refers to corporate image advertising on environmental matters as '*environmental image enhancement, the use of advertising to improve the image or identity of a corporation, reflecting its environ-mental concern or performance*' (p. 376, emphasis in original). He goes on to offer examples of a number of successful and less successful corporate image enhancement campaigns. British Petroleum's (BP) 'Man on the Street' television advertising campaign thus, according to Cox (p. 379) 'appeared to function as BP desired, to build the image of BP in consumers' minds as a company trying to think differently about the future', showing it to be socially responsible and forward-looking in terms of climate change and investment in alternative energy sources. By contrast, ExxonMobil's attempts at using image advertising as a damage-limitation exercise in the wake of the Exxon Valdez oil spill in Alaska in 1989, would appear to have largely failed because of the overwhelming availability in the public news media of images and reports clearly showing delays and poor progress in the process of cleaning up after the extensive oil spill (Benoit, 1995, referred to in Cox, 2006).

In her incisive critique of 'the corporate assault on environmentalism', Sharon Beder (2002) points to the important strategy often adopted by major corporations, namely of creating lobbying or publicity groups or organisations that can do the necessary claims-making, promoting the interests of the corporations behind them, while at the same time appearing to be relatively independent and impartial participants in the public sphere debate. An absolute cornerstone of the public sphere ideal (Habermas, 1989) and of modern parliamentary democracy is of course the clear and transparent separation of individual (or corporate) commercial interests from public and political processes aimed at ensuring the advancement of the 'common good', of what is in the interest of society as a whole rather than of the economically powerful. The power of this ideal is reflected in (healthy) public scepticism of anything that smacks of propaganda or the thinly veiled promotion of particular corporate or commercial interests. Perhaps more significantly for the present discussion, it is reflected in deep-seated journalistic professional antipathy and resistance to anything that looks like attempts at manipulating news coverage and publicity for commercial or corporate gain. It is in this context then that we can understand why it is important – and potentially far more effective than direct campaigning – for business and industry to do their claims-making through 'front' groups. Sharon Beder puts this succinctly in the start to her aptly titled chapter 'Fronting for Industry':

> When a corporation wants to oppose environmental regulations, or support an environmentally damaging development, it may do so openly and in its own name. But it is far more effective to have a group of citizens or experts—and preferably a coalition of such groups—which can publicly promote the outcomes desired by the corporation whilst claiming to represent the public interest. When such

groups do not already exist, the modern corporation can pay a public relations firm to create them.

The use of such 'front groups' enables corporations to take part in public debates and government hearings behind a cover of community concern. These front groups lobby governments to legislate in the corporate interest; to oppose environmental regulations and to introduce policies that enhance corporate profitability. Front groups also campaign to change public opinion, so that the markets for corporate goods are not threatened and the efforts of environmental groups are defused.

(Beder, 2002: 27)

As always, much can be learnt in the field of environmental campaigning from the field of major health controversies, notably the long-running battle over tobacco/smoking – a point well exploited by Al Gore (2006) in *An Inconvenient Truth*. In the UK for example, powerful tobacco interests long since set up a campaign group called Forest (careful naming of course is an essential part of the strategy – as in tobacco advertising, names and images are often deliberately chosen to subvert any negative connotations and instead to promote – in the public mind – associations with freshness, health, nature, etc. – see, for example, Judith Williamson's (1978) elegant and instructive analysis of the 'Kool' brand of cigarettes and of the Marlborough brand). A prime example in the environmental field is the Global Climate Coalition, 'a coalition of fifty US trade associations and private companies representing oil, gas, coal, automobile and chemical interests' (Beder, 2002: 29), whose prime objective was to cast doubt on the evidence for global warming/climate change and to fight scientific, political and legislative initiatives to curb greenhouse gas emissions.

Nor, as Davis (2003), Beder (2002) and others have reminded us, are aggressive uses of PR and lobbying tactics confined to big business/ industry; increasingly, governments are heavily involved in the image management game or political spin, and are deploying the very same tactics in attempts to carefully orchestrate and manage public/political debate and opinion. Beder (2002: 121), for example, highlights the Nigerian federal government's launching of a PR/lobbying campaign in the United States in order to stave off sanctions in the wake of the Nigerian government's execution in 1995 of environmental activist Ken Saro-Wiwa and eight fellow Ogoni activists. The PR/lobbying offensive involved the setting up of 'three US front groups formed to support the Nigerian government – the National Coalition for Fairness to Nigeria, the National Coalition for Fairness in African Policy and Americans for

Democracy in Africa. These groups paid for "advertorials" in key newspapers such as the *New York Times* and courted the black American press.'

In the UK a succession of 'poorly handled' (from a government and public information point of view) public controversies and health scares – from salmonella in eggs and BSE/'mad cow disease' to genetically modified crops/foods and the foot and mouth disease epidemic of 2001 – have inevitably led to an intensification of government attention to the central importance of image and information management in relation to a string of environment, science and health-related issues. While some public inquiries and reports (e.g. Phillips et al., 2000) have examined the government handling of public information in relation to some of these major crises, this is an area that is ripe for further study, particularly into the complex mix of government, business/industry and pressure-group PR. Questions need to be asked about what claims-making and information 'management' strategies are being deployed – and with what success – to influence and manage public unease, concern, opinion and debate regarding environmental, science and health-related issues and problems.

Conclusion

News about the environment, environmental disasters and environmental issues or problems does not happen by itself but is rather 'produced', 'manufactured' or 'constructed'. Environmental news, like other types of news, is the result of a complex set of interactions between claims-makers and media organisations and their operatives. The way these operate is in turn circumscribed by political, economic and cultural factors. Building on the argument of the previous chapter, that environmental issues or problems only become recognised as such through the process of claims-making, this chapter has examined the communication strategies and influence of key claims-makers – including environmental pressure groups, government and business/industry – in environmental debate and controversy.

Key tasks for claims-makers were identified as those of commanding attention, claiming legitimacy and invoking action. These tasks in turn serve as equally useful focal points for the assessment of the effectiveness or success of any claims-making activity or campaign. While extensive media coverage may often be seen as the single most important objective for pressure groups and other claims-makers aiming to get their definitions into the arena of public debate and aiming to influence public and political opinion, it was also noted that an equally important exercise of power is the power to keep issues off the public agenda, away from public scrutiny, with a view to avoiding the mobilisation of opposition or 'counter-rhetorics'.

Key strategies used by pressure groups and other claims-makers for managing and influencing news organisations were examined, including timing, differentiated targeting of media, intelligence gathering for the purpose of 'information subsidising' news media, latching onto or piggy-backing on issues or people already visible in important news forums, and the 'alliance with science' – that is, evidence-based argumentation.

New information and communication technologies have been adopted by claims-makers from all sides, and the internet in particular offers new ways of movement organisation and campaigning, new modes of image management, new ways of engagement with competitor claims-makers, new ways of discursive demarcation and new scope for transgressing or collapsing traditional geographical and temporal communication obstacles and boundaries. Rather than replacing or completely revolutionising traditional modes of communication, new communication technologies have been incorporated as additional layers and complementary to traditional media and communications forms.

While much of the communications research literature has focused on the media and news management strategies of pressure groups, it is important not to lose sight of the equally active – and economically far better resourced – PR and image management strategies of government and corporate business/industry. The final section of the chapter thus briefly examined aspects of government and corporate news management and image enhancement strategies, (Cox, 2006) including the use of 'front' groups.

One of the characteristics of what German sociologist Ulrich Beck has called the 'risk society' (Beck, 1992) – and of post-modern society – is the increasing erosion of public trust in scientific and political authority. This has direct implications for claims-making practices, which are now much less about invoking single authoritative epistemologies (e.g. science, religion) and to a greater extent about the management and manipulation of images, emotions and arguments.

Further reading

Beder, S. (2002). *Global Spin: The Corporate Assault on Environmentalism* (revised edition). Totnes, Devon: Green Books. See, in particular, Chapter 2: Fronting for Industry; Chapter 7: The Public Relations Industry; and Chapter 8: Public Relations Strategies.

Cottle, S. (2006). *Mediatized Conflict : Developments in Media and Conflict Studies*. Maidenhead: Open University Press. See, in particular, Chapter 7: Media, Risk Society and the Environment: A Different Story?

Cox, R. (2006). *Environmental Communication and the Public Sphere*. London: Sage. See, in particular, Chapter 10: Green Marketing and Corporate Campaigns.

Cracknell, J. (1993). Issue arenas, pressure groups and environmental agendas. In A. Hansen (Ed.), *The Mass Media and Environmental Issues* (pp. 3–21). Leicester: Leicester University Press.

Hannigan, J. A. (2006). *Environmental Sociology* (2nd ed.). London: Routledge. See, in particular, Chapter 5: Social Construction of Environmental Issues and Problems.

Rose, C. (2005). *How to Win Campaigns: 100 Steps to Success*. London: Earthscan. Chris Rose, who led the Greenpeace campaign against Shell and the sinking of the Brent Spar and who has worked for Friends of the Earth, WWF International and other organisations, offers highly useful practical insights into the planning, execution and evaluation of campaigns.

Ryan, C. (1991). *Prime Time Activism: Media Strategies for Grassroots Organizing*. Boston, MA: South End Press.

The environment as news: news values, news media and journalistic practices

This chapter:

● Focuses on the roles and 'work' of the media and media professionals in communicating environmental issues.

● Discusses how research on news values, on organisational structures and arrangements in media organisations, on the professional values and working practices of journalists and other media professionals can help explain why some environmental issues become news, while others do not; why some environmental issues become issues for media and public/political concern, while others fall by the wayside.

● Examines the development and significance of specialist environmental journalists and of the 'environment beat' in the creation of environmental news coverage.

● Discusses whether journalism is becoming increasingly re-active, rather than pro-active, and the impact of new information and communication technologies – and associated new source publicity and communication practices – on journalistic work in reporting on environmental issues and controversies.

● Examines the impact of key journalistic values, such as objectivity and balance, and the strategies environmental journalists deploy in order to cope with the scientific uncertainty which often characterises environmental issues and problems.

● The chapter ends with a discussion of the limitations of the sociology-of-news framework, and the ways in which some of these limitations have been addressed through perspectives focusing on cultural resonances in the discursive construction of environmental issues.

Introduction

News coverage of the environment and environmental issues is the result of complex processes of 'construction' (the literature on how news comes about also deploys a number of other and similar terms – 'production', 'manufacture', 'packaging', etc. – to indicate that news is the result of active 'work'), rather than something that just happens by itself or as a result of obvious observable events, accidents or disasters. If we accept the notion of environmental news coverage as actively 'constructed' – and concomitantly and emphatically reject the models of news media commonly referenced in such metaphors as 'a mirror of reality/society' or news as 'a window on the world' – then what becomes interesting from a communications and sociological point of view is to examine the key operatives/agents, the key institutional settings/forums, and other factors which circumscribe and impinge on the processes of news construction.

In the previous chapter, we started this process by looking closely at the publicity and communications practices of some of the principal claims-makers in environmental debate and controversy. In this chapter we extend the focus to the media and media professionals themselves. The chapter discusses how research on news values, on organisational structures and arrangements in media organisations, on the professional values and working practices of journalists and other media professionals can help explain why some environmental issues become news, while others do not; why some environmental issues become issues for media and public/political concern, while others fall by the wayside. If approaches to the study of news can, as Schudson (2005) has elegantly and helpfully argued, be broadly grouped under the following four perspectives: 'economic', 'political', 'sociological' and 'cultural', then this chapter looks predominantly at some of the lessons learnt from the last three of these perspectives.

The environmental news beat and environment correspondents

When scientists, pressure groups, and others first started drawing attention to environmental problems in the 1960s, one of the problems they faced in terms of getting media coverage for these concerns was the simple problem that newspapers and other media did not have an obvious category or rubric for these; they did not have an environmental beat or specialist reporters whose task it was to report on the environment. Thus it was often not clear whether an environmental issue was a job for the medical or health reporter, or for the science correspondent, or for the political or economic correspondent, etc. (Schoenfeld et al., 1979).

This is of course not to say that the environment did not receive media coverage prior to the 1960s; indeed, several historical studies (Krieghbaum, 1967; LaFollette, 1990; Nelkin, 1995) have documented the role of science and technology correspondents in particular in covering issues and events that might now be considered as 'environment' stories. But, as Schoenfeld et al. (1979) argue, the 1960s saw the rise of a new and more holistic approach to the environment in the form of 'ecology', that argued for the need to see everything as connected to everything else, a holistic perspective that very much departed from a view of environmental disasters, events or incidents as isolated occurrences. However, for this kind of perspective to 'fit' with the routine divisions and organisation of news work, it was necessary to create a new specialist category for 'environmental reporting'.

With the creation of specialist environmental beats and the appointment of environmental correspondents toward the end of the 1960s, the media at least became geared up for covering these complex issues which often straddle several subject domains such as science, health, politics and the economy. The appointment of environmental correspondents meant that individual media had reporters who could be on the lookout for environmental news, and this in turn facilitated a marked increase in the amount of coverage.

The importance of specialist environment correspondents to the amount of coverage given to environmental matters in the media seems, perhaps not surprisingly, to be directly reflected in the cyclical trends that characterise long-term media attention to environmental issues. Friedman (2004: 177), in her overview of American environmental journalism, notes that 'the environmental beat has never really been stable, riding a cycle of ups and downs like an elevator. These cycles, and consequent increases or decreases in numbers of environmental reporters and their space or air time, appear to be driven by public interest and events, as well as economic conditions'. The rapid growth in environmental coverage in the British media towards the end of the 1980s – a growth that was to a large extent driven by developments in the political arena, and very particularly by the then prime minister Margaret Thatcher's appropriation of 'environmental issues' as central to the Conservative government's policies – brought with it a rapid expansion of environmental correspondents, including in the British tabloid papers, few of which had a dedicated environment beat prior to 1988.

Many newspapers and broadcast media which were quick to set up environmental news beats and to appoint specialist environment correspondents in the late 1980s, were, however, equally quick to drop these posts as the environment slipped down the political priority list in the early 1990s. Journalism professor Ivor Gaber (2000) notes how, in the early 1990s, the environment suddenly became a 'non-issue' and:

> The ranks of environmental correspondents on the non-broadsheet press were decimated. In May 1989 there were 12 dedicated environment correspondents working on the national press; within two years the only remaining correspondents were on the broadsheet newspapers – even Independent Television News (ITN) decided it no longer required an environmental specialist.
>
> (Gaber, 2000: 119)

Economic conditions in the form of an economic recession were seen as a major contributor to the temporary decline in environmental beats in the UK media in the early 1990s (Gaber, 2000).

Friedman (2004) charts the further development of American environmental journalism in the 1990s, describing the 1990s as the decade that environmental journalism

> [. . .] grew into its shoes, becoming more sophisticated with the help of the Internet and a professional organisation, the Society of Environmental Journalists. The field also matured as stories changed from relatively simple event-driven pollution stories to those of far greater scope and complexity such as land use management, global warming, resource conservation, and biotechnology. Growing into shoes can be painful if they pinch, however, and environmental coverage, like most other journalism faced a shrinking news hole brought about by centralisation of media ownership, revenue losses and challenges from new media. Environmental journalism's dilemma was dealing with a shrinking news hole while facing a growing need to tell longer, complicated and more in-depth stories.
>
> (Friedman, 2004: 176)

Some of the points made by Friedman are also echoed in the findings from a comprehensive national study by Sachsman et al. (2006) of US environment reporters. Sachsman and his colleagues found, inter alia, that: a shrinking news hole was seen as one of the top barriers to environmental reporting, and a greater barrier than interference by editors; that 'newspapers were far more likely than television stations to have a reporter covering the environment on a regular basis' (p. 98); that 'the use of environment reporters tended to increase along with the size of the 550 newspapers examined' (p. 98); that 'most of the environment reporters [. . .] were veteran journalists' (p. 101); that autonomy in story selection was among the top-rated factors among environment reporters; that they relied more often on local and state sources than on national sources; and that most 'felt the need to remain objective, rejecting calls for advocacy or a civic-journalism approach' (p. 93). We shall examine the last two findings in more detail, but let us first see how these characteristics compare with British environmental journalism.

There is little systematic evidence on the ups and downs of the environment beat in the British media from the early 1990s until the present (2008), but present indications are that the environment beat has become well consolidated in the quality press (the 'broadsheets', although the broadsheet/tabloid labels have become somewhat blurred as British newspapers have changed to the smaller tabloid or Berliner format) and major broadcast news channels, while few of the popular (the traditional 'tabloids') newspapers currently have environment correspondents or environment specialist reporters.

Box 4.1

UK media with environment correspondents 2008

The major national broadcast news media and all the national quality or 'broadsheet' newspapers have a specialist environment beat or environment correspondent. Specialist journalists covering the environment have a number of different environment titles: the BBC, for example, has both environment correspondents – for example, Sarah Mukherjee – and an 'Environment Analyst', Roger Harrabin. National quality newspapers likewise often have an Environment Correspondent and an Environment Editor, while the designation 'Environment Reporter' is also used. Occasionally, an additional designation is added, as in *The Times's* Robin Pagnamenta, Energy and Environment Editor.

A search was conducted in the full-text news database Nexis®UK, which contains the full text of all UK national and regional newspapers (as well as the full text of a large number of newspapers from other countries across the globe), for the three months to an arbitrarily picked date, the 23 October 2008. The search looked for any occurrence of the word 'environment' in the byline of all UK national and regional newspapers. As shown in the table below, all the national daily and Sunday quality/broadsheet newspapers – except *The Financial Times* – have journalists designated as Environment Correspondents and/or Editors, but only one of the national popular/tabloid newspapers, *The Express* and its Sunday equivalent, *The Sunday Express* have Environment Editors listed in the byline. By contrast, it is perhaps surprising to see the considerable number of regional newspapers (second column of Table 4.1) with Environment Correspondents or Editors.

Table 4.1 UK newspapers with 'environment' in the byline of articles in the three-month period to 23 October 2008

UK national newspapers[a]	UK regional newspapers[a]
The Times & Sunday Times (75)	Belfast Telegraph (204)
The Daily Telegraph (London) (32)	The Scotsman & Scotland on Sunday (74)
The Guardian (London) (25)	Coventry Newspapers (40)
The Observer (3)	Northcliffe Newspapers (33)
The Independent (London) (13)	Sunday Herald (23)
Independent on Sunday (13)	Huddersfield Daily Examiner (11) Evening News (Edinburgh) (9)
The Express (14)	Middlesbrough Evening Gazette (9)
The Sunday Express (8)	Birmingham Evening Mail (8) Birmingham Post (1)

[a]The numbers in brackets indicate the number of articles bylined 'environment' – correspondent/reporter/editor in the three-month period.

Source: Nexis®UK.

The list below is a selection from the Nexis search on UK national quality/ broadsheet newspapers for the three-month period examined, showing the range of titles used for specialist journalists covering the newspapers' environmental 'beat':

Arctic ice caps are spreading

The Daily Telegraph (London), Thursday, 23 October 2008, NEWS; p. 15, 239 words, Louise Gray, Environment Correspondent

Wealth gap creating a social time bomb: Race behind division in US cities, says UN report Beijing is most egalitarian place in the world

The *Guardian* (London), Thursday, 23 October 2008, GUARDIAN INTERNATIONAL PAGES; p. 21, 973 words, John Vidal, Environment Editor

National: Going, going . . . Britain's vanishing woodland

The *Guardian* (London) – Final Edition, Wednesday, 22 October 2008, GUARDIAN HOME PAGES; p. 11, 328 words, John Vidal, Environment Editor

Heathrow runway 'danger to health'

The Daily Telegraph (London), Tuesday, 21 October 2008, FEATURES; p. 15, 324 words, Louise Gray, Environment Correspondent

Browne warns against media alarmism on biofuels

The Times (London), Monday, 20 October 2008, BUSINESS; p. 41, 758 words, Robin Pagnamenta, Energy and Environment Editor

EU fleets fish bluefin close to extinction

The Sunday Times (London), 19 October 2008, HOME NEWS; News; p. 12, 701 words, Jonathan Leake, Environment Editor

Wind energy becalmed by shortage of finance and fall in the price of oil

The Times (London), Saturday, 18 October 2008, BUSINESS; p. 62, 629 words, Robin Pagnamenta, Energy and Environment Editor

Threat to apples as pollinating bees die

The Express, Friday, 17 October 2008, NEWS; p. 17, 203 words, John Ingham, Environment Editor

How an insect only this big could bring down a giant invader

The Times (London), Tuesday, 14 October 2008, HOME NEWS; p. 25, 427 words, Lewis Smith, Environment Reporter

A 'Green New Deal' can save the world's economy, says UN

The Independent on Sunday, 12 October 2008, NEWS; p. 4, 348 words, Geoffrey Lean, Environment Editor

Wildlife gives early warning of 'deadly dozen' diseases that are spread by climate change

The Times (London), Wednesday, 8 October 2008, HOME NEWS; p. 19, 893 words, Lewis Smith, Environment Reporter, Barcelona

Hutton's move to MoD will clear way for greener agenda

The Independent on Sunday, 5 October 2008, ADVERTISING; p. 8, 261 words, Geoffrey Lean, Environment Editor

Charles: 'I blame GM crops for farmers' suicides'

The Independent on Sunday, 5 October 2008, NEWS; p. 1, 164 words, Geoffrey Lean, Environment Editor

> **Price rises to force cuts in water use**
>
> *The Sunday Times* (London), 5 October 2008, HOME NEWS; News; p. 11, 311 words, Jonathan Leake, Environment Editor
>
> **The swan on song**
>
> *Sunday Express*, Sunday, 5 October 2008, NEWS; p. 32, 107 words, Stuart Winter, Environment Editor
>
> **'Unnecessary' dam project threatens rarest wildlife; Pristine wilderness is home to last significant habitat of Siamese crocodile**
>
> *The Independent* (London), Monday, 29 September 2008, WORLD; p. 26, 668 words, Michael McCarthy, Environment Editor
>
> **Wood pigeons taking over robin's patch: Intensive farming and tasty seeds on offer from homeowners led farmland bird to move to town**
>
> The *Observer* (England), 28 September 2008, OBSERVER HOME PAGES; p. 21, 603 words, Juliette Jowit, Environment Editor
>
> *Source*: Nexis®UK.

Research on environmental journalism (and science/health journalism) has often revolved around the notion that environmental journalism/news is 'different' from other types of journalism/news in that environmental journalists and editors are more likely to be positively disposed toward their subject matter, and towards sources or claims-makers critical of the status quo, than, for example, political reporters or crime reporters. In an early study of environmental journalism in the UK, Lowe and Morrison (1984: 82) thus found that '[i]n interviews, environmental journalists expressed undisguised sympathy for many of the issues raised by environmental groups.'

While journalistic and editorial sympathy towards environmental issues promoted by environmental interest groups has similarly been documented elsewhere (Schoenfeld, 1980; Porritt and Winner, 1988; Linné and Hansen, 1990), the evidence from analyses of media coverage of environmental issues paints a somewhat different picture. The positive attitudes of media professionals towards environmental pressure groups thus does not manifest as an increased presence of pressure groups as primary definers in media coverage. Virtually without exception such analyses have shown that media coverage of environmental issues is essentially no different from media coverage of other types of issues or problems in terms of source orientation and primary definitions.

In terms of 'difference' from other types of journalism, studies of environmental reporters and specialist correspondents in the closely related fields of science, technology, health and medicine have shown, inter alia, that: environment correspondents tend to remain much longer with their specialism than other types of journalist (Hansen, 1994; Friedman, 2004; Sachsman et al., 2006); they are more likely than other journalists to have a science degree, although this is rarely seen by the journalists themselves as a particular advantage in their day-to-day task of reporting – a recurrent refrain from environmental journalists themselves is that they are *journalists first* and *environment/science/medical correspondents second* (Hansen, 1994; Hargreaves and Ferguson, 2000); they often have more contact with fellow environment/science correspondents in competitor media than they do with colleagues in their own medium or organisation – referred to in the literature as a 'competitor–colleague' relationship or as the 'inner club' (Dunwoody, 1980); they have – and value having – a greater degree of autonomy from editorial interference than general reporters, that is, a greater degree of freedom to decide on what to cover and how, although it is also the case that the autonomy of the environmental/science reporter varies considerably depending on the size (e.g. national versus regional or local) of the media organisation and on the type of media organisation (i.e. 'quality' or 'elite' media versus 'popular' or 'tabloid' media) (Hansen, 1994; Sachsman et al., 2006).

Finally, there is a relatively prominent argument in the literature on science and environment journalism that specialist correspondents in these areas tend to develop a deferential and uncritical relationship with their sources in what has been called a 'symbiotic' interdependency (Friedman, 1986; Goodell, 1987; Nelkin, 1995). While the evidence that a relatively close relationship between specialist environmental correspondents and their sources leads directly to a deferential, celebratory or uncritical type of reporting is not particularly strong or convincing, there is indeed considerable evidence, not least from interviews with environment and science correspondents themselves, to suggest that the development of a comprehensive network of 'reliable' and 'trustworthy' sources is seen as a key component of becoming a good reporter (Hansen, 1994; Anderson, 1997). It is also an essential component of the specialist correspondent's strategy for dealing with the uncertainty that often characterises environmental issues, as well as with the controversial and contradictory nature of evidence in public debate about environmental problems. More on this in a moment, but first we examine some of the dynamics of environmental news in terms of whether this comes about principally through the pro-active work of journalists or whether the journalist's role is principally that of the 'gate-keeper' deciding what gets into the news and what 'hits the spike' (White, 1950; Breed, 1955; Shoemaker, 1991).

Pro-active/re-active journalism

Much can be learnt about the production of environmental news by looking more closely at the practices of environmental journalists. It is perhaps tempting to think of the journalist as a detective constantly on the look-out for a news scoop, constantly scouring the key news forums for new information, and vigilantly telephoning a large array of news sources for information, leaks and news about developments. Of course, these are all aspects of journalistic work, but equally important, and perhaps more important, is it to realise that a very large part of journalistic work consists of *responding*, or not as the case may be, to the masses of information which daily flow into the newsroom and land on the journalist's desk (Hansen, 1994). Not only does information pour in in the form of wire services, news agency material, and electronic bulletin boards, but of course also in the form of press releases, video news releases, letters, and telephone calls and emails from publicity agents, press officers, experts, concerned members of the general public, etc.

The role of the journalist then is often one of *reacting* to news, rather than going out searching/scouting for news. A direct implication of this gatekeeping role is that those with the largest publicity resources, other things being equal, stand a much better chance of gaining access to the news than those who have few or no resources for mobilising and pushing information and definitions to the news media.

'Publicity resources' in this context does not simply refer to the quantity of press releases or the volume of media bombardment; it refers also to the ability of sources to package and frame information in ways which resonate well with the perspectives and ideology of the news media, and, at a more direct level, ways which make the journalist's news-writing task easier:

> news is framed by the sources who have the most access to journalists, and who provide a socially constructed interpretation of a given set of events or circumstances that makes a journalist's job easier by providing an acceptable structure for the ensuing news stories. These

> sources exercise social and political power by steering journalists
> toward one particular self-serving way of framing the story.
>
> (Smith, 1992: 28)

There is nothing new about the concern that news sources may have a great deal of influence on what becomes news. Gans (2004 [1979]), in his classic sociological study of news organisations, elegantly described the relationship between sources and journalists as resembling 'a dance, for sources seek access to journalists, and journalists seek access to sources' (p. 116) and he went on to indicate that this was not an equal partnership: 'Although it takes two to tango, either sources or journalists can lead, but more often than not, sources do the leading' (p. 116).

In a pioneering study of environmental news reporting and source influence, Sachsman (1973) notes that environment reporting in the 1940s was often dominated by corporate PR efforts. 'By the late 1960s, however, [. . .] environment reporting was based on conflicting statements from a wide variety of sources, ranging from environmental activists to government officials and business leaders' (Sachsman et al., 2006: 95). Sachsman's (1976) study of environmental news sources and information used by media in the San Francisco Bay area found that over half of environmental news reports originated in or drew directly on source-generated press releases and PR efforts. Sachsman also found that in many cases news reports amounted to little more than a minor rewriting of the press releases that gave rise to the news coverage.

Studies from Canada, the UK, Denmark, Sweden and elsewhere in the 1980s and 1990s have similarly confirmed the tendency for environmental news reporting to rely very predominantly on government and 'authoritative' institutions, on scientists and independent experts, rather than on non-governmental organisations (NGOs) or indeed on environmental pressure groups.

Exercise 4.1

Who sets the news agenda on environmental issues?

Take a look again at the sample of newspaper headlines reproduced in Box 4.1. For each headline, ask: (1) why is this 'news' on this particular day? That is, to the extent that it is possible to tell from the headline alone, whose activity in which news forum has caused this to be considered newsworthy by the environment correspondent? And (2) what sources/claims-makers are quoted, referenced or implied in the headlines? Are environmental pressure groups among the sources/claims-makers referenced?

What do the answers to these questions tell us about who or what drives (rather than perhaps the more categorical sounding 'sets') the news agenda on environmental issues?

Do these headlines seem to confirm the finding from studies of environmental news that environmental pressure groups have a low profile as sources/claims-makers in environmental news coverage?

An answer to the latter question can of course only be highly tentative, given that we are only looking at the headlines here and thus don't see which sources are quoted or mentioned in the full text of these news articles. However, and bearing in mind that newspaper articles tend to follow a very conventional structure that dictates that the most important aspects – and sources – appear at the start, it is possible to discern a tentative trend from these headlines.

In her analysis of environmental coverage in the Canadian press, Einsiedel (1988) found interest group representatives greatly out-numbered by government officials, scientists and private industry as sources used in coverage of environmental issues. Greenberg and his colleagues (1989), in their analysis of television coverage of environmental risk, found that government and industry accounted for 28 per cent and 13.2 per cent of sources, respectively, while advocacy groups were only 6.8 per cent of sources.

In a comparative study of news coverage of environmental issues on British and Danish television, Linné and Hansen (1990) found that despite the generally positive, albeit cautious, attitude of journalists towards certain environmental groups, such groups were not prominently quoted or referred to in the actual coverage. Environmental groups appeared in only 6 per cent of stories, compared with 23 per cent for public body or authority representatives, 21 per cent for government, and 17 per cent for independent scientists or experts.

Similar patterns have been found in many other analyses of environmental and related news coverage (Molotch and Lester, 1975; Wilkins, 1987; Westerstaahl and Johansson, 1987; Hornig et al., 1991; Trumbo, 1996). It is also worth noting, however, that the influence of sources on media coverage may vary significantly from issue to issue: Hargreaves et al.'s (2004) analysis, for example, shows pressure groups to be much more prominent in media coverage of climate change than in media coverage of the measles, mumps and rubella vaccine controversy or of cloning and genetic medical research.

These patterns are confirmed by the findings from a recent large and comprehensive study by Sachsman and his colleagues of environmental print and broadcast journalists in four major regions of the United States:

> State departments of environmental quality, local environmental groups, and local citizens active on the environment were among the most used groups. The results were a bit more varied at the bottom. Greenpeace was one of the least used sources in all four regions. The Chemical Manufacturers Association, the National Health and Safety Council, and the US Food and Drug Administration were near the bottom in two regions, and two national agencies, the National Science Foundation and the US Agency for Toxic Substances, were near the bottom in a single region.

> An examination of the use of all twenty-nine sources in each region showed an emphasis on local and state sources. Among national sources, only the Environmental Protection Agency was ranked between 2.0 (often) and 3.0 (sometimes) in all four regions.
>
> (Sachsman et al., 2006: 105)

The indications from research are that the power balance in the relationship between sources and journalists has shifted increasingly in favour of sources. Lewis et al. (2008) thus argue that 'pressures on journalists to increase productivity, via substantive growths in the pagination of national newspapers across the last two decades, achieved with relatively static numbers of journalists [. . .] have prompted desk-bound journalists to develop an increasing reliance on pre-packaged sources of news deriving from the PR industry and news agencies' (Lewis et al., 2008: 1). In their comprehensive study of UK print and broadcast media, Lewis and his colleagues found that: in broadcast media 'the business world was nearly four times as likely as NGOs or pressure groups to "place" their PR material into news stories' (p. 12); that 'news, especially in print, is routinely recycled from elsewhere and yet the widespread use of other material is rarely attributed to its source' (p. 18). They conclude:

> Our findings do, however, raise questions about the nature and sources of PR. As we have seen, it will favour those, notably business and government, best able to produce strong and effective PR material.

> It would however be unfair to blame journalists for relying on pre-packaged information. It is clear that most journalists operate under

economic, institutional and organisational constraints which require them to draft and process too many stories for publication to be able to operate with the freedom and independence necessary to work effectively. What is clear from this study is that the quality and independence of the British news media has been significantly affected by its increasing reliance on public relations and news agency material; and for the worse!

(Lewis et al., 2008: 18)

While the study by Lewis et al., does not look specifically at environmental news coverage (although see Box 4.2), there are indications from elsewhere (e.g. Allan, 2006; Trench, 2009) that the exponential growth in online and internet journalism, witnessed in the last decade or so, has impacted particularly on science/health/environmental journalism (Trench, 2009: 175). Economic pressures and organisational pressures have led to journalism that is increasingly desk-bound, which in turn has increased the scope for pro-active news sources and news providers to 'subsidise' the work of news organisations and their journalists with ready-packaged and advantageously framed 'information', while at the same time depriving journalists of some of their most traditional networking and source-checking strategies based around 'face-to-face' interviews or contacts with sources.

Box 4.2

PR-driven news?

In their comprehensive study of UK national print and broadcast media, Lewis et al. (2008) provide empirical evidence of the growing influence of PR material and activity on journalistic work and news coverage.

Since the most PR-informed topics are health, business and entertainment, it is not surprising that the main source of PR activity overall (Table 4.2) is the business/corporate world, which originated 38 per cent of the PR material that found its way into press articles and 32 per cent of broadcast news items. This compares favourably with PR from nongovernmental organisations (NGOs) and charities – which might be expected to promote a rather different world view – which was reported in only 11 per cent of press articles and 8 per cent of broadcast news items. In short, when it comes to getting information in the news, the most successful "spin doctors" come from business rather than from NGOs, charities or pressure groups.

(Lewis et al., 2008: 11–12)

Table 4.2 Origins of PR material – excerpt from Lewis et al. (2008)

	Press (n=1343)	*Broadcast (n=236)*
Professional private	38	32
Professional government	21	39
Public body	23	14
NGO/charity	11	8
Professional association	5	4
Citizen(s)	2	3

Their findings further suggest that the news story categories of 'Environment/Domestic Policy', 'Consumer/Business' and 'Health/Natural' rely comparatively much more on PR material than other categories (e.g. 'Crime', 'Politics').

Objectivity, bias/balance and the journalistic construction of expertise

It is not unusual for journalists and media to be made a scape-goat in relation to public debate involving controversial environmental or scientific claims-making, where different claims-making institutions and organisations are competing to promote their particular view. Indeed, a large body of media research, operating from a 'reflection-of-reality' and transmission of information perspective has focused on traditional questions about 'accuracy', 'objectivity' and 'bias/distortion' in media reporting of science and environmental issues (e.g. Tichenor et al., 1970; Tankard and Ryan, 1974; Borman, 1978; Moore and Singletary, 1985; Singer, 1990).

A major problem in criticism of 'media accuracy' is the notion that the perceived inaccuracy is primarily a product of sloppy reporting, inadequate training of reporters, and downright media distortion. What is ignored in criticism of media reporting of controversial issues is the simple fact that the media in their reporting often simply reflect uncertainty, disagreement and controversy in the communities, scientific/industrial/political, on which they report. That pressure groups, industry, government, public authorities, etc. deliberately package their claims with a view to enhancing and promoting their particular definitions of controversial issues should surprise no one. But that scientists and scientific institutions, far from fitting the image as independent establishers of scientific 'truth' and 'fact', are often embarked on similar projects, may be rather more contrary to the conventional wisdom which has guided research on 'accuracy' in media reporting. Yet, as Hilgartner (1990: 531) argues, 'a mountain of evidence shows that experts often simplify science with an eye toward persuading their audience to support their goals.'

Equally important for understanding how and why some issues become news and others do not, is to recognise that there is often competition and downright conflict of interests between the various groups, institutions and agencies who make claims about the environment (Hilgartner and Bosk, 1988). Journalists have a difficult balancing act to perform amid a barrage of conflicting claims about environmental issues. A cornerstone of the professional ideology of news work is the need not to be, or not to be seen to be, simply the extended mouthpiece of any one camp or source. Journalists are generally very dismissive of anything which appears as thinly veiled promotional publicity – of which they receive masses every day from industry and business. They are also – or have become in the last twenty years or so – increasingly cautious about claims made by environmental pressure groups.

But considerable difficulties arise where there is a great deal of scientific uncertainty – as is almost invariably the case – surrounding the various claims made about environmental or associated problems. Climate change (anthropogenic? how fast? what causes? what consequences?) is a classic example of how general scientific uncertainty and disagreement cause considerable problems not just for journalists and media coverage (Bell, 1994b; Wilson, 2000; Zehr, 2000; Smith, 2005; Boykoff, 2008), but indeed more generally for public understanding of the issue (Bell, 1994a; Corbett and Durfee, 2004); but other examples are plentiful, not least from the general fields of public health and food safety (salmonella in eggs, 'mad cow disease' (BSE), genetically modified foods) and bio-genetics (cloning, genetically modified crops and organisms more generally) as well as from nano-technology coverage (Wilkinson et al., 2007).

Journalists, who are of course generally not – nor could they reasonably be expected to be – experts on the science or social science behind the environmental issues and problems on which they report, deploy a number of key journalistic strategies for maintaining the legitimacy and credibility of their reporting. These strategies revolve around the core journalistic value or norm of 'objectivity', which involves, as noted above, abstaining from 'taking sides' and from 'advocating' the case of one claims-maker over another. Objective reporting must be – and more importantly, must be seen to be – balanced, accurate and based on 'facts' originating from credible sources or what Ericson et al. (1987) call the 'authorised knowers' of society.

While specialist journalists reporting on environment, science and health issues generally have considerable ('veteran' in Sachsman et al.'s terminology) experience of reporting on their fields, numerous studies (e.g. Dunwoody, 1979; Friedman, 1986; Hansen, 1994; Conrad, 1999; Stocking, 1999) have shown that they are acutely aware of the (scientific) uncertainties and controversy which often characterise debate about environmental issues. But like journalists in general, and like other types of specialist journalists more specifically, they command an elaborate set of journalistic routines geared towards securing the credibility and 'objectivity' of their reporting. These include judging the credibility of their sources on the basis of such standard clues as qualification, age, seniority and institutional affiliation; using principally senior or top-ranking sources; using 'known' sources (that is, 'known' to the journalist, or to the research council, professional association or other source-conduit that the journalist might use for tracking down relevant sources); they actively seek to cultivate a relationship of mutual trust with their sources, and in particular with a core of regular sources, to whom they turn – time permitting – and use as 'sounding boards' when dealing with new or 'unknown' sources (Hansen, 1994). The importance, to these specialist journalists, of trust and the cultivation of trust in the relationship with their main sources remains a core characteristic of journalistic values (Geller et al., 2005).

Frames and forums

While numerous studies (Dunwoody, 1979; Friedman, 1986, 2004; Hansen, 1994; Stocking, 1999; Sachsman et al., 2006, etc.) of specialist correspondents covering the closely related journalistic beats of science, environment, health and medicine, agriculture, technology, etc. have displayed a remarkable degree of consensus around the journalistic characteristics delineated above, these studies have generally had less to say about the importance of *framing* and *forums* in the journalistic construction of expertise and 'authoritative' coverage. The use of particular frames, settings (Ibarra and Kitsuse, 1993; see also Chapter 2) and forums for constructing or reinforcing the notion of expertise, credibility and authoritativeness is of course especially pronounced in television and other primarily 'image-based' media, although not confined to these – newspapers, for example, have over 2–3 decades become increasingly 'visual' with a much greater use of photographs, images and colour. Yet, while studies in other fields of news journalism (now classic studies of media coverage of industrial conflict or of crime being cases in point – e.g. Glasgow Media Group, 1976; Hartmann, 1976; Hall, 1981) have commented extensively on the importance of framing, settings and forums for the construction of expertise and credibility, less analysis on this aspect of environmental journalism is available (although see Cottle, 1993 and 2000).

Studies on the construction of scientific expertise in television documentary and factual programmes (e.g. Collins, 1987; Murrell, 1987; Hornig, 1990) have, for example, amply demonstrated some of the key narrative conventions and visual props deployed in factual television programmes for conveying the authority of science and scientists. Likewise, it clearly makes a difference to the message which comes across regarding credibility, authority and expertise, if the argument of one side of an environmental controversy is represented by well-dressed, articulate and 'official-looking' government representatives interviewed in the hallowed halls of power, while the other side is represented by cold, wet and perhaps 'scruffy-looking' demonstrators gathered on a muddy verge somewhere near a major airport (see Exercise 4.2 on framing and forums in news coverage of environmental protest).

In their comparative study of environmental news coverage in Britain and Denmark, Hansen and Linné (1994: 381), for example, found that not only do pressure group sources have an overall comparatively low profile, but when they '*do* appear as primary definers, they do so through the forum or news scenario of public demonstration or protest action rather than as legitimate or authoritative sources in their own right.' The construction of 'legitimate' expertise and authority is thus closely linked to questions about the settings, forums or arenas in which sources are 'placed' and filmed/photographed by journalists or with which sources are verbally 'associated' in journalistic print-media reports.

There is clear evidence (Albaek et al., 2003) that journalists increasingly deploy expert and scientific sources in their reporting, and that journalism and media, like indeed other arenas in society, have been subject to an increasing 'scientisation' over the last half century or so (see also Bauer, 1998, on the 'medicalisation' of science reporting since the 1930s).

Paradoxically – perhaps – the increasing journalistic deployment of expert sources parallels a trend of growing public distrust in 'authority' and in experts. As Boyce (2006) comments:

> Many researchers have observed the paradox of the decline in trust of experts and at the same time, the increasing use of expertise in Western society, "(w)e believe less and less in experts [. . .] (but) we use them more and more." (Limoges, 1993: 424)

(Boyce, 2006: 890).

If increasing journalistic use of expert sources is perhaps in part a response to increasing public distrust in authority and experts, then it is also fair to assume that the journalistic task of 'constructing' reliable, credible and believable accounts may need augmenting in other ways as well, namely by way of more elaborate – and perhaps more 'visual' – framings which can lend additional symbolic legitimacy and weight to the 'evidence' presented. Analyses of environmental journalism and environmental news reporting would thus undoubtedly benefit from moving well beyond counts of how 'pro-and-anti' expert testimonies or sources are 'balanced' in media reporting (although these are very useful starting points – see Boykoff and Boykoff, 2004, on objectivity-turned bias (Corbett, 2006) in the climate-change debate, discussed in more detail in Chapter 7, and the much earlier but very similar arguments in relation to media reporting on nuclear power, for example, Rothman, 1990; Friedman et al., 1992) to a more detailed study of how different expert testimonies are imbued with varying degrees of legitimacy and authority, or even in some cases positively undermined, by the setting and other framings deployed by journalists.

Exercise 4.2

Framing and forums: the visual/verbal construction of environmental protest

Using the websites of major television news organisations such as CNN (www.cnn.com) or the BBC (www.bbc.co.uk), identify online news footage of a public protest or demonstration with an environmental component/theme (e.g. airport expansion, genetic modification of agricultural crops, climate change).

What do the images show? For example, orderly, organised and peaceful protest or violent clashes between protesters and police?

How are the protesters/demonstrators portrayed? – for example, does the camera focus on a 'cross-section' (age, dress, ethnic origin, etc.) of protesters or do close-up shots tend to pick out or focus in on 'extreme' or 'unusual' protesters?

Who is interviewed on screen? And where, that is, against what backdrop?

How are interviewees framed visually and verbally? – that is, how are they introduced or labelled? Where are they at the time of interview? What if anything goes on in the background as they are interviewed? How does the reporter's commentary link or juxtapose different interviews/interviewees? How does background noise and/or the reporter's commentary frame or inflect the authority/credibility or 'weight' of what the interviewees say?

The answers to these questions will give an indication of the highly constructed nature of visual news reports, alerting us to the fact that even seemingly straightforward video footage of a demonstration or protest action is essentially a selective construction resulting from a series of deliberate choices about what to focus on, what to juxtapose with what, how to narratively frame and 'give meaning' to that which is portrayed or reported. Ultimately, the answers to the above questions also enable us to determine the general stance and tone of the reporting, that is, whether the protest is portrayed as warranted and legitimate, or alternatively as 'problematic', 'an unnecessary over-reaction', 'a misuse of the right to demonstrate', etc.

Political and economic pressures: local/regional media reporting

Other pressures on the journalist, when deciding on what to cover and on how to frame the coverage, relate to the political and economic allegiances of individual newspapers. Such pressures may include the actual or assumed (by the journalists) concerns of editors and media proprietors that some kinds of environmental coverage may antagonise powerful industries and businesses, whose advertising the media depend on. There is some indication that such pressures apply particularly in relation to media serving smaller regional or local communities.

Although most studies have focused on national prestige media, some studies have examined the coverage of environmental issues in local/regional media (Cottle, 1993, 2000; Gooch, 1996; Campbell, 1999; Lahtinen and Vuorisalo, 2005; Wakefield and Elliott, 2003), highlighting some of the particular characteristics and constraints which govern local/regional media practices and distinguish them from national prestige media. Of particular interest here is the tendency for local/regional media to give more access to ordinary lay 'voices', as sources used in the definition and elaboration of environmental issues (Cottle, 1993, 2000; Crawley, 2007), contrasting with the distinctive authority orientation of national news. However, the greater accessing of lay and oppositional voices is by no means a universal feature of local/regional media coverage of environmental issues, as other studies have confirmed a degree of authority orientation comparable to that usually found in national media (e.g. Corbett, 1998; Taylor et al., 2000).

Local/regional media have also, not surprisingly, been shown to focus on local rather than global problems, to celebrate a nostalgic view of nature and the countryside (Cottle, 2000), and to focus on problems relevant to or arising from the region served by such media. The latter, however, may be paralleled by a somewhat diminished scope for critical, investigative, or adversary reporting, particularly where the 'causes' of environmental problems may be industries or institutions of major significance to the local economy (e.g. Dunwoody and Griffin, 1993). As in other fields of reporting (e.g. education – see Hansen, 2007), local/regional news media are conscious of and sensitised to the way in which local readership feelings may run high in relation to what might be construed as a criticism of local/regional institutions and businesses important to the local economy. Tichenor et al. (1980) and Donohue et al. (1989, 1995) have shown how the scope for critical reporting and for accessing of a wider variety of voices/sources in the media relates closely to the size and degree of pluralism of local/regional communities. In more pluralist communities, the local media thus tend to be less authority oriented, providing a platform for a wider range of viewpoints and positions, while in smaller and more homogeneous communities, the media tend to serve as a sentry not for the community as a whole, but for the dominant groups of power and influence (Donohue et al., 1995).

Event orientation and time in the construction of environmental news

News is largely event focused and event driven, and it is this inherent event orientation which is an important factor in determining which environmental issues get news coverage and which don't. While some environmental issues are associated with spectacular and dramatic events – and thus eminently 'newsworthy' – many environmental issues are characterised by their relative 'invisibility'. The thinning of the Earth's protective ozone layer is invisible to the naked eye; the detrimental effects of carbon dioxide on the Earth's atmosphere are not immediately observable; the link between pollution and an increase in the incidence of respiratory diseases is not immediately obvious, etc.

Schoenfeld et al. (1979) add to this observation that the timescale of most environmental problems is ill-suited to the 24-hour cycle of news production. Many environmental problems take a long time to develop; there is often uncertainty for years about the causes and wider effects of environmental problems (climate change, again, is an obvious example, as is BSE or 'mad cow disease') and even where a scientific and political consensus may emerge, the 'visualisation' for a wider public audience of what is happening requires a great deal of skilful journalistic and communicative 'work'. In a recent historical analysis, Julie Doyle (2007) offers a comprehensive mapping of Greenpeace's strategies for visualising climate change and she demonstrates that the visualisation – for campaigning purposes – of climate change is a highly selective and skilled process of image construction. The importance of 'visualisation work' in making environmental problems newsworthy has also been extensively analysed by DeLuca (1999, 2000).

While some of the most prominent environmental issues in the media over the last few decades have been, intrinsically, neither particularly visible, nor well matched to the conventional timescales of news work, their prominence in the news is testimony perhaps that with the right kind of claims-making, visualisation, exploitation of journalistic and news values and exploitation of news routines any potential environmental issue or problem can be packaged and constructed in ways that will attract the news media. Insight into the intrinsic event orientation of news and news work is thus strategically important for environmental claims-makers in that the ability to link campaign objectives and claims-making to events (e.g. upcoming national or international political, economic or cultural meetings or otherwise scheduled gatherings or negotiations) that predictably will attract news attention is a good guarantor of news coverage. Ungar (1992) uses the apt term or analogy of 'piggybacking' – 'environmental claims are most often honored when they can piggyback on dramatic real-world events' (Ungar, 1992: 483). However, the real-world events of course need not necessarily be 'dramatic' – although, in news value terms, drama certainly helps – but can simply be the kind of events taking place in those forums (e.g. parliament, the courts, international politics) which by definition are attended to by journalists and news organisations.

It is not sufficient for environmental claims-makers to stage newsworthy events or protests that merely coincide with routine newsworthy diary events. For piggybacking to work effectively, 'linking' to routine news diary events or to routine news forums needs to be done in a way that is meaningful and visible to news organisations. Otherwise the strategically timed co-incidence of events may affect environmental claims-making negatively, in the sense that the limited 'carrying capacity' (Hilgartner and Bosk, 1988) leads to environmental events or news items being pushed off the media agenda to make room for routine diary events or routine developments in established news forums.

Cultural resonances and frames in media coverage of environmental issues

If traditional approaches to the study of media and news coverage can throw some light on the relationship between the immediate actors involved in the production of such coverage, it is to the wider notion of *cultural resonances* that we must turn in order to account further for the very different careers and media presence enjoyed by different environmental problems.

Schudson (1989), Gamson (1988) and Hilgartner and Bosk (1988) have all argued for the importance of complementing traditional organisational perspectives on media coverage and news production with a wider view which takes into consideration how the 'cultural givens' of society both facilitate and delimit the elaboration and coverage of issues. In order to gain prominence in the public sphere an issue has to be cast in terms which resonate with existing and widely held cultural concepts (Gamson and Modigliani, 1989).

Developing their public arenas model to explain the rise and fall of social problems, Hilgartner and Bosk (1988: 64) similarly note that selection principles of all institutional arenas, including the mass media, are 'influenced by widely shared cultural preoccupations and political biases. Certain problem definitions fit closely with broad cultural concerns, and they benefit from this fact in competition.'

Among the 'cultural givens' within which much media reporting on the environment is anchored are the beliefs in 'mastery over nature' (or 'nature as object', see Evernden, 1989) and in 'progress through science and technology'. Both of these may help explain why media discourse on the environment is to a large extent a 'science' discourse drawing on scientists as the primary arbiters of right and wrong, true and false, real and imagined.

As Gamson and Modigliani (1989) maintain, for each cultural theme there is a counter-theme, and this principle is perhaps particularly evident in much environmental coverage with a heavy science component. The pro-science optimism which finds expression in themes and terms such as 'progress', 'development', 'industrialised', 'rational', 'efficient' finds its counter-expression in numerous mediated forms, including perhaps most prominently, in popular films which stress the dangers of man's hubris and associated tinkering with nature (from *Frankenstein* and *The Island of Dr Moreau* to *Jurassic Park* and *The Lost World*). Indeed, a raft of studies across Europe as well as in the United States have found, *inter alia*, the deep-seated cultural themes of 'Pandora's box', 'runaway technology/science' and 'tampering with nature' to be prominent – albeit to varying extents over time – in much news coverage of developments in genetic modification and biotechnology (Bauer et al., 1999; Nisbet and Lewenstein, 2002; Ten Eyck and Williment, 2003; Hansen, 2006).

The notion of 'cultural resonance', as a contribution to understanding why some issues gain currency in public and media debate more easily than others, can be extended further to include questions about the ease with which some issues link into powerful, historically established, symbolic imagery. This marks out nuclear power issues and a host of genetic or biotechnology-related issues with environmental dimensions from some other environmental issues (e.g. ozone depletion, climate change, deforestation, species extinction, etc.). Patterson (1989), for example, drawing on psychological and risk studies, notes the deep-seated public fears ('Atom-Angst') associated with anything nuclear. Others have pointed to the powerful and deep-seated images of mass destruction associated with the use of nuclear bombs in the Second World War. Spencer Weart (1988), in an impressive historical analysis of the origins and inflections of 'nuclear images', traces the fear and angst-ridden imagery much further back to the discovery of radiation, to 'alchemistic' connotations associated with the new science of atoms and nuclear radiation, and to the key theme of 'mutation/transmutation' – themes which are all equally central to the rapid developments witnessed in biotechnology and genetic modification in the last few decades.

Metaphorical anchoring and linking of arguments to widely available cultural values and images give such images more potency in the public mind and in public debate, and in turn they serve to *frame* public perception and debate about their subject matter. Patterson's (1989) analysis of American and other Western news coverage of the Chernobyl nuclear accident similarly notes the important ideological implications of the ways in which the accident was framed. Principally, the accident was framed in terms of the dangerous technological incompetence of the Soviet Union, a frame which placed the blame firmly on the particular design of Soviet nuclear technology and the (in-)competence of its engineers, operatives, and bureaucrats, while specifically diverting attention away from Western nuclear technology ('it could not happen here') or suggestions that civil nuclear energy generation is inherently dangerous and prone to 'normal' accidents.

Much framing and the activation – through vocabulary and metaphor choice – of particular cultural resonances start with the claims-makers who make claims about environmental issues. But, as we have seen in the highly skewed use of sources, the media play a key *gatekeeping* role through their control over the *selection* of sources, information and arguments. In addition, they do further 'ideological work' by adding their own discursive spin or framing to the issues on which they report.

> [. . .] the media can impose its own meaning frames and symbols to a given event. By calling a policy 'controversial', by highlighting a dispute, by suggesting a benefit and excluding risk information, the media can legitimate positions and project images with considerable power [. . .] Lee (1989) [. . .] demonstrated the significant role played by opposing sides in framing the debate [about seal hunting] in strong moral terms. More interesting, however, was the additional role played by the media in injecting its own voice in the debate. The opponents to the seal hunt lead by Greenpeace claimed the hunt was a 'slaughter' of 'endangered baby seals'; the hunters, on the other hand, succeeded in gaining support for their cause by presenting the attempts to stop the hunt as 'cultural genocide'. Lee further demonstrated that the largest amount of moral keywords presented were not from the competing claimsmakers but in the reporters' own voices. He concluded thus: 'the moral reality of the seal hunt is communicated in the apparently objective voice of the news reporter rather than [. . .] in the voices of the moral contestants, a profoundly significant comment on the power of the newspaper to construct moral social reality'.
>
> (Einsiedel and Coughlan, 1993: 136–37)

In their analysis of nuclear discourse, Gamson and Modigliani (1989) point out that different, and often competing, frames may co-exist simultaneously in different forums of meaning-making (e.g. policy-making forum, the media, public opinion, etc.). Smith (1992: 109) examined this phenomenon in relation to media coverage of the Exxon Valdez oil spill in Prince William Sound, Alaska, and found that the event was framed variously as 'environmental catastrophe' and 'as a fable about a drunken sea captain and a mighty oil company that couldn't clean up after itself.'

Daley and O'Neill (1991: 42) point perhaps even more succinctly to the ideological implications (what causes, who to blame, what appropriate remedial action) of the various frames or narratives used in media coverage of the Exxon Valdez oil spill. From their analysis of media coverage they conclude that 'mainstream narratives naturalise and individualise the spill, turning ordinary members of the public into victims, while minority narratives offer a competing conception of nature'. They identify three mainstream frames or narratives (a disaster narrative, a crime narrative, and an environmental narrative), and one marginalised minority frame (a subsistence narrative) in the coverage:

> The disaster narrative naturalized the spill, effectively withdrawing from discursive consideration both the marine transport system and the prospective pursuit of alternative energy sources. The disaster narrative overtly moved the discourse away from the political arena and into the politically inaccessible realm of technological inevitability [. . .] The disaster narrative also drew upon a few widely available cultural metaphors – Faustian bargains, Frankensteinian nightmares – to transform a specific social and historical event into a tale of natural or technological inevitability [. . .] The disaster narrative and journalistic practice in general facilitate the categorisation of accidents as abnormal, thus deflecting attention away from production-driven systemic problems.
>
> (Daley and O'Neill, 1991: 53)

The *crime* narrative framed the event in terms of individual failure and incompetence, focusing attention on the drink problem and personality of the captain, and on legal proceedings against him. The *environmental* narrative focused on environmental spokespersons contesting the statements and practices of industrial spokespersons and government – but rather than highlighting the threat which the oil spill posed to the livelihood of Native Alaskans (the marginalised *subsistence* narrative), this was a frame which drew on traditional binary oppositions of messy high-tech industrial exploitation versus a (largely romanticised) view of nature as a place of tranquil and pristine beauty.

> This narrative frequently offered visually compelling photos of soiled birds or cuddly sea otters, domesticated before our eyes and for our eyes. They were offered as pathetic human interest stories, not as animals who exist in their own right in fragile marine ecosystems. The spectator role scripted for the public by the environmental

narrative is at odds with Native Alaskans' subsistence relationship
with nature. Because Native Alaskans see themselves as a part of this
system, they see no need to anthropomorphize animals.

(Daley and O'Neill, 1991: 54)

Not all environmental issues or problems engage with, or 'benefit' from, a
culturally deep-seated imagery of the same symbolic richness as
genetics/biotechnology or as 'nuclear/radiation-related issues', and they
are disadvantaged by this in competition for elaboration in media and
other meaning-creating forums. But it is precisely the extent to which
they can be anchored in and made to activate existing chains of cultural
meaning which helps determine whether they become successful claims,
gain prominence in media coverage, achieve legitimacy in public arenas,
and influence social and political action.

Conclusions

News coverage of the environment and of environmental issues is the
result of complex processes of construction. Research on the 'sociology
of news' since the 1950s has indicated how factors such as news values,
organisational structures and arrangements in media organisations,
economic and political pressures on news organisations, the professional
values and working practices of journalists, etc. all influence to varying
degrees what is reported and how it is reported.

The organisational arrangement of having an 'environment beat', staffed
by specialist 'environment reporters', has been shown to considerably
influence the amount and nature of coverage of environmental issues.
Studies of specialist reporters in the fields of science, environment and
health reporting have added further to our understanding of how and why
these areas are reported. They have pointed to the complex strategies that
journalists deploy in order to deal with the pervasive 'uncertainties'
characteristic of issues in these areas, including by 'balancing' opposing
sources and by cultivating relationships of trust with sources, by drawing
on recognised, 'credible' and 'authoritative' sources.

Recent studies have shown how technological advances and increasing
economic pressures on news organisations combine to change the nature
of news gathering and news work generally, and how this has impacted
particularly on specialist areas of reporting such as science and the
environment. The evidence discussed in this chapter thus points towards
environmental journalism which is under increasing pressure, resulting –

through a combination of technological advances, economic pressures as well as a changing political and 'publicity driven' climate – in a shifting balance of power between journalists and their sources, in the direction of sources. Gans' observation of thirty years ago that the relationship between journalists and sources is like a dance, but while 'it takes two to tango [and] either sources or journalists can lead, [. . .] more often than not, sources do the leading' (2004 [1979]: 116) thus seems to be truer than ever before.

Studies of media organisations and different types of media (broadcast versus print media, national versus regional/local media, 'quality/elite' versus 'popular' media) have provided further evidence of the complex factors which impinge on what is and can be said about environmental issues; particularly interesting – although as yet insufficiently researched and understood – are perhaps the very different obligations, responsibilities or pressures which characterise regional/local media compared with large national and international media, particularly when it comes to the balancing of economic, employment and environmental considerations with particular relevance to regional/local communities.

The final part of the chapter aimed to go beyond the focus on organisational characteristics and arrangements of news media and the professional values and practices of journalists to indicate how wider cultural factors also impinge on the nature of environmental news. Put simply, certain environmental issues or stories 'resonate' more easily with common cultural narratives or preoccupations than others; certain ways of 'saying things' (choice of words, metaphors, images) or reporting on issues/problems sound more familiar and perhaps therefore more plausible and trustworthy to media publics than others. In the next chapter we shall pursue these 'cultural packages' and cultural resonances further by tracing their origins in and perpetuation through media and popular culture more generally, that is, beyond the present chapter's particular focus on news and news media.

Further reading

Cottle, S. (2006). *Mediatized Conflict : Developments in Media and Conflict Studies*. Maidenhead: Open University Press. See, in particular, Chapter 7: Media, Risk Society and the Environment: A Different Story?

Friedman, S. (2004). And the beat goes on: the third decade of environmental journalism. In S. Senecah, S. Depoe, M. Neuzil, and G. Walker (Eds.),

The Environmental Communication Yearbook, vol. 1 (pp. 175–87). London: Lawrence Erlbaum Associates.

Friedman, S. M. (1986). The journalist's world. In S. M. Friedman, S. Dunwoody, and C. L. Rogers (Eds.), *Scientists and Journalists: Reporting Science as News* (pp. 17–41). New York: The Free Press.

Stocking, S. H. (1999). How journalists deal with scientific uncertainty. In S. M. Friedman, S. Dunwoody, and C. L. Rogers (Eds.), *Communicating Uncertainty: Media Coverage of New and Controversial Science* (pp. 23–42). Mahwah, NJ: Lawrence Erlbaum Associates.

Trench, B. (2009). Science reporting in the electronic embrace of the internet. In R. Holliman, E. Whitelegg, E. Scanlon, S. Smidt, and J. Thomas (Eds.), *Investigating Science Communication in the Information Age: Implications for Public Engagement and Popular Media* (pp. 166–80). Milton Keynes: Oxford University Press and The Open University. Brian Trench focuses primarily on science reporting but most of what is said here applies equally to environment reporting.

5 Popular culture, nature and environmental issues

This chapter:

- Discusses the notions of scripts, cultural packages, interpretive packages and cultural resonance, and explores their significance for understanding the nature and potential 'power' of popular media representations of nature and the environment.
- Traces the particular interpretive packages which have been – and continue to be – prominent in media and popular culture constructions of nuclear power and the new genetics, genetic modification and biotechnology.
- Explores some of the core frames and cultural assumptions which are in play in media and public sphere discussions about the environment, nature and environmental issues.
- Looks beyond the conventional focus on *news coverage* of the environment to explore how nature and the environment are constructed ideologically in other media genres, including television entertainment programming and more particularly in wildlife film and television nature programmes.
- Explores the significance of lexis or word choice in media constructions of environmental issues, and the similarly significant contribution of narrative analysis to uncovering the deeper ideological values communicated through wildlife film and nature programming.
- Discusses the historical changes in narrative and stylistic formats, and explores the relationship between socio-historical circumstances and media constructions of nature and the environment.

Introduction

Images of nature and the environment extend far beyond news media reporting. As indicated at the end of the previous chapter, the 'success' of environmental claims in the news media will often depend on the extent to which such claims engage or resonate with deeper cultural images, beliefs and perceptions. This chapter therefore focuses on research on the kind of deeper-lying cultural and interpretive packages which can be seen to inform media and public images of nature, the environment and environmental issues. Drawing on studies of a range of popular media genres the chapter will show how deep-seated cultural narratives have reflected, and in turn shaped, particular ideological interpretations of nature and the environment, including changing dominant interpretations of the environment as either an object of control and exploitation or as something to be protected.

Much of communications research focusing on the media coverage and media reporting of the environment and environmental issues has focused mainly on news coverage (on the – often implicit – understanding that news coverage is the main influence on everyday political opinions, public understanding, etc. of socially constructed issues like environmental controversy). Likewise, such analyses have often been concerned with traditional questions about the amount of coverage, accuracy and balance/bias in coverage, 'primary definers' (i.e. the key sources quoted or referred to in news coverage) and major thematic emphases of coverage. These are all important aspects of any analysis of news coverage. They are also categories that are generally well grounded in relevant theoretical frameworks for understanding the nature and social functions of news. Thus, an emphasis on balance and bias in news coverage relates to key concerns in theories about the role of news media and their watchdog role in society, as well as to core ideas about the professional practices and the required – by professional ideology – objectivity and impartiality in news reporting; the emphasis on 'primary definers' relates closely to social constructionist concerns about claims-making as well as to wider – often Marx and/or Gramsci-inspired – concerns about hegemony, inequality and the maintenance of power structures in society. But by focusing on these – perhaps more obvious and conspicuous – dimensions of news coverage, the deeper-lying and perhaps taken-for-granted assumptions, myths and ideologies which form both the basis and contexts for 'what is or can be said' about certain problems or issues have been less in focus and less fore-grounded in analyses of media coverage of environmental issues and problems.

The rise since the early 1990s in the application of framing theory has provided a major impetus for a refocusing of media and communication research on these deeper-lying structures and messages, and this has helped in particular in throwing light on such key questions such as why it is that some types of claims about environmental problems are or become much more successful in the public sphere than others. As we saw in Chapter 2, the types of rhetoric deployed (e.g. rhetoric of loss, rhetoric of calamity, rhetoric of unreason – see the discussion of Ibarra and Kitsuse, 1993, in Chapter 2), simple lexical choice, and the types of metaphors used reference, invoke or signal deeper-lying ideological 'scripts' or cultural narratives, that articulate – as ideological clusters – a particular perspective, world view, assumption or understanding.

In his excellent analysis of the deeper historical and cultural images which inform much of the current debate about genetic modification and biotechnology, Turney (1998: 6) notes the power of such scripts:

> Once a script has been laid down, a single cue can evoke an entire story, as an interpretive frame or context for what is being discussed. In this sense, the *Frankenstein* script has become one of the most important in our culture's discussion of science and technology. To activate it, all you need is the word: *Frankenstein.*

As argued in the previous chapter, some environmental problem formulations 'resonate' more easily or better with deep-seated cultural assumptions and anxieties than others, and they benefit from this in their public sphere careers. Likewise, some ways of making claims about the environment 'resonate' or 'fit' better with established or conventional journalistic and news 'templates' than others, and consequently they stand a better chance of, first, gaining media attention, and second, of gaining favourable and legitimating media coverage.

The key objectives of this chapter are twofold: (1) to explore further some of the core frames and cultural assumptions which are in play in media and public sphere discussions about the environment, nature and environmental issues; and (2) to look beyond the conventional focus on news coverage of the environment, and to begin to show that these frames and cultural assumptions permeate throughout – and are in some respects the bedrock of – a broad range of different media genres and types of content. In this chapter we shall look particularly at the interpretive packages and frames furnished by the science fiction genre (literature and film), wildlife/nature films and popular television nature programming. In the next chapter we shall focus more specifically on the genre of advertising and the articulation of environment and nature in this particular persuasive genre.

Cultural packages, assumptions and frames (in media reporting on the environment)

Cultural packages, scripts, schema or narratives can be regarded as a 'reservoir', indeed they could be seen as the reservoir of world views which helps us understand how things work and what counts as appropriate or acceptable within any given culture. The notion of a reservoir of world views or perspectives, readily available to members of a particular culture, is akin to another sociological metaphor, namely Ann Swidler's notion of culture 'as a "tool kit" of symbols, stories, rituals, and world views, which people may use in varying configurations to solve different kinds of problems' (1986: 273). But while the reservoir or tool kit may be *always available*, it is also the case of course that not all parts of it are activated or drawn upon equally often (just as one – to continue the analogy – would rarely have all the tools out of the tool bag all at once, nor indeed would all of the tools be called upon equally frequently).

Moreover, the meaning, relevance and usefulness of particular clusters within the cultural reservoir change – or are deliberately changed – over time. As Gamson and Modigliani (1989: 2) put it, 'Packages ebb and flow in prominence and are constantly revised and updated to accommodate new events'. Changes in packages and their relative prominence in the public sphere depend on historical, social and political factors, and of course also on the more media-specific factors to do with the organisational, professional, technological and economic dimensions discussed in the previous two chapters.

In their now classic and oft-quoted article from 1989, Gamson and Modigliani offer an exemplary analysis and map of the *cultural packages* which have served as interpretive frameworks for media and public discussion about nuclear issues and nuclear power since 1945. As indicated in Chapter 2, Gamson and Modigliani offer a useful approach to frame analysis, and as we shall see in Chapter 7, they also offer a particularly helpful way of conceptualising the relationship between media coverage and public opinion.

Here, however, I wish to focus on their core proposition that analysis of media and public debate needs to move beyond the quantitative measurement – characteristic of much communication analysis of media coverage of nuclear power and related concerns about the media's (negative) influence on public opinion about nuclear power – of whether media coverage is positive or negative, for or against, nuclear power.

Analysis needs to take into account the broader scripts or interpretive packages, which make up the reservoir of scripts, storylines, idea clusters, core propositions, etc. from which both media and public draw to make sense of issues, in this case of nuclear power. As Gamson and Modigliani (1989: 1–2) argue,

> Nuclear power, like every policy issue, has a culture. There is an ongoing discourse that evolves and changes over time, providing interpretations and meanings for relevant events. An archivist might catalog the metaphors, catchphrases, visual images, moral appeals, and other symbolic devices that characterize this discourse. The catalog would be organized, of course, since the elements are clustered; we encounter them not as individual items but as interpretive *packages*.

Packages, in Gamson and Modigliani's argument, are not intrinsically about positions for or against an issue; rather they provide the building blocks *and* a guide-structure or frame for viewing a particular issue. They thus, for example, identify the *progress package* in the nuclear power discourse as a package that 'frames the nuclear power issue in terms of society's commitment to technological development and economic growth' (Gamson and Modigliani, 1989: 4). But not all packages 'speak to' or resonate equally powerfully with the underlying culture:

> Certain packages have a natural advantage because their ideas and language resonate with larger cultural themes. Resonances increase the appeal of a package; they make it appear natural and familiar. Those who respond to the larger cultural theme will find it easier to respond to a package with the same sonorities. Snow and Benford (1988) make a similar point in discussing the 'narrative fidelity' of a frame. Some frames 'resonate with cultural narrations, that is, with the stories, myths, and folk tales that are part and parcel of one's cultural heritage.
>
> (Gamson and Modigliani, 1989: 5)

The progress package thus benefits from its resonance with deeper American values, in many respects overlapping with the protestant ethic (Weber, 1930) of many European countries. It also resonates with a broader utilitarian enlightenment perspective emphasising efficiency, technological innovation, a frugal, rational and logical approach, science and – perhaps most importantly of all in the context of environmental issues – mastery over nature as the key to progress.

Gamson and Modigliani identify seven key packages in the public discourse on nuclear power from 1945 onwards:

- The *progress* package – a package that 'frames the nuclear power issue in terms of society's commitment to technological development and economic growth' (p. 4).
- The *energy independence* package – a pronuclear package stressing nuclear power as a guarantor of American energy independence in the face of problems with Arab oil supplies and concerns about dwindling oil reserves.
- The *devil's bargain* package – a package that conflates pronuclear packages with the *runaway* package, and evokes the classic Faustian legend of folktales.
- The *runaway* package – nuclear power is seen from a fatalistic and resigned position, it has an antinuclear flavour, but the gallows humour by which it is frequently expressed suggests resignation and fatalism more than opposition: 'grin and bear it' is more the message than 'no nukes' (p. 20).
- The *soft paths* package – offered by environmental groups, this package stresses the dangers of nuclear energy and emphasises the need to pursue alternative, decentralised, ecologically safe and renewable sources of energy (p. 16).
- The *public accountability* package – a populist and principally anti-corporate package, emphasising the profit-driven nature of the nuclear power industry as a serious obstacle to the development of alternative energy sources, and stressing the lack of control over and lack of public accountability in relation to the nuclear power industry (p. 16).
- The *not cost-effective* package – a pragmatic, cost-benefit-focused package, emphasising the empirical fact that in simple cost-benefit terms, nuclear power does not compare well with other types of energy.

As argued in previous chapters (see, in particular, Chapters 2 and 3), a key to understanding the dynamics of the claims-making process is the recognition that for every claim there's a counter-claim (or in Ibarra and Kitsuse's (1993) wording, a 'counter-rhetoric'). Gamson and Modigliani similarly make this point, and do so in a way which succinctly articulates one of the key concerns of this chapter, namely the focus on deeper-lying cultural scripts which can be evoked and drawn upon in the public discourse on environmental issues. In relation to the technological 'progress' values delineated above, they thus identify the equally deep-seated counter-values in Western culture, namely the emphasis on harmony with and protection of nature rather than exploitation of it and control over it, the valuing of 'small-scale' harmony and quality rather than intrusive maximisation, efficiency and quantity. And if the progress theme is prominent – as Gamson and Modigliani demonstrate –

in media and public discourse, the countertheme finds equally powerful expressions in popular culture:

> Much of popular culture features the countertheme: Chaplin's *Modern Times,* Huxley's *Brave New World,* and Kubrick's *2001* and countless other films about technology gone mad and out of control, a Frankenstein's monster about to turn on its creator. If *progress* benefits by its resonance with the theme, two of its competitors, *runaway* and *soft paths* [. . .], draw much of their symbolism from different parts of the countertheme.
>
> (Gamson and Modigliani, 1989: 6)

Spencer Weart (1988), in his pioneering archaeology of nuclear images in popular culture, shows one of the core scripts in relation to public images and discourse on nuclear power to revolve around deep-seated public fear about the interference with nature or the natural order in ways, which are both unpredictable and potentially highly devastating. Weart argues that public narratives of the mid-twentieth century about nuclear bombs polluting fish, causing birth defects, or influencing the weather system all amounted to saying that nuclear energy 'violated the order of nature' (Weart, 1988: 187–88):

> This idea was bound up with one of the strongest of primitive themes: contamination. In most human cultures the violation of nature, and forbidden acts or things in general, have been directly identified with contamination. According to the anthropology theorist Mary Douglas, whatever is 'out of place', whatever goes against the supposed natural order, is called polluting.
>
> (Weart, 1988: 188)

Weart is discussing nuclear technology, but, as Turney (1998) and others have noted, the fundamental fear that scientific progress and science's interference with nature or with God's creation may spiral 'out of control' and produce dangerous outcomes that are both 'wrong' (an ethical discourse) and unpredictable, is equally central to much of the history of genetic manipulation and biotechnology. As with public fears about nuclear power, public fears about genetic manipulation draw from a cultural reservoir, originally expressed in literature and then in wider popular culture products, not least film. Mary Shelley's *Frankenstein,* H.G. Well's *The Island of Dr Moreau* and Aldous Huxley's *Brave New World* – and popular films based on these novels – are perhaps the most prominent expressions and sources of such fundamental fears. Weart points to how public and popular images draw on culturally deep-seated ideas about contamination:

Most important was the fact that radiation could cause genetic defects. This fact resonated with certain old and widespread ideas about contamination. Traditionally, defective babies were a punishment for pollution in the broadest sense, violations such as eating forbidden food, looking at something that should not be seen, or breaking a sexual taboo.

(Weart, 1988: 189)

On occasion the ideas were openly invoked. As early as 1950, liberal newspaper and radio commentators had exclaimed that hydrogen bombs, wrongfully exploiting the 'inner secrets' of creation, would be 'a menace to the order of nature'. On receiving news of the BRAVO test, the conservative publisher William Randolph Hearst told millions of readers that such explosions 'could cause dangerous changes in the orderly processes of natural law'. Even Pope Pius XII, in Easter Sunday messages heard over the radio by hundreds of millions on every continent, warned that bomb tests brought 'pollution' of the mysterious processes of nature.

(Weart, 1988: 190)

As in the public discourse on nuclear power, so too has the increasingly prominent media and public discourse on genetic modification and biotechnology been characterised by broadly two opposite discourses, each with deep cultural resonances: one, celebratory and enthusiastic about the immense potential of scientific and technological progress, and the other concerned and fearful about the dangers and potential for 'out-of-control' damage inherent to scientific and technological development.

Longitudinal analyses of media coverage of biotechnology and genetics both in the UK and the United States (Durant et al., 1996; Bauer et al., 1999; Bauer, 2002; Nisbet and Lewenstein, 2002) show how the polarisation of public discourse on genetics and biotechnology became particularly pronounced in media coverage from the latter half of the 1990s onwards. Bauer (2002) and Nisbet and Lewenstein (2002) thus point to a significant change in the overall 'symbolic environment of biotechnology' in the 1990s in the form of a deepening polarisation between 'desirable' biomedical research/applications and 'un-desirable' agri-food biotechnology, although it needs to be noted that there are deep cultural differences between Europe and the North America in terms of relative prominence of these discourses.

Drawing closely on Gamson and Modigliani's notion of framing and their typology of cultural packages, communication research in Europe, Australia and the United States (e.g. Bauer et al., 1999; Petersen, 2001;

Nisbet and Lewenstein, 2002; Ten Eyck and Williment, 2003) has mapped key trends in media coverage of the new genetics and biotechnology, including the rapid advances in genetic manipulation of both plants and animals. Not surprisingly, as it is in the nature of cultural packages that they articulate general ideas and principles rather than issue-specific characteristics, many of the same cultural packages identified in the nuclear power discourse, are equally prevalent in the media and public discourse on genetic engineering and manipulation. Thus, the 'progress' package (celebrating the rapid advances, breakthroughs, and developments in genetic research and science) features prominently, as does the 'economic prospect' package. But also present, and in some cases increasingly so as the coverage moves into the more recent period, are the 'fear-and-concern'-related packages such as 'nature/nurture', 'Pandora's box' and 'runaway technology/science'.

Turney (1998), Huxford (2000) and others have persuasively argued that environment and science correspondents as well as journalists generally rely heavily on readily available cultural scripts and frames, particularly when reporting on new and unfamiliar developments in science and environmental issues. Likewise, much communication research – although more so in the fields of science and medicine, than in the field of 'environment' – has pointed to the central significance of metaphor in news reporting (see also the discussion in Box 5.1). This is not surprising, as the very purpose of metaphor is of course to make the unfamiliar familiar, or in other words, to help us understand that which we don't know by explaining it with reference to what we know and are familiar with. Invoking familiar scripts, interpretive packages, schema or metaphors serves the purpose of transferring ('transfer' is the literal meaning of the Greek root of 'metaphor': metapherein) meaning from what we know to what we don't, as yet, know. Importantly, however, the process is not simply a matter of conveying information or establishing comprehension, but also significantly carries with it a particular 'view' or 'perspective', a particular way of framing the unknown, and with these, a potential attitude or stance on things. Journalists invoking particular frames or scripts is often 'more to do with cueing certain cultural fears' (Huxford, 2000: 192), as embodied in popular culture, than with providing an understanding of environmental or scientific developments or phenomena.

But while our cultural reservoir is replete with both utopian and dystopian perspectives on nature, the environment and science, it is often the scary and dystopian, rather than the optimistic and utopian, scripts from literature, film and other popular culture that are invoked and drawn upon in media and public discourse on environmental and scientific developments. This is particularly the case, where – as with nuclear power and with the new genetics – genuine fears, concerns and worries are fuelled by scientific uncertainty or controversy. Like Turney (1998), Huxford (2000) thus, for example, demonstrates the prominence of particular science fiction frames or scripts in media reporting on cloning:

> The use of the science fiction frame was extremely common in this coverage, both in Britain and in the United States. In a sample of 204 articles in which cloning was the principal focus, ninety-two (46 per cent) carried such associations. Of these, the tone of the vast majority was negative, raising fears of the future use of the technology.
> (Huxford, 2000: 191)

Huxford's analysis shows the three most prominently referenced science fiction works to be Aldous Huxley's *Brave New World* (mentioned in thirty-two of ninety-two articles referencing science fiction), Mary Shelley's *Frankenstein* (referenced in twenty-one of ninety-two articles) and *The Boys From Brazil* (thirteen of ninety-two articles). The analysis shows, argues Huxford (2000: 197),

> the way that science fiction frames, employed by the media during the clone coverage, brought with them largely negative narratives that cued a series of oppositional couplings: religion versus science, man versus institution, the individual versus society, high culture versus low culture, past versus future. In each case the former was privileged—but shown to be threatened through cloning—by the latter.

The largely negative scripts identified in Huxford's analysis as readily used frames for media coverage of cloning interestingly bear many similarities with some of the dominant interpretive packages identified by Gamson and Modigliani in relation to popular culture narratives about nuclear power. Like the frames informing popular culture narratives about the new genetics, those concerned with nuclear power can similarly be divided broadly into the dichotomy of dystopian and utopian scripts/frames or narratives. But as shown in Gamson and Modigliani's analysis the relative prominence of different interpretive packages varies across different genres of media and popular culture output.

This is further confirmed by Podeschi's (2002) analysis of environmental discourse in science fiction film from the latter half of the twentieth century. Podeschi thus demonstrates a marked change in this particular genre's nuclear discourse, from scary foreground narratives – often metaphorically transcoding and expressing the communist and cold war fears of the time – in the 1950s and 1960s, to a *naturalisation* and back-grounding of nuclear power as an innocuous and abundant power source for the futuristic societies commonly depicted in science fiction film. As Podeschi notes, such portrayal is at odds with both the rise of public resistance to nuclear power evidenced during the 1970s and 1980s, with the flood of news coverage brought on by the high-profile nuclear accidents at Three Mile Island (1979) and Chernobyl (1986), and with non-science-fiction film discourses on nuclear technology:

> Unlike the film *The China Syndrome* (1979) which transcodes fears about nuclear power, science fiction films [after 1970] are comfortable with the technology.
>
> Concern about nuclear weapons and concern about technology that unites with humanity are the strongest threads of resistance in the entire sample. Taken together, they cover the entire period, one largely prior to 1970 and one largely after 1970. Combined with the naturalisation of nuclear power that is also evident after 1970, these films may be articulating a shift in societal anxiety, from the tangible fear of radiation and nuclear war to explorations of futures in which computer technology is central and powerful in our lives.
>
> (Podeschi, 2002: 288)

Exercise 5.1

Interpretive packages in the current nuclear power and climate-change debate

Media images and public perceptions regarding nuclear power have a turbulent history, characterised by ups and downs in both levels of interest and in the 'climate of opinion' surrounding this technology. Following comparatively low levels of media and public interest in nuclear power during the 1990s, the start of the new millennium witnessed renewed interest:

> At the start of 2000, however, new focusing events began to shift the interpretative packages and mental categories applied to nuclear energy. In 2001, in reaction to rising energy costs and rolling blackouts in California, the George W. Bush administration launched a communication campaign to promote nuclear power as a *middle way path* to energy independence. The terrorist attacks of September 11, 2001, dampened the viability of this frame package, as experts and

media reports focused on nuclear power plants as potential terrorist targets. But since 2004, as energy prices have climbed and as U.S. dependence on overseas oil has been defined by political leaders as a major national security issue, a renewed emphasis on the energy independence interpretation has surfaced.[. . .]

The effort by the second Bush administration and the nuclear energy industry to reframe the relevance of nuclear energy has been complemented by an attempt to similarly sell nuclear energy as a *middle way* solution to greenhouse gas emissions.

(Nisbet, 2009: 13)

Similar trends to those identified in this quote in relation to the United States can be seen in the UK and other European countries.

Using the Google search engine and the search term 'nuclear power and climate change' (or equivalent terms or search combinations), identify from the first 2–3 pages of Google hits, a selection of relevant news and other internet items (e.g. pressure group statements, blogs, etc.) that refer to or discuss the role of nuclear power in relation to public and political concern about action on climate change.

Which major 'cultural packages' (e.g. *progress, energy/economic indepen-dence, runaway/Pandora's box, public accountability, soft paths/middle way, not cost effective,* etc.) are in evidence?

Comment: note that the individual package descriptions given earlier in this chapter, for example, in relation to Gamson and Modigliani's analysis, should be taken, not as definitive categories, but rather as tentative indications of the general focus of each particular package. Thus, the manifestation of a package such as the progress package in current discourse may well 'look' slightly different from its main articulation in public discourse of, say the 1960s. For example, the 'progress package' traditionally cast nuclear power generation and technology as a symbol of modernity and society's progress; in its current version, it is probably more likely to appear simply as affirmation of the belief that technological innovation and prowess is the best solution to tackling and moving forward on problems such as climate change.

Which packages seem to be most prominent in the current discourse?

Comment: note particularly that the relative prominence of different packages does not equate with or translate in any simple way into stance, that is, the *progress package* or the *soft paths/middle way* package may be prominent both because they are being used to promote nuclear power and/or because they are being refuted or used/referenced in arguments against nuclear power.

Significant changes over time in the relative prominence of different cultural narratives and interpretations of nature and the environment are also the central focus of Glenda Wall's (1999) detailed and illuminating study of a very different – from science fiction film, that is – genre, namely television documentary. Wall examines the changing discourses of science, nature and environment in the Canadian documentary series *The Nature of Things* over the extended period from 1960 to 1994. Her analysis shows that a bio-economic outlook dominated the 1960s, that is, a perspective which saw nature as an exploitable source of resources and wealth, a domain to be studied, understood, controlled and managed by science, and a place 'where one could go to renew oneself and escape the alienating effects of city life' (p. 61). This view changed gradually, moving in the 1970s towards an increasing emphasis on nature 'as vulnerable and fragile, with parts of it being under attack as a result of technological growth' (p. 64), and with an increasing focus on the complexity evident in nature. At the beginning of the 1990s, 'the idea that nature will respond with a vengeance to the abuses piled upon it' (p. 68) became prominent.

Wall's longitudinal analysis thus shows how discourses of nature in the television documentary changed, from the 1960s to the early 1990s, from a view of nature as a resource to be controlled and exploited, to a view of nature as fragile, but also potentially vengeful, and as deserving of respect and protection.

But while nature and the environment may have featured prominently for a long time in particular science or nature-oriented types of programming (e.g. the Canadian *The Nature of Things* analysed by Wall, or long-running documentary series such as the American *Nova* or the British *Horizon*, or indeed – as discussed in more detail below – a long tradition of wildlife films and nature programmes), analyses of mainstream television entertainment programming show a very different picture. James Shanahan and his colleagues, in a series of studies (Shanahan, 1996; Shanahan and McComas, 1997, 1999; McComas et al., 2001) of the portrayal of nature, the environment and environmental issues in television entertainment programmes broadcast on the main American television networks in the 1990s, thus found not only that popular television entertainment programming gave little attention overall to the environment as an issue or a problem, but also that such attention declined considerably and rapidly after the peak of environmental public concern in the very early part of the 1990s.

Nature and the environment were thus rarely – in television entertainment programming – in the foreground as a key theme or narrative component, that is, rarely foregrounded as something to be discussed or problematised. Moreover, Shanahan and McComas found that, while environmental issues and those speaking up on environmental issues may have been portrayed with some conferral of legitimacy in the early 1990s, by the mid-1990s environmental claims and claims-makers had either been absorbed within the general consumerist ideology of television or had been marginalised, 'acquired a bit of the air of the lunatic' as they put it (1999: 103).

Viewers of entertainment television programmes are, in the words of Shanahan and McComas (1999: 102–3) encouraged to see the environment as (in no particular order):

• A beautiful alternative to city life.
• A 'problem' to be solved through citizen action.
• A political commitment for socially marginal types.
• A source of jokes.
• A source of trivia (a nostalgically fading issue that characterised a particular era).
• A test and challenge for human resourcefulness.

Mainstream television entertainment programming thus taps into and reinforces many of the same cultural resonances identified in relation to film and popular culture generally. But perhaps the key lesson to be drawn from studies of television entertainment programming is that to the extent that the environment is seen as a 'problem' or a topic for debate and discussion at all, its 'meaning' is largely framed in terms which fit the overall objective of commercial television – to promote consumerism. Television entertainment programming thus offers a symbolic environment which denies legitimacy, or at least any sense of urgency, to the notion that there may be a 'problem' with how we interact with nature and the environment, while at the same time affording legitimacy to consumer culture that is potentially highly detrimental to nature and the environment.

The key lessons that can be drawn from the various studies and analyses referred to so far can be summarised as follows:

1. Media coverage of environmental issues, science and technology draws on, evokes and articulates readily available cultural and interpretive packages, which in turn set particular frames or boundaries for how issues are and can be discussed and understood.

2. Cultural and interpretive packages (also often referred to in the literature as, *inter alia*, scripts, schemas, frames, narratives or discourses) are, by their very nature, *always available*, but some resonate more readily than others with widely held beliefs, fears and concerns, and such resonances change over time.
3. While deep-seated cultural packages can be drawn upon or evoked across widely different types of media and popular culture output, their articulation and inflection varies considerably with the genre, narrative and other (e.g. journalistic and organisational) conventions of different types of media and media content.

The latter point also redirects our attention to differences between large national or international 'mainstream' media and regional/local or 'alternative' media – a distinction that, as we have seen in the previous chapter has important implications for how environmental issues are reported, and for how 'blame' and 'solutions' are constructed. An important recent study by Widener and Gunter (2007) demonstrates this very clearly through an analysis of the coverage of the aftermath and environmental recovery after the Exxon Valdez oil spill in Prince William Sound in Alaska in 1989. Their analysis focuses on the '*Tundra Times,* an Alaska Native newspaper based in Anchorage and established in 1962' (p. 769) and compares its coverage of the long recovery after the 1989 oil spill with coverage in Alaskan mainstream newspapers (*The Anchorage Daily News* and *Anchorage Times*).

Using Gamson and Modigliani's notions of interpretive packages and cultural resonances, they demonstrate a clear hierarchy of source use, that is, that the mainstream media draw on traditional authority sources, while the *Tundra Times* gives proportionally more space and access to the voices of both native and non-native 'ordinary' people (confirming, as we have seen in Chapters 3 and 4, the findings of many other studies that mainstream media are notoriously 'authority oriented'). And they go on to show how who gets quoted has direct implications for the relative prominence of different interpretive packages and related cultural resonances.

> In this case, scientists sought precise measures of wildlife decline, reflective of a scientific worldview that shapes the image of news as objective. In our examination of the *Anchorage Daily News*, coverage of recovery was confined principally to measurable entities such as financial compensation and wildlife.[. . .]
>
> In contrast, the *Tundra Times* sought to connect damage with broader themes of respect, duties, and the betrayal of trust from the oil industry

and the state government to the people of Alaska. For example, the 'Voice of the Times' claimed primarily that 'objective science' had been lost following the spill, indicating that scientific research that demonstrated prolonged damage lacked objectivity. On the other hand, the *Tundra Times* never limited the debate to such narrow terms. Rather, the focus in the *Tundra Times* was on the cultural meaning of the spill through a wide range of devices, including stylistic features such as poems and fables.

(Widener and Gunter, 2007: 775)

The mainstream newspapers thus give priority to a science-based, expert-driven, quantitative and 'objective' measurement-oriented discourse, while the alternative *Tundra Times* affords prominence[8] to an interpretive package that stresses the subjective-lived experiences of people affected, loss of trust and quality-of-life issues, as well as deploying a more general 'rhetoric of loss' (see also the discussion of Ibarra and Kitsuse, 1993, in Chapter 2) – a rhetoric which activates notions of a past pristine idyllic utopia and pits this against notions of a damaged, spoilt, 'broken', dysfunctional present and future. The 'alternative' interpretive package, prominent in the *Tundra Times*, was further activated and consolidated through the use of culturally resonant symbols such as 'Mother Earth' versus 'Father Oil',[9] 'Black Death' and 'Holocaust', as well as comparisons of the oil spill with the AIDS epidemic 'to draw attention to the massive and tragic nature of their loss' (Widener and Gunter, 2007: 778).

Widener and Gunter's confirmation of the well-known finding from a large body of media research on source access and source hierarchies, that 'alternative' voices and marginalised groups are largely excluded from large mainstream media but may find a platform in smaller regional/ local or 'alternative' media, points to an important dilemma for claims-makers seeking to gain a hearing for their claims in the public sphere:

> Marginalized groups turn to alternative media because their voices are excluded from mainstream media, while in turn the very 'unconventionality' of their voices prohibits a connection to the mainstream.
>
> (Widener and Gunter, 2007: 780)

This suggests that if marginalised groups wish to gain access to mainstream media, not just to alternative media, they must rhetorically *re-package* their claims in terms that resonate with and conform to the dominant culture and dominant interpretive packages. But, and this is the crucial question, can such *re-packaging* be done without loss of the fundamental and defining strands and principles of a package?

The point about access to alternative media is also relevant to considerations – see Chapter 3 – about how environmental activists and pressure groups might exploit new media technologies (internet, mobile communications technology, etc.) for campaigning purposes. Essentially, successful claims-making is not merely or even predominantly about securing access to just any public sphere outlet (e.g. an alternative medium, an email list, a website, etc.), but it is crucially about 'breaking into' mainstream media and dominant discourses, and this, I would argue, is often done more effectively by *engaging* with, chipping away at (which would include subtle acts of rhetorical re-definition or re-framing), dominant interpretive packages rather than by merely placing alternative frames or interpretive packages alongside dominant packages.

Box 5.1

Word-matters/words matter: changing lexis/metaphor to change public connotations

Words matter. A single well-chosen word is often enough to evoke an entire readily available cultural script or frame (see Turney, 1998, at the beginning of this chapter). There is no such thing as 'neutral' language. Communication – whether in scientific articles in peer-reviewed journals, or in news reports, or press releases – is in some way or form about persuasion. Environmental issues are not – and perhaps can never be – described in a completely value-free or objective fashion. As argued in previous chapters, claims-makers (whether scientists, environmental activists, politicians or simply concerned 'lay' citizens) and media professionals are fully aware of the importance of lexical choice and are fully conscious that successful communication in the public sphere is an act that requires careful attention, not just to the general thematic content or the general legal, ethical, scientific, economic, etc. 'rights' and 'wrongs' pertaining to particular issues, but also crucially to the connotations and cultural scripts that are or may be evoked through the choice of vocabulary, the choice of particular words for describing the issue and for making claims about it.

Public and media communication about environmental issues is not then so much about information or indeed about education as it is about competition between different claims-makers and between different claims or constructions of these issues. The language used, the choice of vocabulary, is key to what we may call the ideological management of competing discourses in the public sphere. The vocabulary generally and the metaphors more specifically chosen to describe existing and newly emerging environmental problems are thus anything but arbitrary: they are, to use Günther Kress's

(1997) term, highly 'motivated'. That is, they are deliberately chosen with a view to, of course, making them intelligible beyond a specialist audience by connoting or evoking some phenomenon, perspective or explanatory frame that is already widely known or familiar, but more importantly with a view to framing what are often contentious and controversial issues in such a way as to promote and strengthen particular arguments, interests and discourses.

When scientists and others first started drawing attention to the thinning of the ozone layer, something that was and is wholly invisible to the naked eye, the term 'hole' in the ozone layer was much more effective in raising public alarm and concern because it resonated much more widely with public perceptions and fears, and was simply easier to comprehend, than the process of 'thinning' (which of course raises difficult-to-answer questions such as 'how much' or 'how fast', 'how widespread'?) (Ungar, 1992, 2003; Mazur and Lee, 1993). It is of course not only the choice of words that is important to successful claims-making, but also – crucially for an issue which could not be visualised in conventional terms by filming it directly – the scientific graphs and computer graphics 'designed' to visualise the problem. In the early claims-making about global warming, both scientific graphs and computer graphics thus played a key role in visually constructing this as an important and urgent environmental problem requiring immediate public and political action (Mazur and Lee, 1993).

The construction of climate change as a key – the key – environmental issue of our time similarly has an interesting linguistic history. When the recent, as in the last 20–25 years, round of claims-making about the potentially catastrophic outcome of rapidly rising carbon dioxide levels in the atmosphere started in the 1980s, this phenomenon was of course widely referred to as the 'greenhouse effect' and as 'global warming'. The term 'the greenhouse effect' was particularly evocative, because of its instant appeal to something that virtually everybody could relate to as a direct sensory experience, that is, humidity and heat, and although the word image could potentially evoke positive connotations of lush and fertile growth, it also potentially carried the negative connotations of unpleasant and stifling humidity and heat.

While the terms 'greenhouse effect' and 'global warming' may have been effective lexical choices for 'sounding the global alarm' (Mazur and Lee, 1993), it also became increasingly clear during the 1990s that these were rather misleading terms that failed to capture the diverse impacts of climate change and maybe even were counterproductive in terms of raising public awareness and more importantly in terms of persuading a reluctant politics that action was urgently needed. Thus the term 'global warming', for example, potentially handicapped claims-makers, like the Intergovernmental Panel on Climate Change (IPCC), who tried to argue that climate change was anthropogenic – caused by humans – and instead afforded room for counter-claimants to argue that climate change was merely a 'natural' part of the Earth's long history of cycles of colder and warmer periods.

'Global warming' and 'greenhouse effect', in claims-making terms were also disadvantaged by the fact that the period preceding the rise of concern and claims-making about climate change in the late 1980s, had seen a degree of prominence given to cold-war-related scientific concerns about a 'nuclear winter', the notion that a major nuclear exchange between the then superpowers would cause enough dust and particle pollution in the atmosphere to shut out sunshine and send the earth into a prolonged period of much colder temperatures. The fact that the terms 'global warming' and more particularly 'greenhouse effect' have receded from prominence in public debate since the mid-to-late 1990s is thus an example of what discourse analysts would call successful 're-lexicalisation', a deliberate change of terms for the purpose of promoting a particular view, understanding or perspective (while also, in this case, removing the basis on which many of the counter-claims were built).

But perhaps one of the most active domains of 're-lexicalisation' – indicative of the deep-seated uncertainties and public anxieties which characterise this field – is that of the new genetics, of biotechnology and the manipulation of genes/genetic material in both plants and animals. Bauer et al. (1999) thus describe the significant lexical changes, symptomatic both of public/cultural sensitivities and of claims-maker interests:

In the early days, the term biotechnology itself was hardly used. Instead, the English-speaking world commonly referred either to 'genetic engineering' or – in more technical discourse – to 'recombinant DNA (rDNA) technology'. With time, however, what came to be perceived as the negative connotations of 'genetic engineering' led to the introduction of two new terms: first 'genetic manipulation', and then (as this term, too, came to be viewed with suspicion) 'genetic modification' (GM). Recently, in what may be a borrowing from the German-speaking world, there has been a noticeable increase in the use of the term 'gene technology' (Gentechnologie).

(Bauer et al., 1999: 217)

More recently, Condit et al. (2002: 69) have provided a systematic longitudinal analysis of the changing meanings of the word 'mutation' in US mass magazine articles about genetics published between 1919 and 1996. They concluded that:

the term 'mutation' has become increasingly negative in its connotations through time. [. . .] Increases in the negative contextualisation of 'mutation' were initially associated with reports of genetic damage to humans from nuclear radiation after 1956. Later increases in negative connotations appear to arise from more diffuse sources.

The particular value of the study by Condit and her colleagues is the clear demonstration that meanings and connotations associated with key terms in popular and media discourse on genetics change over time, leading in some cases, as Bauer et al. (1999) argue, to a deliberate substitution of terms. These arguments help sensitise us to the idea that media and public discourse on genetics does not, of course, just arise naturally, as it were, but is ultimately the result of deliberate rhetorical, linguistic and framing 'work' undertaken by stakeholders in the debate. Perhaps the key rhetorical task for genetic research and science in the last forty to fifty years has been to separate and distinguish – in the public mind – the endeavours, achievements and goals of the New Genetics from the wholly negative historical legacy of images and connotations associated with eugenics (Hansen, 2006: 816).

Wildlife films and nature documentaries: reading popular constructions of nature and the environment culturally

Wildlife films and nature documentaries may at first sight appear to belong to the more pleasant, wholesome, aesthetic, innocently entertaining and educational end of popular culture, far removed from the harsh, politicised, controversy-saturated and often violent realities of, for example, everyday mainstream news output. Such a perception would not be entirely accidental, as indeed it has often been one of the major explicitly stated objectives of producers of wildlife films and nature documentaries to project exactly such an image. In his impressive historical tour of American wildlife film and programming, history professor Greg Mitman (1999) thus quotes from the stated objectives of the producers of the popular wildlife series *Wild Kingdom* of the late 1950s and early 1960s, that it would carry 'no vestige of political, ideological, or governmental conflict or controversy' (Mitman, 1999: 155–56). Bousé (1998) similarly notes the 'absence of overt history or politics' as one of the defining features of the much more recent mode of nature programming known as 'blue chip' programmes (see Box 5.2).

The particular relevance of Mitman's historical analysis of wildlife and nature programming to the arguments of this chapter concerns his clear exposition of how such programmes provide a carefully 'constructed' view of nature and the environment, a view which both resonates with and in turn impacts on wider social and cultural perceptions and attitudes regarding life in general and nature/the environment in particular. Because of the longitudinal and historical scope of his analysis, Mitman is also able to indicate some of the kind of dialectical and interactive nature of the relationship between media packages, public climates of opinion and wider cultural packages.

In a very simplified form one could sketch these dialectics along the following lines: wildlife films and nature documentaries are popular with their audiences to the extent that they succeed in 'speaking to' and – implicitly – engaging with deeper public anxieties, worries and concerns; wildlife films and nature documentaries project, channel and re-construct wider abstract social and cultural concerns within a frame which offers particular core values and world views as 'solutions' and exemplary modes of conduct; over longer periods of time, the frequent repetition of such core values and world views impacts on public views – and ultimately on political and policy debate in the public sphere – by providing first and foremost a discursive frame or interpretive packages which define what is and can be said about, for example, nature/environment protection and conservation versus exploitation of nature/the environment (I shall return, in Chapter 7, to a more extended discussion of the conceptualisation of media 'influence' or roles inherent in this type of model).

Mitman persuasively demonstrates how some of the most popular wildlife films and nature series of the 1950s – many of them created by Disney – essentially reinforced and reworked the romantic view of nature from the eighteenth and nineteenth centuries to engage with, accommodate and reinforce dominant American cultural values of the 1950s. Mitman (1999) particularly reads Disney's nature films of the early 1950s as speaking directly and soothingly to the painful public memories of war:

> To a wider public, Disney's nature – benevolent and pure – captured the emotional beauty of nature's grand design, eased the memories of the death and destruction of the previous decade, and affirmed the importance of America as one nation under God. (p. 110)

> Disney not only captured the aesthetic beauty of nature, he transformed it into a commodity with a set of values pertaining to democracy and morality that appealed to the American public. (p. 124)

Not only then did wildlife and nature films of the time allow a public, horrified by the atrocities, violence and devastation of the Second World War to immerse itself, in an almost escapist fashion, in a highly selective and aestheticised construction of nature as spectacle, but the 'nature-world' on display at the same time metaphorically emphasised and affirmed a particular ideological view of society. Disney, in particular, used nature as a frame into which to project core American values, while at the same time lending to those very same values the power and legitimacy of 'natural-ness'. In the wake of the destruction and violence of the Second World War, and amidst growing public anxiety about communism and the escalating Cold War, Disney, argues Mitman, 'offered a persuasive vision of the American way of life rooted in individualism, traditional family values, and religious morality' (1999: 129). The supreme ideological achievement of the selective and particular construction of nature in the wildlife and nature films of the 1950s was indeed to *naturalise* core values built around the nuclear family and religion, traditional gender roles, democracy and the social order of the time.

Mitman demonstrates how this particular visualisation and construction of nature was anything but natural, in the sense that it presented a highly selective portrait of nature and the environment, a construction with a very clear convergence of particular ideological, commercial and not least ethnic and class-specific interests. Nature, in the Disney films and other popular programmes of the 1950s and early 1960s, was a sanitised version of nature emphasising the environment and nature as beautiful, idyllic, harmonious and above all 'pristine' – untouched and unspoilt by humans – and carefully devoid of graphic portrayals of animal violence and of any direct focus on animal sex.

> Like pristine nature, childhood, conceived as a time of innocence, offered a place of grace from the horrific acts of destruction and degenerative influences wrought by modern civilisation. Both were hallowed spaces in American society that needed to be preserved. Much of natural history films were the respectable alternative to less wholesome films in the early motion picture industry, animal shows on 1950s television offered entertaining and educational subject matter that the whole family could enjoy. In television shows like *Zoo Parade*, the construction of sentimental nature and childhood in postwar American society were closely intertwined. (p. 135)

> In sheltering young, be they animal or human, from nuclear annihilation, the threat of communism, and the more insidious side of commercial culture, Americans in the 1950s upheld the nuclear family as a safe haven. Animal behaviour stories, especially those that focused on themes such as courtship, nest-building, parenting, and development of the young, universalised the family as a natural unit. The ideal of universality conformed precisely to the marketing needs of national television advertisers, who sought to project an image of the white, middle-class American family in which ethnic and class differences were homogenized. (pp. 141–42).

(Mitman, 1999: 135)

The appreciation and popularisation of wildlife and nature engendered through the 1950s' aesthetically pleasing images of a pristine and natural order, and through the construction of nature as the natural home of core cultural values, received a further twist towards domestication of animals/wildlife and spectacle in the 1960s. Mitman notes how the rise of pet keeping and the growth of tourism in the 1960s was exploited by wildlife and nature film producers, with further implications for the campaigning strategies of environmentalists. Thus, programmes worked to establish associations between wild animals and domestic pets, and animals were imbued with personality and charisma in anthropomorphic fashion, in ways which lent themselves not only to the use of animal characters for marketing purposes, but to the marketing of 'the value of wildlife' (Mitman, 1999: 153).

> By transforming wildlife into domestic pets, animal rights groups and environmental organisations could appeal to pet owners in America [. . .] for support. In the 1960s, as the environmental movement gained political ground, footage and logos of charismatic species such as harp seals, dolphins, and panda bears became common in the political campaign strategies of animal rights groups and environmental organisations such as the International Fund for Animals, Greenpeace, and the World Wildlife Fund.
>
> (Mitman, 1999: 154)

By the late 1970s, the sanitised and harmonious constructions of nature in perfect balance had long since given way to an altogether more violent, sensational, dramatic and dramatised depiction of nature. The historically and culturally rooted change – and the dialectic interplay, alluded to earlier in this section, between media constructions of wildlife and nature, public tastes and demands, and social and political values – can then be broadly summarised as follows:

> The immediate postwar years saw an explosive growth in nature audiences [. . .]. War-weary Americans looked to nature for wholesome entertainment for their children. When the baby-boom generation came of age, these childhood experiences became the seeds of 1960s environmental activism. The environmental movement in turn sparked even greater audience demand for natural history shows. [. . .] By the mid to late 1970s, however, television networks filled programming slots with less expensive and equally popular game shows as costs for more sophisticated technological productions of nature programs kept pace with viewers' increasingly exacting taste for more dramatic, hyperreal scenes of wildlife.

[. . .] Furthermore, by dramatizing sex and violence found throughout the animal kingdom, such shows as *Fangs, Predators,* and weekly specials like *Shark Week* engaged new generations of enthusiasts with graphic, close-up scenes of animals copulating or predators killing prey.

(Mitman, 1999: 205)

Box 5.2

Nature as narrative – narrativising nature

In Box 5.1, we looked at the key significance and power of individual terms or words in evoking or triggering chains of connotations and associated meanings. Here, I wish to draw on Bousé (1998) to move beyond the word level of analysis to point to the equally important role of narrative and narrative structure as a conveyor of ideological meanings in media texts.[10]

Bousé argues that the defining master stroke of Disney's contribution to wildlife films was the act of imposing a conventionalised narrative framework upon them, including the use of dramatic and comic plots often reflecting familiar mythic patterns deeply ingrained in Western cultural traditions (p. 130). As Bousé points out, the demand of media organisations in the 1990s continues to be for 'well-plotted, dramatic storylines and strong character development', a successful formula that was well established in the Disney productions of the 1960s and has since been exported and adapted worldwide, including in British natural history films.

> This 'classic format' for wildlife films, with its 'rules' and narrative conventions, has also been flexible and adaptable enough over the years to accommodate stories about domesticated animals, from Disney's *The Incredible Journey* (1963), to its recent Japanese rip-off *The Adventures of Milo and Otis* (genially narrated by Dudley Moore). It has also survived intact without voice-over narration in films like Jean-Jacques Annaud's *The Bear* (1989), and Disney's *Homeward Bound* (1993; also a reworking of *The Incredible Journey*).
>
> (Bousé, 1998: 132)

The core narrative formula thus runs along the following lines – note the similarity with the classic folk/fairy-tale formula identified by structuralists such as Vladimir Propp (1968), Roland Barthes (1977a) and others:

> The story typically opens in spring, and centers on a protagonist (sometime more than one) who is either orphaned, abandoned, or separated from family or community. It then faces a perilous journey or struggle to survive so that the lost primal unity of family and/or community can be regained. Present in this 'family romance' are such

mythic narrative elements as departure, separation, quest, initiation, and triumphant return or re-union. Though the perilous journey motif has given way in recent years to the perilous ordeal, such as weathering the dry season, or surviving attacks by predators (or humans), the relation of these events to the theme of youthful initiation remains central.

(Bousé, 1998: 132)

As a result largely of economic and media-organisational pressures to maximise audiences, the tendency today, argues Bousé, is in the direction of what has become known as 'Blue Chip' films. In terms of 'constructions of nature', perhaps the key point that stands out is the way in which several of the core features combine to project and reinforce an image of nature as a pristine and unspoilt 'Eden on Earth', devoid of the politics, controversies, problems and stresses of modern civilisation, yet serving, through the narrative and anthropomorphic depiction of animals, to 'naturalise' and reinforce particular cultural and social values and arrangements.

Bousé (1998: 134) offers this helpful characterisation of the key features of 'Blue Chip' nature programming:

1. *The depiction of mega-fauna* – lions, leopards, tigers, bears, sharks, and other large predators, although elephants, whales and few other non-predators are also included.

2. *Visual splendour* – magnificent scenery, beautiful sunsets, and stunning panoramas as a background to the animals, all of which suggest a still unspoiled, primeval wilderness.

3. *Dramatic narrative* – this can entail the classic, animal protagonist-centred narrative, or some version of the 'family romance', or even a narrative centring on the film-maker's encounter with the animals, but in any case usually includes some dramatic chases and escapes.

4. *The absence of history and politics* – no overt [. . .] propaganda on behalf of conservation issues and their causes.

5. *The absence of people* – although the film-maker can occasionally appear as a character to provide the point of view, more than one or two people can spell the introduction of scientific and technical conservation efforts that spoil the 'natural' picture.

6. *The absence of science* – while perhaps the weakest and most often broken of these 'rules', the discourse of science can entail its own narrative of research (see Silverstone, 1984), with all its attendant technical jargon and seemingly arcane methodologies, which, like history and politics, spoil the picture of nature in all its 'natural' splendour.

Thanks to the excellent – often longitudinal and historically focused – analyses of wildlife films and nature documentaries by the likes of Mitman (1999), Bousé (1998, 2000), Davies (2000a, 2000b), Cottle (2004), Aldridge and Dingwall (2003), Dingwall and Aldridge (2006) and others, we now have a relative comprehensive understanding of the narrative formats, key values and associated constructions of nature and the environment in this popular genre, particularly for the post-war period and up until the late 1990s. As I have argued above, one of the most interesting aspects of analysing wildlife films and nature documentaries concerns their ideological content. That is, the way in which they both express and ideologically reinforce particular and selected social values and world views, while also in the longer term contributing to changes in social and public perceptions and attitudes to nature. What is fascinating is the intricate web of interaction between material and social realities, their representation and articulation in media and popular culture, and changes in public and personal views about the environment, including about how we relate to, treat, use and protect nature and the environment in ways that are both 'sustainable' and (ethically) responsible.

Exercise 5.2

Constructing nature and naturalising social/cultural values?

Analyses (including those by Mitman and Bousé referred to earlier) of wildlife films and nature documentaries have emphasised the way in which the narrative and format conventions of these types of programmes require and work towards a view of nature as separate and distinct from mankind or civilisation. The illusion created for us is nature programmes as a 'window' on nature, a passive observer of animals and nature going about their business. Major nature documentaries of the last decade or so would appear, however, to have deliberately broken with this traditional mould by devoting, for example, the last ten minutes of an hour-long episode to a 'behind-the-scenes' sequence focusing on the patience, stamina and technological ingenuity required by camera crews and on the trial-and-error process of capturing nature in what Bousé (above) refers to as its 'natural splendour'.

Consider one of the most prestigious, most expensive and most widely viewed nature documentary series of recent times, *Planet Earth*. Here is Wikipedia's introductory overview:

Planet Earth is a multi award-winning 2006 television series produced by the BBC Natural History Unit. Four years in the making, it was the most expensive nature documentary series ever commissioned by the BBC, and also the first to be filmed in high definition. The series was co-produced by the Discovery Channel and NHK in association with CBC, and was described by its makers as "the definitive look at the diversity of our planet".

Planet Earth was first broadcast in the United Kingdom on BBC One in March 2006, and premiered one year later in the USA on the Discovery Channel. By June 2007, it had been shown in 130 countries worldwide. The original BBC version was narrated by David Attenborough and produced by Alastair Fothergill. For Discovery, the executive producer was Maureen Lemire, with Sigourney Weaver's voiceover replacing Attenborough.

The series comprises eleven episodes, each of which features a global overview of a different habitat on Earth. At the end of each fifty-minute episode, a ten-minute featurette takes a behind-the-scenes look at the challenges of filming the series.

Source: http://en.wikipedia.org/wiki/Planet_Earth_(TV_series)

Watch one or more episodes of *Planet Earth* and explore how far the various characteristics delineated in this chapter, for example, with reference to Mitman and Bousé's analyses, apply:

- Does the sheer 'visual splendour' suggest 'unspoiled, primeval wilderness'?
- Are people and other signs of civilisation's intrusion absent? Is the impression conveyed that we as viewers are simply spectators, voyeurs 'looking in' on nature?
- Does the 'behind-the-scenes' addition at the end of each episode effectively alert us, the viewers, to the constructedness of what we see? Does it matter if it does or doesn't?

Comment: it would be fair to assume that one reason why a series such as Planet Earth has been so successful is precisely because it excels on all the normal criteria (technical, visual, aesthetic, narrative, etc.) and viewer expectations of what a nature documentary should do and should look like. The implicit criticism in much of the research on nature documentaries seems to be that these conventions carry with them and perpetuate an idealised – maybe romanticised – and environmentally perhaps 'un-realistic' view of our natural environment.

- What kinds of story-telling or narrative devices are used?

Comment: note particularly the importance of visuals, sound/music and, of course crucially, the voice-over narration which tells us what the visuals 'mean' and provides narrative continuity.

- Does the narrative structure/formula conform – in whole or in part – to the 'core narrative formula' described above with reference to Bousé?

Comment: does the narrative formula follow the seasonal (spring, summer. . .) and/or life cycle of a central protagonist (an individual animal, a nuclear family or larger unit of a particular species, etc.), construed along such key narrative elements as 'departure, separation, quest, initiation and triumphant return or re-union' (Bousé, 1998: 132)?

- What values or ideologies are communicated through the narrative structure and the visual/verbal characterisation of wildlife?

Comment: are animals imbued – for example, through the voice-over narration – with human characteristics and values. If so, which values and can these values be seen to relate to a particular social class, religion, age or ethnic group, or culture?

- Depending on the answer to the previous question, is it possible to argue that the programme effectively 'naturalises' or 'universalises' values and views which are perhaps not universal but rather specific to particular social, ethnic, cultural or philosophical groups?

While several studies have examined and commented on the very considerable technological, narrative and other format changes which have impacted on the genre of wildlife and nature programming in the most recent 15–20 years, we know rather less – than is the case for the period from the 1940s to the late 1980s – about how or whether these changes have significantly altered the ideological messages of this important and popular genre, or indeed in a wider sense, engaged with and/or influenced public and popular views of the environment and nature.

Advances in film, television and visual technology seemingly went hand in hand with changes in public tastes and public demands of the genre of wildlife and nature programmes to move away from the sanitised narratives of the 1950s and early 1960s towards, as Mitman and Bousé and others have noted, a more graphic, dramatic and raw mode of portrayal. But while this change could be seen at face value as a move away from the highly constructed and structured narrative form in the Disney mode of the 1950s and 1960s towards a more realistic and realist – perhaps more documentary-like and factual – mode, the real change is more likely away from the realist illusion of the earlier decades to a postmodernist preoccupation with spectacle and multiple representational modes, with little or no concern for 'facts' or 'reality'.

Bagust (2008: 219), drawing extensively on Scott (2003), thus notes:

> For Scott (2003), the 'computer generated extravaganzas' of the
> Walking with . . . documentary 'franchise' represent the nature film

(sub-?) genre's desperate attempt to maintain a foothold in an
increasingly global, fragmented and profit-driven television market.
To do this, she suggests, producers are increasingly looking away
from traditional 'blue-chip' wildlife film conventions (with their
pretence that they access 'unmediated reality') towards a product that
jumps generic boundaries and 'ups the representational ante' through
the use of high-tech visual effects to create a level of spectacle which
'produce[s] a visceral response in the viewer by way of the sheer
audacity of the image itself'. (Scott 2003: 30)

If the emphasis of the postmodernist wildlife and nature programmes is
on the visually spectacular and impressive, rather than on conventional
story-telling or the communicative construction of nature in terms of
recognisable and culturally widely shared value sets or packages, how
does this impact on public perceptions, attitudes and actions with regard
to nature and the environment?

Conclusion

Moving beyond the specific focus on *news* reporting of the environment,
this chapter has examined the notions of scripts, cultural packages,
interpretive packages and cultural resonance, and explored their
significance for understanding the nature and potential 'power' of popular
media representations of nature and the environment. We have seen how
media representations of environmental issues, science and technology
draw on, evoke and articulate readily available cultural and interpretive
packages, which in turn set particular frames or boundaries for how issues
are and can be discussed and understood in the public sphere.

Cultural and interpretive packages (also often referred to in the literature
as, *inter alia*, scripts, schemas, frames, narratives or discourses) are, by
their very nature, *always available*, but some resonate more readily than
others with widely held beliefs, fears and concerns, and such resonances
change over time in response to changes in socio-historical conditions as
well as in economic pressures, organisational arrangements and
technology (including media technology).

While deep-seated cultural packages can be drawn upon or evoked across
widely different types of media and popular culture output, their
articulation and inflection varies considerably with the genre, narrative
and other (e.g. journalistic and organisational) conventions of different
types of media and media content. As we have seen in this chapter, much
is known about narrative and stylistic formats of wildlife films and nature

programming from the post-war period until the 1990s, *and* about the wider cultural values and views of nature and the environment evoked and expressed in these. While a growing body of research has charted many of the significant changes of the more recent period in narrative and stylistic formats, in 'character' development and in thematic content, there is still much work to be done on the question of how these changes have impacted on the media and public ideological constructions of nature and the environment.

The following chapter continues the examination of how constructions of nature and the environment change over time, but pursues the investigation by focusing particularly on another important media genre: advertising.

Further reading

Allan, S. (2002). *Media, Risk and Science*. Maidenhead: Open University Press. See, in particular, Chapter 2: Science Fictions and Chapter 3: Science in Popular Culture.

Bousé, D. (2000). *Wildlife Films*. Philadelphia: University of Pennsylvania Press. Like Mitman's (1999) *Reel Nature*, Bousé provides an impressive and comprehensive analysis of the long history of wildlife and natural history film-making with a keen focus on production dimensions as well as on the conventions and ideological messages of the films themselves.

Corbett, J. B. (2006). *Communicating Nature: How We Create and Understand Environmental Messages*. Island Press. See, in particular, Chapter 5: Leisure in Nature as Commodity and Entertainment.

Turney, J. (1998). *Frankenstein's Footsteps: Science, Genetics and Popular Culture*. London: Yale University Press. See, in particular, the Introduction and Chapter 10: Conclusion: The Human Body Shop.

Selling 'nature/the natural': Advertising, nature, national identity, nostalgia and the environmental image

This chapter:

● Explores how concepts of 'nature' are historically specific and constructed.

● Explores the ideological uses of nature in advertising and other media output.

● Shows that while environmental themes and 'green' advertising come and go, appeals to nature and the natural have featured prominently in advertising since the early days of advertising itself.

● Examines the key 'uses' of nature in advertising and the extent to which they reflect changing historical constructions of nature, social change and changing views of society.

● Explores media uses of nature in relation to the concepts of nostalgia and national/cultural identity.

● Examines whether increasing globalisation in advertising is at odds with culturally specific concepts/images of nature and environment.

Introduction

Nature imagery and ideas regarding 'the natural' form, as we have seen in previous chapters, an important part of media and popular culture generally. Such images are also prevalent in the particular media genre of advertising. In contrast to the now relatively infrequent advertising appeals to environmental protection and 'green' or 'sustainable' consumption, nature imagery and cultural notions of nature continue to figure prominently in advertising discourse. Advertising is perhaps particularly interesting in this regard because it effortlessly and seamlessly draws on culturally deep-seated, ontological and taken-for-granted meanings of nature and the natural, and reworks these in ways which promote consumption, particular world views and particular identities.

Starting from the recognition that nature is socially constructed, and that its social construction changes over time, this chapter explores the key ways in which advertising and other media use and articulate ideas of nature. There is much literature to suggest that constructions of nature are nationally and culturally specific. There is also evidence from the communications research literature to suggest that media constructions of nature – including in advertising – often significantly draw on and in turn reinforce notions of national and cultural identity. These arguments and suggestions are examined in light of the trends of globalisation and homogenisation in advertising.

The chapter examines the nature discourses deployed in advertising content, the extent to which these resonate with environmental concerns, and the extent to which they articulate and reinforce culturally specific identities. It is argued that advertising, in its uses of nature, makes an important contribution to ongoing public definitions of the environment, consumption, and cultural identity. Tracing the discourses of nature uncovered in a number of studies, an attempt is made to examine how these change over time and to explore how advertising articulates and reworks deep-seated cultural categories and understandings of nature, the natural, and the environment, and in doing so, communicates important boundaries and public definitions of appropriate consumption and 'uses' of the natural environment.

Constructed nature and ideology

A discussion about nature and identity in advertising perhaps needs to start by reiterating the simple recognition of the complex and historically changing meanings associated with 'nature'. Not only does nature figure prominently in our cultural vocabulary and in popular culture, but it means different things, at different times to different people. Cultural critic Raymond Williams called nature 'perhaps the most complex word in the language' (Williams, 1983: 219), and he noted how dominant cultural views of nature have changed over time, from, for example, the Enlightenment view of nature as something to be studied, understood and controlled, to Romanticism with its emphasis on nature as pure, spiritual, sublime, authentic, and pristine. Particularly relevant to studying the uses of nature in advertising and other media is Williams's observation that,

> one of the most powerful uses of nature, since the late 18th century, has been in this selective sense of goodness and innocence. Nature has meant 'the countryside', the 'unspoiled places', plants and creatures other than man.
>
> (1983: 223)

The power and semantic complexity of nature derives not only from the fact that dominant interpretations of nature change historically, but perhaps even more so from the contemporaneous co-existence – within the range of meanings associated with the word – of a rich cultural reservoir of binary opposites: 'nature was at once innocent, unprovided, sure, unsure, fruitful, destructive, a pure force and tainted and cursed' (Williams, 1983: 222). Referencing or using nature thus offers potentially rich interpretative flexibility (to the extent that we as members of a culture have access to the repertoire of meanings culturally and conventionally associated with nature), while at the same time appearing to render things ontological, permanent and beyond questioning. References to nature or what is regarded as 'natural' are key rhetorical devices of ideology in the sense that they serve to hide what are essentially partisan arguments and interests and to invest them with moral or universal authority and legitimacy.

The ideological power of nature-referencing derives, as Armitage (2003) – drawing on Williamson (1978) – has argued, from the archetypal binary opposites of culture versus nature:

> What is 'natural' has a dual, even contradictory, role in advertising. Nature is given meaning through culture, but its significance lies in the fact that nature is understood to be outside or even the very opposite of culture. The cultural messages attached to nature thereby appear to have an authority independent of and superior to any particular culture.
>
> (Armitage, 2003: 75)

Contrary to its surface appearance of being beyond culture, beyond that which has been culturally created and constructed for particular ideological purposes, the appearance of referencing something stable, permanent, authentic, inviolable, and god-given, nature can be, and has been, used for lending authority to particular ideas, interests and political objectives. Evernden (1989: 164), with reference to Marshall Sahlins (1977), refers to 'the general and possibly essential propensity of human societies to invent the nature they desire or need, and then to use it to justify the social pattern they have developed'. Nature, Evernden continues, 'is used habitually to justify and legitimate the actions we wish to regard as normal, and the behaviour we choose to impose on each other'.

Thompson (1990: 66), in his comprehensive discussion of ideology, culture and media, refers to this as the 'strategy of naturalisation' and others, like Fairclough (1989) and Stuart Hall (1982), have similarly noted the ideological character and centrality of a discourse of naturalisation in media and political rhetoric. Stuart Hall offers a particularly succinct observation of the way in which television, both as 'content' and as (visual) 'medium', hides its own highly selective representation of 'reality' through a process of naturalisation:

> Much of television's power to signify lay in its visual and documentary character – its inscription of itself as merely a 'window on the world', showing things as they really are. Its propositions and explanations were underpinned by this grounding of its discourse in 'the real' – in the evidence of one's eyes. Its discourse therefore appeared peculiarly a naturalistic discourse of fact, statement and description. But [. . .] it would be more appropriate to define the typical discourse of this medium not as naturalistic but as *naturalized*: not grounded in nature but producing nature as a sort of guarantee of its truth.
>
> (Hall, 1982: 75)

If nature-referencing and naturalisation are key rhetorical components of the way in which ideology is communicated, then the semiotic linking of a (romanticised) view of nature *with* a rural (idyllic) past *with* national identity has undoubtedly been one of the most potent ideological uses in the modern age, used in the early parts of the twentieth century for naked political propaganda and mobilisation for war, and in the second half of the twentieth century for commercial purposes:

> More insistent in recent times has been the commercial recourse to the 'rural imaginary', in order to reconcile us to the activities of multinational companies and to solicit our custom for their commodities. Today, it is the marketing rather than the political propagandist potential of nature that is more exploited, and the clichés of nationalist rhetoric have become the eco-lect of the advertising copywriter.
>
> (Soper, 1995: 194)

The use of nature and referencing of the natural in advertising may be partly to do with ideological power (selling products or corporate images by invoking the qualities of goodness, purity, authenticity, genuineness, non-negotiability (Cronon, 1995)) and partly to do with the format constraints of the advertising genre. Thus, the time constraints of the advertising format calls for the use of easily identifiable and recognisable shorthand symbols, or what Gamson and Modigliani (1989) aptly refer to

Box 6.1

Nature commodified as warranty of goodness, authenticity and health

Figure 6.1 *Original Source bath foam.*

Figure 6.2 *Jordans Superfoods: Mother Nature (The original Superhero).*

as 'condensing symbols', and nature and the natural are perhaps among the most universally recognisable such symbols. This is not to say that appeals to nature and what is regarded as natural are insignificant in other genres; quite the contrary, they play a powerful role in much media and public discourse – see, for example, the frequent references to nature in arguments and public controversy about biotechnology and genetics (Hansen, 2006). But it is to suggest that their uses in advertising may be more frequent and perhaps also more heavily stereotypical in the sense of relying on a narrower and more limited range of essential 'nature/natural' icons.

What particularly distinguishes the use of nature in advertising is the seamless way in which, in its predominant use, it blends in 'naturally' (for want of a better expression) and almost unnoticeably. It is thus its relative inconspicuousness, combined with the deep-seated – culturally and historically specific – values/views which its uses represent, that give nature its ideological power. The ability of advertising to forge signification links which convey such key nature-related values as freshness and health onto cigarettes and smoking (Williamson, 1978) is perhaps one of the clearest examples of the semiotic flexibility and power of uses of nature in advertising. An equally powerful reminder that there is something here worthy of critical attention comes from corporate image advertising, which succeeds in converting or 're-framing' a tainted association – in the public mind – with pollution, risk, environmental degradation, ruthless exploitation of natural resources, etc. into connotations of responsible sustainability and the image as protector and custodian of the environment (see Exercise 6.1).

Environment and nature in advertising and other media

Leiss et al. (1997), in their excellent and comprehensive historical study of 'social communication in advertising', touch briefly on the signifying uses of nature in advertising, but perhaps surprisingly, representations of nature and the environment are not among the many key variables that they systematically analyse either in the present or historically. A number of studies have, however, begun to reveal some of the current or longer-term representations of the environment, nature or environmental issues in advertising. Comparing a sample of American television advertisements from 1979 with a sample a decade on, 1989, Peterson (1991) thus found that explicit environmental or ecological messages were used in less than a tenth of advertisements, although slightly more frequently in 1989 than in 1979.

Numerous studies have documented the considerable increase in media reporting (and public concern) about environmental issues which happened in the latter half of the 1980s and very early 1990s (e.g. Einsiedel and Coughlan, 1993; Hansen, 1994; Mazur, 1998; Shanahan and McComas, 1999). Several studies from the mid-1990s (e.g. Iyer and

Banerjee, 1993; Banerjee et al., 1995; Buckley and Vogt, 1996; Kilbourne, 1995; Beder, 1997) indicate that this 'green boom' was also reflected in advertising, where so-called 'green advertising' or 'green marketing' became prominent. Much of this advertising latched onto general public concerns by labelling products as 'green' and 'eco-friendly' or by emphasising measures taken to reduce the potential impact that advertised products might have on the environment. The trend also extended to corporate image advertising stressing the environmental credentials of large companies, and to advertising more directly in the tradition of persuasive information/education campaigns in the form of government and local authority advertising campaigns designed to promote recycling initiatives or environmentally responsible behaviour (Rutherford, 2000).

> While little has changed in terms of product association with nature and 'the natural', in the case of corporate image advertisements, there has been a major shift since 1970. During the past twenty years companies have begun to portray themselves as nature's caretakers; environmentally friendly, responsible, and caring. This has resulted in the use of more scenes from nature [. . .] and an almost total elimination of the factory and machinery visuals which were standard fare in the corporate image ads of the 1950s.
>
> (Howlett and Raglon, 1992: 55)

Although little is available in the way of systematic longitudinal research like that of Howlett and Raglon (1992), it nevertheless seems clear that the trend they identify has, if anything, become even more pronounced since their study was published in the early 1990s. As climate change has gradually assumed paradigmatic status as the 'umbrella' issue which subsumes and overshadows all other environmental issues, or, more accurately, has become the master discourse for interpretation and construction of all other issues, so corporations, businesses and advertisers have sought to promote themselves as variously 'environmentally friendly', 'nature's caretakers', 'environmentally responsible', etc. As Rutherford (2000), Beder (2002) and others have shown, oil companies have a long history of promoting a corporate image of themselves in this way. What is new – and interesting – in this type of corporate promotion then is not so much the fact that companies promote themselves as 'environmentally friendly' or as 'nature's caretakers', but rather the way in which such traditional discourses have been cleverly adapted to the emerging public and political language of climate change.

Exercise 6.1

Packaging corporate business as Nature's Caretaker

Take a look at the websites of selected major oil companies (e.g. Shell, BP or Exxon Mobil) and consider:

1) To what extent are the images used to represent/symbolise the 'environment', 'iconic' and global images of pristine nature, lush nature, un-touched nature? Is nature principally shown on 'its own' and separate from humans or human artefacts?
2) Is there discursive, and ideological, re-conciliation between, on the one hand, the environment/nature as a resource to be mastered and controlled, and, on the other, the environment/nature as a fragile and precious system to be protected? Consider particularly the significance of language use, e.g. the deliberate choice of words such as 'protect', 'responsible', 'stewardship', 'respect', 'sustainable', 'challenge', 'responding', 'helping', 'local', 'community', 'people', etc.
3) Do the images and messages projected on oil-company websites 'fit' into such ideological categories as the 'techno-fix' or the 'progress package'? (Gamson and Modigliani, 1989; see also the discussion in Chapter 5).

A new vocabulary as well as, in some respects, a new iconography has emerged and become part of the promotional language of advertisers as well as of the public idiom, although much of the visual and verbal vocabularies consist of 'classic' environmental and nature imagery. Characteristically, the new vocabulary associated with climate change (itself a relatively recent master term for what used to be principally referred to not so long ago as 'global warming' or the 'greenhouse effect') has quickly been adopted by corporate advertisers in a way that assumes (and asserts) clear meanings and definitions when none exists (see Box 6.2).

While 'green' advertising and explicit environmental campaign messages in advertising may have enjoyed some considerable prominence in the late 1980s and early 1990s, explicit environmental messages and themes in advertising seem to have followed and reflected the general flow and ebb of media interest in and coverage of the environment.

A recent study of British television advertising (Hansen, 2002) thus showed that while nature imagery was deployed in no less than 28 per cent of advertisements, the sample did not turn up any advertisements

Box 6.2

Regulating green advertising

Firms to get green advertising guidelines

As British Gas criticises green advert ban watchdog insists it is working to clarify what claims are acceptable

Written by James Murray

BusinessGreen, 30 Jan 2008

Firms confused over how to use green terms in their advertising and marketing campaigns without falling foul of customers or regulators will receive new guidance later this year.

The Committees of Advertising Practice (CAP), which are responsible for the UK's advertising codes, are currently working on a series of guidelines for advertisers in the wake of a series of rulings from the Advertising Standards Authority (ASA) that have criticised firms for making misleading claims about their green credentials.

Advertisers have repeatedly criticised the watchdog's rulings, insisting their green claims are being made in good faith and that any confusion is the result of a lack of clear definitions for new environmental terms, such as zero carbon or offsetting, rather than a deliberate attempt to mislead customers. [. . .]

British Gas today reacted angrily to an ASA ruling banning a TV and newspaper advert for its Zero Carbon energy tariff. The ASA ruled the adverts were misleading as the TV ad claimed the energy was zero carbon when the tariff relied on offsetting schemes and the print advert claimed it was 'the greenest domestic energy tariff', despite there being no standard methodology for measuring tariffs' greenness.

A spokesman for British Gas said the company 'fundamentally disagreed' with the ruling, arguing that it had stated in the TV advert that the tariff used carbon offsetting schemes and that the print advert made it clear the claim was based on independent data from the energywatch website.

'It is disappointing that the ASA has underestimated how commonly used and understood the term "zero carbon" is, especially considering we consulted the Broadcast Advertising Clearance Centre (BACC) when we produced the [TV] advert,' he said.

Source: www.accountancyage.com/business-green/news/2208426/
firms-green-ad-guidelines [accessed 29 February 2008].

with an explicit environmental message, that is, there were no advertisements specifically encouraging consumers to 'save energy', 'recycle', 'use alternative modes of transport', 'purchase environmentally friendly products' nor did the sample contain any 'green' corporate image advertising.

The study further showed that the most prominent discourses of nature in British television advertising are ones which celebrate nature as: intrinsically good; fresh and pure; a guarantor of genuineness and authenticity; a place of beauty and a space for human relaxation and recreation, but also, albeit less frequently, simply a space to be traversed.

Box 6.3

Nature in television advertising

Table 6.1 shows the primary images or uses of nature in television advertisements sampled from the main UK independent television channel, ITV, during March and April of 2000 (Hansen, 2002).

Point to consider:

Not a single advertisement in this sample had 'the protection of fragile or vulnerable nature' as its primary image or theme. It would be fair to assume that the growing public and political concern, seen in the last decade, about climate change may also have impacted on advertising images. How far do current advertising images of the environment and nature portray these as fragile and in need of care and protection?

Table 6.1 Primary images/uses of nature in television advertisements

Categories	Frequency	Percentage
Nature as intrinsically good (e.g. healthy, fresh)	43	32.6
Human mastery/power over nature	28	21.2
Nature as a nice place to be	25	18.9
Recreational function of nature	11	8.3
Nature as distance/space traversed/the in-between/obstacle	9	6.8
Nature as a threat	5	3.8
Nature as a metaphor for life's journey	4	3.0
Nature as a symbol of freedom	2	1.5
Nature as a spectacle, packaged (TV) spectacle	2	1.5
Nature as global, big, awesome, impressive	2	1.5
Nature as a challenge/sport/manhood/endurance	1	0.8
Total	132	100.0

Nature is seen as strong (i.e. *not* in need of protection) and is very predominantly positively valorised, with only occasional foregrounding of its threatening qualities. While nature is predominantly cast as the countryside or wild/uncultivated nature, a substantial proportion of advertisements equate it with the domesticated/tamed/controlled nature of the garden (Hansen, 2002).

The occasional image of 'nature as threat' or vengeful is, as also noted by several other studies (e.g. Elbro, 1983; Rutherford, 1994; Budd et al., 1999), closely allied to, but slightly distinct from, a related image, namely 'nature as challenge'. This is an image which emphasises the testing qualities of nature, and it serves by extension to demonstrate the manhood, stamina, or physical prowess of characters, or the reliability, sturdy quality, and durability of products.

A particularly useful hint of how images of nature in advertising may have changed over time comes from a study of a very different genre, the television documentary. In a systematic study of the Canadian documentary series *The Nature of Things*, over the period 1960–94, Glenda Wall (1999) demonstrates how images of nature and the environment changed significantly during this period. In the 1960s, the dominant perspective was a bio-economic outlook which constructed nature as an exploitable resource, to be studied, understood, and then controlled and used. At the same time nature was also portrayed as a place 'where one could go to renew oneself and escape the alienating effects of city life' (p. 61). The 1970s saw an increasing emphasis on nature as vulnerable, fragile and complex (p. 64). Nature was portrayed as being under attack from unchecked and indiscriminate technological growth. By the beginning of the 1990s, the portrayal of nature in *The Nature of Things* had shifted towards 'the idea that nature will respond with a vengeance to the abuses piled upon it' (p. 68). This trend is also echoed in Cottle's (2000) analysis of British television news of the 1980s and 1990s.

How prominent are representations of nature in advertising and how far have they followed a similar path of change to that identified by Wall in relation to television nature/science/environment documentaries? Several studies suggest considerable parallels with the trend identified by Wall, but there are also some exceptions. Thus, Elbro (1983) in his survey of Danish and German advertising seems to imply that nature imagery was little used in advertising prior to the 1970s, other than in what he terms a background decorative function. Others (Howlett and Raglon, 1992; Goldman and Papson, 1996; Rutherford, 2000; Corbett, 2002), however, note that while 'environmental' or 'green' advertising may come and go, nature imagery has played a prominent part since the rise of modern advertising. Thus, Goldman and Papson (1996) persuasively argue that:

> [f]rom its inception, modern advertising used nature as a referent system from which to derive signifiers for constructing signs. Nature's landscapes were used to signify experiences or qualities that urban-industrial life failed to provide. [. . .] Advertising suggested that civilisation's deficiencies could be ameliorated by consuming commodities that contained the essence of nature.
>
> (p. 191)

Drawing on a number of historical analyses (including Marchand, 1985), they argue that nature was prominently used in advertising in the 1920s and 1930s in a nostalgic way that was itself a response to the economic and the social-psychological crisis of the 1920s. Tracing the general trends in uses of nature in advertising up through the twentieth century, Goldman and Papson note that '[t]he nostalgia for nature evident in the advertising of the 1920s and 1930s gave way to the fetish of gadgetry' (p. 191) for the middle decades of the twentieth century, and not until the 1970s did nature once again take a central position in advertising. While nature is thus seen to have been prominent in advertising throughout the twentieth century, Goldman and Papson also point out that the genre known as 'green' advertising did not emerge until the 1980s.

Taking his point of departure in the now famous Crying Indian advertisements of the early 1970s, historian Kevin Armitage (2003) shows how (American) popular culture has long used the stereotype of the noble savage to epitomise and articulate a nostalgic view of unspoilt nature and of an idealised past of harmony between man and nature. Armitage persuasively argues that 'The fascination with nature and the primitive that marked turn-of-the-twentieth-century American culture was rooted in a larger ambivalence about modern life' (p. 73) – not unlike the disillusion with modernisation identified by Raymond Williams (1973) in the British context – but crucially, as Armitage argues, the fascination with nature and the primitive 'did not involve a rejection of civilisation, but rather an accommodation to modern life that was simultaneously nostalgic and progressive, secular yet spiritually vital' (pp. 73–74). Armitage shows that the idealised referencing of nature – through or with representations of the American Indian – in advertising was well under way towards the end of the nineteenth century.

In their exemplary systematic (and in this respect, quite unique) survey of advertising from 1910 to 1990, Howlett and Raglon (1992) similarly note that there is nothing particularly new about business using natural imagery to sell products.

> What the survey does reveal as 'new' in the 1990s is the desire of companies to create corporate images which are environmentally friendly or benign. This contrasts sharply with [. . .] public images of business from earlier decades which were more likely to associate business with the 'leading edge' of consumptive, nature-defying, modernity.
>
> (p. 54)

Wernick's (1997) comparison of 1950s and 1990s advertising adds further confirmation of the changes in the ways in which nature imagery has been deployed in advertising. Where the 1950s advertisements celebrate 'the fruits of industrial civilisation' (p. 209), gadgetry, technology, science and progress, the 1990s adverts appeal to nostalgic ideas of nature and the past, a nature and a past that exist only in myth:

> The Good identified as the essence of its product is located in the past, not in the future. It [. . .] is something to be recovered rather than attained
>
> (p. 210)

Drawing on the arguments presented by these authors, it seems then that a key difference in the uses of nature between advertising of the 1940s–1970s and advertising of the late twentieth century is one of perspective: the adverts of the middle part of the twentieth century in short *look forward*, with optimism even, to the progress and prosperity of the techno-scientific urban society, while the perspective of the late twentieth century is one of *looking back* – to recover a lost idyll, harmony, authenticity and identity of a mythical past. Wernick refers to the 'progress myth' of the 1950s advertising; others, notably Gamson and Modigliani (1989) in their study of the framing of nuclear power since the mid-twentieth century in popular culture and in public opinion, refer to this as the 'progress package' – a common and prominent frame in media and popular culture accounts involving the relationship between technology and nature, and valorising technological, economic and scientific progress above concerns for the environment or nature. Wilson (1992) likewise identifies this period as one in which the relationship with nature was one of domination and greed, where the urge to 'acquire and consume' (p. 14) far outpaced any hint of concern about the environment, limited resources or the protection of nature.

Rutherford (2000) introduces his own label for advertising celebrating the progress myth: 'Technopia'. In his historical sweep of what he broadly terms 'advocacy advertising', he implies a similar trend to that identified by Wernick, Goldman and Papson and others. He contrasts the 'Technopia' type of advertising – advertising which principally promotes a belief in the scientific and technological control and domination of nature as synonymous with progress and development – with what he terms 'Green Nightmare' advertising. 'Green Nightmare' advertising is advertising which stresses and calls public attention to the 'Dystopia' – the destruction of nature, the environment and our entire habitat – resulting from the unchecked and wasteful production and consumption practices characteristic of late modernity.

In very general terms, Rutherford's analysis maps onto the time-line indicated above, namely with 'Technopia' advertising most prominent in the 1960s–1980s, and 'Green Nightmare' advertising prominent from the 1970s onward. If Rutherford's categories seem to overlap considerably, it is perhaps confirmation not only of a diversification of discourses on nature, but of a public sphere marked increasingly by discursive competition over the framing and meaning of nature generally, and more specifically of the framing of science, technology and progress in relation to public conceptions of nature.

In summary, then, it would seem from the work of the authors discussed above that nature imagery has been a feature of advertising since at least the early part of the twentieth century. It is also clear that the particular deployment and constructions of nature in advertising and other media have, broadly speaking, oscillated between, at the one extreme, a progress-package-driven view of nature as a resource to be dominated, exploited and consumed, and, at the other extreme, a romanticised – and often retrospective – view of nature as the (divine) source and embodiment of authenticity, sanity and goodness, to be revered and protected (or to use a more current invocation: 'not to be tampered with').

Nature, identity and nostalgia

Nature imagery in advertising of the late twentieth century is, as we have seen above, often deployed in relation to a retrospective look, a yearning for the 'idyllic past'. Nature imagery in this context is used to construct a mythical image of the past (including childhood) as a time of endless summers, sunny and orderly green landscapes, and, perhaps most importantly of all, as a time and place of community, belonging and well-defined identity. Several researchers have referred to this view as one of 'nostalgia':

> Nostalgia became, in short, the means for holding onto and reaffirming identities which had been badly bruised by the turmoil of the times. In the 'collective search for identity' which is the hallmark of this postindustrial epoch – a search that in its constant soul-churning extrudes a thousand different fashions, ecstasies, salvations, and utopias – nostalgia looks backward rather than forward, for the familiar rather than the novel, for certainty rather than discovery
>
> (Davis, 1979: 107–8)

The nostalgic view of the past, as enacted through the use of nature imagery in advertising, is not merely a longing for a mythic past, but it is very much also a romanticised view of the past. In its use of nature imagery, it draws particularly on the romantic view of the countryside, the view constructed not least by the poets (e.g. William Wordsworth, Samuel Taylor Coleridge) and painters (e.g. John Constable, J.M.W. Turner) of the Romantic period. As Williams (1973) has pointed out, the growing cultural importance of a romanticised view of the countryside perhaps not surprisingly coincided – at least in Britain – with a period of immense social upheaval, urbanisation, migration to the cities and the rapid decline of a rural/agrarian economy.

This argument easily extends further to the early part of the 1900s and perhaps helps explain why, as Goldman and Papson (1996) argue, advertising of the 1920s and 1930s used nostalgic nature imagery. As 'mass society' theory (Swingewood, 1977) would have it, and as sociologists and historians generally agree, the period between the two world wars was one of tremendous social, economic and political upheaval – following on from the devastating carnage and destruction of the First World War. It was also one of alienation associated with the increasing separation of the sphere of work from the sphere of family and community, an uprooting from the stable and ordered rural hierarchies and communities to the anonymity of the urban masses. Against this background, it seems hardly surprising that advertising should respond with romanticised images of a more natural, rural, countryside past, where identities seemed more firmly fixed, if only through 'knowing one's place' in the highly hierarchical structure of rural society. What is particularly ideological about this reconstructed past is the way in which the deeply hierarchical structures are either glossed over *or* romanticised and portrayed as indeed natural, desirable and harmonious.

Exercise 6.2

The nostalgic natural authenticity and simplicity of the past/the country

Examine a selection of current or recent advertisements for food, drinks, financial and insurance-related products or services, Consider the interplay of images, text and type of product.

While appeals to naturalness and referencing of nature may not seem so strange in relation to food, why are these also frequently used in the advertising of financial and related products?

How do the uses of colour and light add to the 'message' in these advertisements? Soft focus or a hazy look may for example be used to invoke tranquility, idyll or perhaps nostalgia, but these values can also be achieved by other means, such as enhanced tonal/light contrasts or the tendency towards sepia in the Jack Daniels advertisement reproduced below.

Figure 6.3
Jack Daniel's whiskey.

WITH ALL DUE RESPECT TO PROGRESS,
THE WORLD COULD USE A LITTLE LESS PLASTIC.

JACK DANIEL'S NO7 TENNESSEE WHISKEY

To what extent and *how* are values such as 'simplicity', 'small scale', 'local-ness', 'tranquil'/'idyllic', 'rural', 'happiness', 'authentic', 'traditional' communicated or expressed?

Comment: advertisements, like other types of communication but perhaps more so, 'work' through juxtaposition, through what semiologists call a structure of 'binary oppositions'. Thus, when food advertisers are increasingly stressing 'organic' -ness or 'local'-ness as something positive, they automatically – without having to mention it explicitly – activate a chain of associations regarding its binary opposite (e.g. fertilizer/pesticide intensive farming and/or large-scale national / international production, and everything 'negative' – at least in the current prevailing climate of opinion – associated with such modes of production). Likewise, the intended reading of the image in the Jack Daniels advertisement as a warrant of 'traditional' quality and craftsmanship is secured through juxtaposition with the rhetorically dismissive reference to 'progress' in the text. It is the textual anchoring (Barthes, 1977b) of the image, that steers us away from reading the image as, for example, an image of undesirable, messy, outmoded, uneconomic, inefficient production practices in the whisky industry.

The romanticised construction of nature and the uses of idyllic nature in advertising are then not just a matter of advertising responding to a public sense of alienation or a public search for identity. They are an ideological reconstruction in the sense that they naturalise, and sometimes even celebrate, a deeply stratified society. There are, in other words, important social class, race and gender dimensions to these uses of nature.

Phillips et al. (2001) in their analysis of the construction of rural/countryside/nature imagery in British rural television drama thus show that the dominant construction of a rural idyll goes further to 'also enact particular social identities, including, but not exclusively, those of class' and that the class identity enacted is predominantly a middle-class identity. Others (Thomas, 1995; Scutt and Bonnet, 1996) have similarly commented on the social class, race and gender dimensions of television and print media constructions of countryside and nature, and their associations with 'Englishness':

In order for rural areas to continue to represent Englishness, it is essential that they are ideologically and physically separated from those groups who do not conform to stereotypical images of the English. Social and racial exclusion can, therefore, be seen as intrinsic to the maintenance of the countryside as a cultural reservoir [. . .].

(Scutt and Bonnet, 1996: 8)

In a similar vein, but with a particular focus on racial exclusion in American magazine advertising from 1984 to 2000, Martin (2004) points to the racial dimension to nature imagery: 'Advertisements taking place in the Great Outdoors or featuring models participating in wilderness leisure activities rarely include Black models, while advertisements featuring White models regularly make use of Great Outdoors settings and activities' (p. 513). He notes that the dominant view of nature/wilderness in advertising is a white Eurocentric view which finds little resonance among Black and Native American audiences.

Nature and national identity

A considerable body of literature has pointed to the links between particular constructions of nature and national identity. Macnaghten and Urry (1998), drawing on a broad range of work from geographers, sociologists and historians, note how every nation celebrates its particular nature. 'National natures' may not seem particularly 'constructed' where these bear a seemingly obvious relation to the particularly striking features of those natures (the Alps of Switzerland, the fjords of Norway, the forests and lakes of Finland, etc.). However, on closer historical scrutiny, it becomes clear that 'national natures' are indeed very much 'constructed'. This is made particularly clear in historian Simon Schama's insightful analysis of *Landscape and Memory* (Schama, 1995), in which he demonstrates the particular historicity and political role and construction of nature in the culture and politics of a range of nations (with examples ranging as widely as the 'forest' in German culture and history to 'wilderness' and national parks in the United States). Geographers, historians, sociologists and media researchers in Britain have commented on the close links forged, from the 1800s onwards, between national identity and a romantic view of nature. More specifically, this is a view which constructs the 'green and pleasant land' of William Blake's famous hymn, *Jerusalem*, as both the true home and the essence of Englishness:

> Between 1880 and 1920 the conviction that English culture was to be found in the past was stabilised. Images of rolling hills, winding lanes, country cottages and the concept of an organic community of days of yore were offered as the source of English culture and the physical setting of ideologies of Englishness.
>
> (Scutt and Bonnet, 1996: 5)

Since the late 1800s then, the dominant image of Englishness in literature, art and popular culture generally has become one of equating

Englishness with the countryside, the countryside as the true home of the English (seen as white and middle class) and the essence of Englishness. However, as Thomas (2002) among others has noted, the 'association of national identity with a country's rural roots is not confined to Britain, and may be connected to the cultural homogenisation which is one of the outcomes of globalisation' (p. 34).

Following a similar line of argument, Creighton (1997), looking at domestic tourism and popular culture in Japan, demonstrates a renewed search for authentic Japanese identity as manifested in the increasing popularity of 'traditional' rural Japan. She describes the 'retro boom' – a looking back to the past and a search for authentic Japanese identity – experienced in Japan since the 1970s as a reaction to 'the perceived threat of cultural loss to which the processes of modernisation and Westernisation have subjected modern Japan' (p. 242). As in British advertising and popular culture, the 'place' of authentic national culture is seen as the countryside or traditional village:

> This retro boom has romanticized Japan's agrarian heritage, allowing the domestic tourist industry to capitalize on travel promotions featuring rural hamlets that were formerly considered unsophisticated and boring.
>
> (p. 241)

For the alienated urban masses, the search for identity is perhaps answered through the travel – or pilgrimage, even – 'back' to the true time and place of Japanese culture and identity, the romanticised rustic countryside setting. But, as Creighton demonstrates, this journey is increasingly commodified in popular culture, department store displays and consumer goods, so that the busy urban dweller need never leave the city in order to consume – or buy into – the retro boom construction of Japanese cultural identity.

As in the West, the achievement of advertising deploying this kind of nature imagery is to channel the yearning for authenticity or identity or the pure goodness of nature into consumption: purchasing the advertised product becomes a means of 'buying into' the identity or the authenticity ostensibly anchored in the idyllic rural past.

While, as indicated by Macnaghten and Urry (1998) and others, there are different 'national natures', it is perhaps testimony yet again to the semantic flexibility hinted at by Williams (1983), when he suggested that 'Nature is perhaps the most complex word in the language', that some have implied a degree of global universality in 'nature imagery' and cultural constructions of nature. Howlett and Raglon (1992) thus note that:

> Elements of nature have long provided humans with the symbols and metaphors that have helped order and explain the world, and these symbols and metaphors are extraordinarily resilient, long-lived, and in some cases at least, seem even to transcend specific cultural and linguistic borders.
>
> (p. 60)

In their view then, the attractiveness of nature imagery and symbolism to advertisers stems from the simple recognition that '[n]atural symbols and metaphors are among any culture's most easily understood ones' and they 'tend to be long-lived and their meanings widely accessible' (p. 61). The similarities noted above between British and Japanese linking of national identity with a (romanticised) rural, idyllic, countryside past likewise suggest an element of culture-transcending universality. In a comparative study of cultural values in American and Japanese advertising, Barbara Mueller (1987) found that on the two nature-related dimensions investigated ('oneness with nature appeals' and 'manipulation of nature appeals') there was remarkably little difference between the advertising of the two countries:

> Themes emphasizing the goodness of nature are found in both Japanese and American advertisements. A subtle difference in the application of this appeal exists: U.S. advertisements in this category focus on natural as opposed to man-made goods, while the Japanese advertisements emphasize the individual's relationship with nature.
>
> (p. 56)

In her study of cultural values in Chinese and American television advertising, Carolyn Lin (2001) notes that previous studies have shown that 'advertisements in China are more likely than Western advertisements to use appeals of traditional values such as status and oneness with nature, whereas U.S. advertisements reflect such values as individualism and manipulation or control over nature' (pp. 86–87). Her own study likewise confirms that Chinese advertisements are more likely to use oneness with nature appeals than US advertising.

Cho et al. (1999) identified three categories of appeals involving nature in American and Korean advertising: Manipulation of Nature, Oneness with Nature, and Subjugation to Nature. They found that only Oneness with Nature featured prominently in the advertising of both countries, while Manipulation of Nature and Subjugation to Nature were comparatively rarely used. While the differences between the two countries were not statistically significant, Cho et al. found 'non-significant directional support for the contention that oneness-with-nature is found more often in Korean commercials and that manipulation-of-nature is found more often in U.S. commercials' (p. 68). Another study of Korean advertising, in a comparison with Hong Kong advertising (Moon and Chan, 2005), found a greater – but still relatively small – use of appeals to the natural in Korean advertising than in Hong Kong advertising, but, as in the study by Cho et al., the difference was not statistically significant.

There is, however, considerable evidence from elsewhere (e.g. Kellert, 1995) to suggest that the uses and interpretation of nature do indeed vary across different cultures, that nature is indeed not only culturally constructed but also culturally specific in its construction/interpretation. Any apparent similarity, across (Occidental and Oriental) cultures, in advertising and other popular culture constructions/uses of nature are thus more likely to be symptomatic of the increasing globalisation, Westernisation and homogenisation characteristic of modern advertising trends than of some universality of nature as a sign and metaphor.

A particularly interesting – but somewhat different – inflection of nature and national identity in advertising is the use of national stereotypes. Advertising, as Armitage (2003) has shown, has long articulated and exploited the popular culture stereotype of the American Indian as the idealised 'child of nature', epitomising a nostalgic anti-modern sentiment and a yearning for a lost harmony between man and nature. But this type of inflection also extends beyond peoples (the American Indian) to national stereotypes. A particularly potent example is the referencing of the Irish and Irishness in the global marketing of Irish Spring soap by the American Colgate-Palmolive company. Elbro (1983) and Negra (2001) both offer insightful analyses of the ways in which the Irish Spring advertisements draw on and reinforce the (stereotypical) linking between nature (pure, cleansing and untainted by modernity), the (idyllic) past, nation and national (Irish) identity. As in much other popular culture construction of national identity (see Creighton on Japan, referred to above), nostalgia plays a key role, in that the linking or association also implies that Ireland is a place where the (natural) qualities of the past can still be found, visited and consumed, or alternatively, bought into through consumption of the advertised product.

The Irish Spring soap advertisements have used, for example, idyllic images of the Irish countryside (winding lanes, hedges, fresh and green) and the Irish (jolly courting couples in rural attire) to associate the qualities of freshness, authenticity, genuineness, romance, etc. with the advertised product. The advertisements trade on and reinforce a nostalgic stereotypical image of Ireland as a 'non-industrialized paradise populated by simple country folk' (Negra, 2001: 86) and of Irishness as synonymous with honest, authentic, natural, uncomplicated, pure and romantic qualities. Condensing-symbols of nation and national identity linked to landscape and the natural environment are of course widely exploited in tourism advertising (see e.g. Urry, 1995, 2001; Negra, 2001; Nelson, 2005), and very likely increasingly so, as the popularity of 'nature-tourism' and 'eco-tourism' continue to rise.

Although there is a large and growing body of comparative research on the cultural values reflected in advertising across different cultures, only a small number of these have touched specifically on nature imagery or the uses/constructions of nature in such advertising, and this is clearly a field ripe for further investigation. Research needs to compare the uses/constructions of nature and environment in television and other media advertising of several different countries. It further needs to examine how far, in a time of increasing globalisation (not least in marketing and advertising), constructions of nature are either increasingly universal, homogeneous (or Western perhaps) or alternatively, how far advertisers in their use of nature imagery seek to reflect and appeal to regionally, nationally or culturally specific understandings of nature.

Conclusion

Raymond Williams argued that 'nature is perhaps the most complex word in the language' – the present review of how nature has been used and appropriated in media discourse essentially confirms this. It testifies to the signifying flexibility of nature, and to the historically changing underlying views of nature. It is only by examining how discourses of nature change over time that we can begin to understand how they are used ideologically for promoting everything from national identity, nationalism, consumerism and corporate identity to framing and circumscribing what kinds of questions can and should be asked about the environment, environmental issues and (sustainable) development.

Invoking nature/the natural in advertising and other public discourse is a key rhetorical device of ideology in the sense that referencing something as 'of nature' or as 'natural' serves to hide what are essentially partisan arguments and interests and to invest them with moral or universal authority and legitimacy. Nature, as Evernden (1989: 164) so succinctly puts it, 'is used habitually to justify and legitimate the actions we wish to regard as normal, and the behaviour we choose to impose on each other.'

While explicit environmental messages and 'green' advertising seem to come and go, with some periods of prominence in advertising since the early 1970s, it is clear from the literature examined here that nature and appeals to the natural have been a significant part of advertising since at least as far back as the early 1900s.

The particular deployment and constructions of nature in advertising and other media have, broadly speaking, oscillated between, at the one extreme, a progress-package-driven view of nature as a resource to be dominated, exploited and consumed, and, at the other extreme, a romanticised – and often retrospective – view of nature as the (divine) source and embodiment of authenticity, sanity and goodness, to be revered and protected, 'not to be tampered with'.

On the continuum between these extremes lie, as we have seen, a wide range of 'constructions' of nature, including: nature as resource, good, authentic, idyllic, healthy, spiritual, enchanting, the 'home' of identity, fragile, a threat, a 'proving ground' for both human and product qualities, vengeful, etc. Several authors have indicated that the dominant construction of nature in advertising and popular culture of the late twentieth century is one which draws heavily on nature imagery of the Romantic period. It is also one which invokes a nostalgic view of the past, with implications for the public construction of social class, gender, race and, not least, national identity.

There are contrasting – and possibly contradictory – indications from a number of studies regarding the extent to which advertising and other media constructions of nature are culturally or nationally specific. Cross-cultural comparisons of advertising show relatively small differences in the views/constructions of nature in Occidental and Oriental advertising, and indicate that traditional – and well-documented – differences in views of nature may be subsumed under the homogenising influence of globalisation. But the evidence is very tentative and further research should focus specifically on the construction of nature to examine the extent to which the discourses of nature in advertising are culturally and nationally specific.

Further reading

Armitage, K. C. (2003). Commercial Indians: Authenticity, nature and industrial capitalism in advertising at the turn of the twentieth century. *Michigan Historical Review, 29*(2), 71–96.

Howlett, M., and Raglon, R. (1992). Constructing the environmental spectacle: green advertisements and the greening of the corporate image. *Environmental History Review, 16*(4), 53–68.

Rutherford, P. (2000). *Endless Propaganda: the Advertising of Public Goods.* Toronto: University of Toronto Press. See, in particular, Part IV: Progress and Its Ills, pp. 179–227.

Williamson, J. (1978). *Decoding Advertisements: Ideology and Meaning in Advertising.* London: Marion Boyars. See, in particular, Chapter 4: 'Cooking' Nature and Chapter 5: Back to Nature, pp. 103–37.

Media, publics, politics and environmental issues

This chapter:

- Examines selected measures of public concern for or interest in environmental issues, noting the long-term parallels between public opinion and media coverage regarding the environment.
- Discusses some of the major approaches which have been used for researching media influence on public and political opinion and political decision-making.
- Reviews the evidence on media influence produced by major approaches such as agenda-setting research, framing analysis and cultivation analysis.
- Explores the referencing and use of 'media coverage' for rhetorical and political purposes in public environmental controversy, arguing that this can be seen as an important type of 'effect' or influence, albeit one much less commonly thought of in general discourse on media influence.
- Concludes, via a brief discussion of alternative approaches to studying media roles in relation to public understanding(s) of environmental issues, by emphasising the 'circulation of claims' perspective over a linear perspective on media roles and by emphasising the complex and multiple ways in which media coverage interacts with other 'forums of meaning-creation' (Gamson, 1988) in society.

Introduction

Ultimately, the assumption, whether explicit or implicit, behind most research into media representations of environmental issues is that these play a role in shaping and influencing public understanding/opinion and political decision-making in society. Perhaps regrettably, concerns about the 'effects' or role of the media are often construed in relatively simplistic terms which assume a simple relationship between media coverage and general public belief, attitude and behaviour, while ignoring the diverse chains of influence which characterise the media's role and function in society. This problem is by no means unique to 'environmental issues' and the media, but in fact has a far longer pedigree in discussions about the media and politics, crime, violence, terrorism, international conflict, race and ethnicity, etc.

While the tradition of studying the social role and effects of the media has long since moved away from simplistic notions of 'direct effects' of the media, public and political discourse on the media and the environment frequently appear to still operate with tacit assumptions about 'vulnerable' publics easily manipulated or swayed by 'powerful' media. The rhetoric of powerful media and vulnerable publics is indeed itself a key player in the framing – for public consumption and debate – of political arguments about environmental issues (see Box 7.3). Although undoubtedly instances and circumstances can be found where something approximating a powerful and immediate media impact on public beliefs can be found, the aim of this chapter is not to dwell on anecdotal examples, but rather to examine some of the wider research evidence on media roles in relation to the dynamics of public and political discussion and action on environmental issues.

This chapter then discusses some of the major frameworks and approaches which have been used for examining media influence on public understanding, public opinion and political decision-making. It explores the evidence, from a variety of research approaches and frameworks, for how media representations of environmental issues influence political processes or are interpreted and used by different publics.

Public opinion and the environment

Public opinion, attitudes, understanding and behaviour in relation to environmental issues have been the subject of research, as indeed has media coverage, since the emergence of the 'environment' as an issue for public and political concern in the 1960s. As noted in earlier chapters, this is of course not to say that environmental issues and problems did not exist before the 1960s, but merely to stress that the more holistic way of thinking about – and labelling – seemingly diverse issues/problems such as air, soil and water pollution, waste disposal, overpopulation, excessive exploitation of natural resources, etc. as inter-connected and part of ecology only began to crystallise in the 1960s.

While surveys of public opinion and attitudes regarding the environment have not generally been focused on the specific role of the mass media, they have relatively consistently confirmed: (1) that there is considerable public interest in being informed about science/technology/environment issues (e.g. MORI, 2005); (2) that the mass media are a major – in some cases *the* major – source of public information and knowledge about the science and scientific evidence involved in major environmental and health-related issues (Hargreaves et al., 2004; MORI, 2005), particularly where these are new and rapidly developing issues; (3) that the extent to which publics are influenced by, draw on and/or use media information/images is determined by local knowledge, first-hand experience and availability of other – more direct – sources of information (Chapman et al., 1997; see also the discussion below about 'unobtrusive' issues in agenda-setting research).

Studies of public opinion and attitudes on environmental issues suggest that public awareness and concern about the environment in Western countries has waned and waxed in 'cycles' not dissimilar to the up-and-down cycles of media coverage of environmental issues. In very general terms these cycles can be described as follows: public concern about the environment developed during the 1960s and reached an initial peak around 1970, then fell back during the 1970s; a second cycle started with a gradual increase in public concern during the 1980s, reaching a peak around the early 1990s, and then waning again from around 1992 onwards, while the early 2000s would appear to have witnessed yet another resurgence centred, in particular, around an increased sense of urgency about climate change.

However, although there are some superficially tantalising parallels, in trends for the last fifty years, between the up-and-down cycles of media coverage of environmental issues and the ups and downs of public concern, as measured through opinion polls, it would be a mistake (although one often made) to attempt to draw any simple conclusions about cause and effect regarding the relationship of media coverage and public concern.

In a wide-ranging review of evidence on public opinion and attitudes on environmental matters, Lowe and Rüdig (1986), for example, point out that longitudinal and more comprehensive surveys have shown public concern about the environment to be relatively resilient, stable and widespread. Like many others before them (e.g. Funkhouser, 1973), they suggest that the fluctuations registered by more superficial opinion polls may merely reflect 'the immediately prevailing preoccupations of the mass media' (Lowe and Rüdig, 1986: 514), rather than the public's actual concern about environmental issues.

Perhaps the clearest evidence against a simple notion of media coverage of environmental issues *causing* public concern about the environment comes from the trends uncovered by media analyses and public opinion surveys in the recent two–three decades. While longitudinal studies of media coverage of a range of environmental matters have demonstrated considerable fluctuations – characteristic, as argued in earlier chapters, of the news-value orientation and other factors impinging on the media communication of social issues – studies of public opinion have generally pointed to a greater degree of 'stability', and indeed to slow but steady increases, in the public's concern about the environment (Dunlap, 1991, 2006; Park et al., 2001):

> People in Europe are concerned about the state of the environment, confused as to whom to believe, disenchanted with governmental attempts at all levels to deal with the problems of pollution and ecological degradation, and ready for radical action. The public's view is shared by elite opinion as well, including, significantly, legislators at Westminster and at the European Parliament.
>
> (Worcester, 1994)

Surveys in England and Wales on attitudes to the environment have shown clear increases between 1986 and 2001 in the percentages of people who were 'very worried' about a broad range of environmental issues (Social Trends 29, 1998, and Social Trends 32, 2002). Thus 'the fifth Survey of Public Attitudes to the Environment in England, carried out in 2001, found that concerns about the environment have increased across all types of issues in the last 15 years' (Social Trends 32, 2002: 180), including (listed in declining order of prominence) concern about: the disposal of hazardous waste; effects of livestock management methods (including BSE); pollution in rivers and seas; pollution in bathing waters and on beaches; traffic exhaust fumes and urban smog; loss of plants and animals in the UK; ozone layer depletion; tropical forest destruction; climate change and global warming, etc. (Social Trends 32, 2002).

On a wider European scale the regularly conducted Eurobarometer surveys similarly indicate increasing concern about environmental issues among citizens of the European Union countries, while also showing – as one would reasonably expect – some very considerable country-by-country as well as wider regional variations. A recent Eurobarometer survey published in 2008 and comparing results of surveys in 2004 and in 2007, thus shows that not only do European citizens attach great value to the environment, but that they are also increasingly aware of the role that the environment plays in their lives (see Box 7.1).

Box 7.1

Attitudes of European citizens towards the environment (Eurobarometer, 2008: 7)

2.2 Europeans are most likely to be concerned about global environmental issues

Since **climate change** is already associated with the concept of environment in general, it is not surprising that it ranks as a top concern among Europeans with the absolute majority (57%) mentioning it among their top five environmental concerns. Water pollution (42%) and air pollution (40%) are mentioned by around two in five respondents. At the bottom of the ranking one can find items that can be seen as directly linked to **people's behaviour** such as consumption habits (11%) and transport choices (12% for impact of current transport modes and 15% for urban problems).

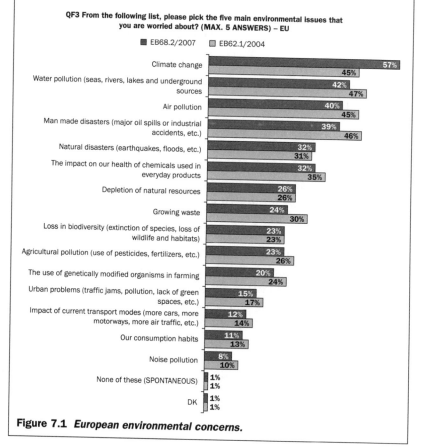

Figure 7.1 *European environmental concerns.*

The survey shows that the range of environmental issues that people are concerned about has changed little, but the rank order of the top four concerns shifted considerably between 2004 and 2007, with 'climate change' moving into the top spot as the single issue that most people express concern about. Again, and as noted previously, it is of course tempting to speculate about whether such changes merely reflect people's awareness of major publicity events (the release of Al Gore's *An Inconvenient Truth*, the amount of media publicity generated in this context, the award of the Nobel Peace Prize to Al Gore and the IPCC in 2007, etc.) or whether they signify more genuine changes in public concern.

Other evidence of increasing public concern about environmental issues comes from membership figures for a range of environmental organisations. While membership of Greenpeace fell quite dramatically from a peak in 1991 to a comparatively low point in 1999, it had recovered considerably by 2002. Other major environmental organisations, including the Friends of the Earth, the World Wide Fund for Nature (WWF), and the Royal Society for the Protection of Birds, experienced relatively sustained growth, and indeed in some cases (e.g. WWF) impressive increases (see Box 7.2 from Social Trends 33, 2003).

On a wider global scale, a recent forty-seven-nation survey (The Pew Global Attitudes Project, 2007) has similarly confirmed that concerns about environmental problems have been growing on a global scale during the first decade of the new millennium. In a report comparing 2002 survey results with 2007 survey results, The Pew Global Attitudes Project found 'a general increase in the percentage of people citing pollution and environmental problems as a top global threat' with evidence of concern rising sharply in Latin America and Europe, as well as in Japan and India. On a comparative scale, comparing concern about environmental issues with other key areas, they also found the largest increase between 2002 and 2007 to be in public concern about pollution and environmental problems: in 2002 only two out of forty-seven countries nominated pollution/environment as the greatest danger, while in 2007 this figure had risen to top place (replacing 'Nuclear weapons' in this place in the 2002 survey) with twenty countries nominating pollution/environment as the area of greatest concern/danger.

While opinion poll surveys at both national and global level thus seem to confirm that public concern about the environment is both well

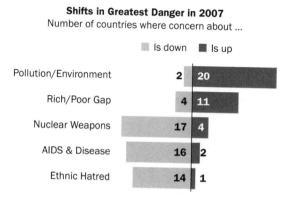

Shifts in Greatest Danger in 2007
Number of countries where concern about ...

Pollution/Environment — 2 | 20
Rich/Poor Gap — 4 | 11
Nuclear Weapons — 17 | 4
AIDS & Disease — 16 | 2
Ethnic Hatred — 14 | 1

Figure 7.2 *Changes in global concerns.*

embedded and indeed shows signs of having increased considerably during the first decade of the new millennium, it is also clear from international surveys such as the Eurobarometer surveys and the Pew global forty-seven-nation surveys that huge variations exist across countries and regions of the world. Moreover, while the longer-term trends do indeed confirm that public concern about the environment is here to stay and remains among the major issues on public agendas, we should also be aware of the continued shorter-term ups and downs of the major issues competing for public attention in the public arenas. As we have seen with regard to media agendas, issues compete with each other for prominence on the public opinion agenda, and all such arenas are furthermore characterised by their limited carrying capacities – when one issue moves up on the agenda, others have to move down or give way altogether. It is one thing to try and determine the interaction of different issues on the public opinion agenda; it is a different, and somewhat more complex, problem to try and map the interaction of different public agendas (e.g. 'public opinion', 'media coverage', 'government and political agendas', etc.). In the remainder of this chapter, I examine some of the theories and approaches which have been used for studying these relationships.

Box 7.2

Membership of environmental organisations (from *Social Trends*)

Table 7.1 *Membership of selected environmental organisations, 1971–2002*

UK	Thousands					
	1971	1981	1991	1997	1999	2002
National Trust[a]	278	1,046	2,152	2,489	2,643	3,000
Royal Society for the Protection of Birds	98	441	852	1,007	1,004	1,022
Civic Trust[b]	214	–	222	330	–	330
Wildlife Trusts[c]	64	142	233	310	325	413
World Wide Fund for Nature	12	60	227	241	255	320
The National Trust for Scotland	37	105	234	228	236	260
Woodland Trust	–	–	63	60	63	115
Greenpeace	–	30	312	215	176	221
Ramblers Association	22	37	87	123	129	137
Friends of the Earth	1	18	111	114	112	119
Council for the Protection of Rural England	21	29	45	45	49	59

[a]Covers England, Wales and Northern Ireland.
[b]Latest Civic Trust data are for 2001.
[c]Includes the Royal Society for Nature Conservation.
Source: Organisations concerned.

The United Kingdom has a history of dense civic networks with clubs, unions, leagues, societies, commissions and committees set up for a host of social, political and environmental activities and causes. In general, average membership levels among most kinds of voluntary organisations have risen at least enough to keep pace with population growth since the Second World War. Some types of voluntary organisations, such as environmental organisations, have experienced very high levels of growth in membership. The National Trust had a membership of 3 million in 2002, which is more than ten times the number in 1971. This represents a significant growth in membership, well above the 5 per cent growth in the United Kingdom population over the same period.

Source: Social Trends 33, 2003.

Exercise 7.1

What do public opinion surveys really tell us about public concerns?

In Chapter 2, I raised the question of whether the economic downturn that began to manifest itself in 2008, would have a similar detrimental effect on media and public concern about the environment as the economic downturn of the early 1990s seemed to have. A recent Pew survey in January 2009 seems to suggest an affirmative answer to this question:

> Of the twenty issues people were asked to rate in both January 2008 and January 2009, five have slipped significantly in importance as attention to the economy has surged. Protecting the environment fell the most precipitously – just 41% rate this as a top priority today, down from 56% a year ago.

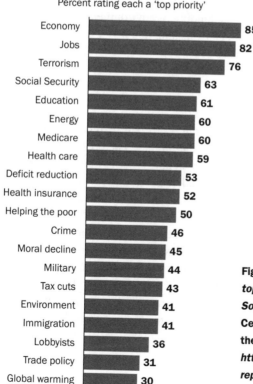

Top Priorities for 2009
Percent rating each a 'top priority'

Issue	Percent
Economy	85
Jobs	82
Terrorism	76
Social Security	63
Education	61
Energy	60
Medicare	60
Health care	59
Deficit reduction	53
Health insurance	52
Helping the poor	50
Crime	46
Moral decline	45
Military	44
Tax cuts	43
Environment	41
Immigration	41
Lobbyists	36
Trade policy	31
Global warming	30

Figure 7.3 *Pew survey of top priorities for 2009. Source*: **The Pew Research Center for the People and the Press, 2009.** *Available: http://people-press.org/ report/485/economy-top-policy-priority*

What does a graph like this 'really' tell us? The question is an invitation – as a pre-amble to some of the issues that I discuss in the remainder of this chapter – to think about how we might reconcile the indications from this graph with the indications from the previously mentioned findings showing increasing concern about the environment and increased media coverage of global warming and related issues since the start of the current millennium. Does the graph thus primarily confirm the fickleness of public opinion? Does it show what the public is genuinely concerned about or does it merely show the public's awareness of what media and politicians are preoccupied with? Do the Pew survey findings give any clues about why public priorities, particularly regarding the environment, might have seemingly changed so dramatically between January 2008 and January 2009?

Major communications approaches to media and public opinion

While a multitude of approaches have been used, the main approaches in media and communication research which have contributed to examining the relationship between media coverage of the environment and public/political understanding of environmental issues, are agenda setting, framing, cultivation analysis and, to a lesser degree, the 'quantity of coverage' hypothesis.

Agenda-setting research

The starting point for agenda-setting research is commonly seen to be Cohen's (1963: 13) formulation that 'The press may not be successful much of the time in telling people what to think, but it is stunningly successful in telling its readers what to think *about*'. The first empirical test of the formulation, however, was not published until nearly a decade later in McCombs and Shaw's (1972) study of agenda setting during the American presidential campaign of 1968. Interestingly, the agenda-setting paradigm thus emerged in mass communications research at around the same time as the environment and environmental issues began to emerge as issues for public and political concern, and it is perhaps not surprising, although probably quite coincidental, that agenda setting has been a relatively prominent approach to studying the role of the media in relation to environmental issues since the late 1960s/early 1970s.

Thus, Funkhouser (1973) in his study of the 'issues of the 1960s' found a tantalisingly close match between many of the issues/news stories, including 'Environment', dominating American news magazines of the

1960s and the issues, nominated in Gallup surveys of the American public as 'the most important problem facing America', while also concluding that 'the news media did not give a very accurate picture of what was going on in the nation during the 1960s' (p. 73).

> The data cited here suggest that the amount of media attention given to an issue strongly influences its visibility to the public. However, the amount of media attention does not seem to relate as closely to public attitudes concerning the issues and related policies. The Gallup item, "What is the most important problem facing America?" may in effect be an indirect content analysis of the news media, showing us the surface of public opinion but not its depth.
>
> (p. 74)

Similar trends have been confirmed in a string of agenda-setting studies since (Atwater et al., 1985; Iyengar and Kinder, 1987; Protess et al., 1987; Ader, 1995; Mikami et al., 1995; Dearing and Rogers, 1996; Yin, 1999). These studies have shown the ability of the media to raise general public and political awareness about environmental issues, although identifying the specific ways in which media agendas and public agendas co-vary over time has proven a more elusive task. Fan et al. (1994) showed how German television news in 1986 influenced the public agenda on energy supply and other issues. Their analysis showed that television coverage of the Chernobyl accident and other issues influenced and contributed to the public agenda and helped increase public concern about energy supply.

In an earlier publication, Brosius and Kepplinger (1990), in a complex agenda-setting study in Germany, similarly found evidence of relatively strong agenda-setting effects on the issues of energy supply and environmental protection. They also, however, noted some of the complexities in interpreting the findings arising from their research: they noted, for example, the very different agenda-setting timescales applying to the development of general perspectives such as environmental protection, compared with awareness of specific events (e.g. the Chernobyl accident) within a wider issue.

Christine Ader's study, published in 1995, provides particularly strong evidence for the agenda-setting role of the media on the issue of environmental pollution. The study is noteworthy not only for the extended period of time analysed, 1970–1990, but also for its careful comparison of media and public agendas with 'real-world' conditions or indicators of environmental pollution. Where much agenda-setting research has thus been relatively narrowly focused on the relationship between two agendas, the media agenda (as determined through systematic content analysis) and the public agenda (as determined through surveys of public opinion), Ader convincingly argues for the need to 'control' for the possibility that any observed co-variation between the media and public agendas may be caused by a third exogenous factor.

Like researchers both before (e.g. Zucker, 1978) and since (see Soroka, 2002, discussed below), Ader points out that there are particularly good reasons for expecting the media to have an agenda-setting effect in relation to environmental issues: environmental issues are often – although certainly not always – what agenda-setting researchers call 'unobtrusive' issues in the sense that they are often not easily observed or experienced first hand. It is this relative absence of direct observation, experience or indeed of more immediate sources of information, which makes it possible for the media to 'step in' as the main source of information (and potentially 'influence') for the public.

At the face of things, it looks as if climate change is very much not an unobtrusive issue, in the sense of agenda-setting researchers, that is, climate change is all around us for everybody to observe and experience first hand. However, it is clearly important to remember that whatever 'symptoms' of climate change, that we see around us, they are of course only just that because we have been told (often through the media) that this is what they are, manifestations of climate change. It is not so long ago that a whole host of natural phenomena such as flooding, hurricanes, droughts, hot summers, etc. would *not* automatically have triggered references to global warming or climate change in the way that has now become more or less customary.

Ader's study, comparing the press and public agendas over the period 1970–1990, while controlling for the impact of real-world conditions, found strong support for the agenda-setting power of the media. Thus, the study confirmed that the level of public concern about environmental pollution was influenced by the amount of media attention devoted to this issue, and further that:

> When the effects of reality were controlled, the correlation between the media agenda and the public agenda was strengthened. As predicted, this study found that real-world conditions do not influence the media or public agendas directly. The public needs the media to tell them how important an issue the environment is. Individuals do not learn this from real-world cues. Also, the media are not effective at determining the importance of this issue from real-world cues.
>
> (Ader, 1995: 310)

Where early agenda-setting studies of media coverage and environmental issues were principally focused on the relationship between amount of media coverage and issue importance as designated by public opinion surveys, more recent agenda-setting research has focused on the complex interactions among several public 'agendas', including media agendas, political/policy agendas, 'real-world cues' and public opinion. In a longitudinal study of the agenda-setting process in relation to global warming, Trumbo (1995) found that the influence of media coverage on politicians (members of the US Congress) was considerably more pronounced than media influence on the public opinion agenda. In a particularly sophisticated design, Soroka (2002) similarly examined interactions of the agendas of Canadian newspapers, public opinion polls, formal political forums and legislative initiatives from 1985 to 1995.

He found different agenda-setting dynamics for each of the three issues examined (inflation, environment, and debt/deficit) and, importantly, showed that the agenda-setting dynamics of issues is linked to issue attributes. Not surprisingly, as this has long been recognised in studies of media coverage and public perceptions (first suggested by Lippman, 1922, and since confirmed in many studies and overviews of mass media effect, e.g. Klapper, 1960; Wade and Schramm, 1968), Soroka's study confirms that the media are less influential on issues or topics that the public can 'access' through direct experience or through more immediate, possibly more trusted, sources of information:

> The media's role is stronger for environmental and debt/deficit issues. For the environment, effects between media, public, and policy agendas appear to be multi-directional, suggesting that the increased salience in the late 1980s was not simply a product of media emphasis. Nevertheless, further analysis suggest that the media played an especially important role. [. . .]

> In sum, the issues surveyed here suggest three different agenda-setting dynamics – in Canada, from 1985 to 1995, inflation was real-world-driven, environmental issues were media-driven, and debt/deficit issues were policy-driven.

(p. 281)

Contrasting with the conventional 'media-to-public-opinion' direction of influence in agenda-setting studies, Lindahl (1983) in his analysis of media coverage of nuclear power in Sweden argued that, rather than the media setting the agenda for public opinion, journalists generally responded to their perceptions of the public mood on nuclear power and attuned their coverage accordingly – in other words, public opinion indirectly seemed to be setting the agenda for media coverage. Another Swedish study (Gooch, 1996) found that 'the alleged agenda-setting role of the regional newspapers in environmental issues is not pronounced [. . .] personal experience of local environmental problems, interpersonal communication and levels of trust for news sources, may have more substantial effects on the public's perceptions of local environmental risks than information communicated through the press' (Gooch, 1996: 107). This study again then confirms the findings of Ader (1995), Soroka (2002) and others, that media-agenda setting is most pronounced in relation to unobtrusive issues. It further suggests a geographical dimension to this, namely that media may impact on public opinion considerably more in relation to national/global issues than in relation to local environmental issues.

Mazur's 'quantity of coverage' thesis

Most environmental issues are characterised, at least in their early stages of becoming defined as issues for public and political concern, by considerable degrees of scientific uncertainty and disagreement, as well as by public controversy about appropriate ways to deal with them. In this context, a particularly tantalising model of media influence is the 'quantity of coverage' model suggested in the early 1980s by American sociologist Alan Mazur. In a seminal – and much quoted – article published in the *Journal of Communication* in 1981, Mazur suggested that increased media coverage of scientific controversies seemed to have at least one simple influence on public attitudes: 'When media coverage of a controversy increases, public opposition to the technology in question (as measured by public opinion polls) increases; when media coverage wanes, public opposition falls off' (Mazur, 1981: 109).

This was not only a beautifully simple but also quite a brave statement to make at a time when the tide of media and communication research had long since (i.e. since the 1940s and 1950s) turned emphatically against any notions of such simple cause–effect relationships between media coverage and public opinion. Interestingly, and this perhaps explains some of its general appeal within the research community, Mazur's suggestion was not far removed from the agenda-setting hypothesis (which also, as we have seen, focuses on general rather than specific influences, on 'what people think *about*' rather than on 'what they *think*') and, indeed, relied on the very same methods and type of data, that is, content analysis of media coverage and surveys of public opinion. But where agenda-setting research has developed in the direction of ever further differentiation of media content and the particular framing of media messages (e.g. McCombs and Bell, 1996), Mazur takes the agenda-setting hypothesis in the opposite direction by suggesting that it is the sheer quantity and intensity of media coverage, not the balance of positive and negative messages within such coverage, that essentially determines public reaction, and that increased coverage (whether positive or negative) leads to increased public opposition:

> My thesis is that the amount of reporting about an environmental or technological hazard, rather than what is reported about the topic, is the primary vehicle of communication about such risks, and that the beliefs of the audience follow directly from the intensity and volume of reporting.
>
> (Mazur, 1990: 295)

In addition to the evidence provided by Mazur's own studies of the relationship between media reporting of nuclear power/waste, fluoridation, chemical waste, etc. and public opinion, a number of other studies have provided further support. Wiegman et al. (1989), in a study of Dutch newspaper reporting and reader reactions regarding technological and environmental hazards, found that increased exposure to media coverage correlated with negative public reactions. Frewer (2002), in a study of the media reporting and public risk perception in relation to genetically modified foods, found that increased media reporting led to increased public perceptions of risk and related negative consequences. When media reporting declined, public perceptions of risk likewise reduced. Studies of media reporting and public attitudes to biotechnology have pointed in a similar direction, although not as strongly (Gaskell et al., 1999; Gutteling, 2004).

Cultivation analysis

Cultivation research, first articulated and developed by George Gerbner and colleagues in the late 1960s (see e.g. Gerbner et al., 1994), centres on the simple and intuitive hypothesis that the more audiences (and here the original cultivation analyses as well as most cultivation analyses since have focused on television viewers) are exposed to media content, the more likely are they to hold beliefs about reality that are consistent with the media's portrayal of reality. The fundamental assumption of the cultivation argument is that for all its apparent diversity, television essentially offers a relatively consistent and repetitive set of narratives, images and values, and that, over time, viewers come to see these as the dominant narratives, images and values of society, as 'reality'.

The application of cultivation analysis to media and environmental issues was first pioneered by Shanahan in the early 1990s (Shanahan, 1993) and has since been applied by Shanahan and colleagues in numerous studies. One problem for the use of cultivation research in relation to environmental issues is, that rather than systematic over-representation – as in the case of depictions of violence, crime and law enforcement – the 'environment' has not generally been a prominent focus in television entertainment, leading to what Shanahan (1993) calls 'cultivation in reverse'.

> Using a cultivation approach, Shanahan, McComas and their collaborators have found that heavy viewers of television viewing are less likely to be environmentally concerned and less willing to pay more (either through taxes, prices, or a lower standard of living) for the environment, although only in the absence of controls. Heavy television viewers also displayed lower levels of trust in science and technology and less environmental knowledge than lighter viewers of less television: relationships that generally withstood controls. [. . .] (Shanahan 1993; Shanahan and McComas 1997; 1999; Shanahan et al. 1997). Holbert, Kwak, and Shah (2003) recently showed a positive relationship between environmental concern and attention to television news and nature documentaries while also finding no evidence of a relationship between environmental concern and three different types of attention to entertainment television.
>
> (Besley and Shanahan, 2004: 864)

Framing

While cultivation analysis proper focuses on the general, long-term and consistent trends and messages of media content, research on narratives and framing in media depictions of environmental issues has emphasised how individual (news or entertainment) stories are structured to, as it were, produce a particular response or conclusion in the minds of viewers.

Framing research in particular has drawn attention to how the principles of 'selection' and 'salience' (Entman, 1993) in media content help structure audience responses by directing attention to: (1) what the issue/problem is; (2) who/what is responsible; and (3) what is to be done about the issue/problem, that is, what the solution is (Ryan, 1991). Research on media reporting of risk has thus demonstrated that the media tend to give prominence to the reporting of potential harm, while offering little or no contextual information within which to realistically assess the likelihood of harm actually occurring (Friedman et al., 1992).

Likewise, the media have tended to misrepresent the 'balance' of scientific opinion – or more accurately, the degree of scientific consensus/dis-sensus – on a host of controversial environmental issues, from nuclear power and genetically modified crops to climate change, leading, so it is argued, to public perception of widespread scientific uncertainty and disagreement persisting long after scientific – and even in some cases, political – consensus has been reached (Boykoff, 2008; see also the discussion in Box 7.3).

Although not presented as a framing analysis per se, Speers's (2005) study of media coverage and public opinion regarding climate change makes an interesting observation about what is essentially an outcome of the media's structuring or framing of stories about climate change. She notes that when the media repeatedly juxtapose particular explanations about climate change, such *associations* often filter through to the public as *causal* relations: 'What is, in media coverage, merely a juxtaposition (under the general heading of human-made environmental problems) undergoes a cognitive leap in public understanding, so that it is understood as a causal relationship' (Speers, 2005: 133).

Box 7.3

A different kind of 'effect'

Like public opinion, media coverage itself often becomes a central referent in the rhetoric of public controversy. Selective use of media stories as 'evidence' is both tempting and easy for the simple reason that the media are so highly visible and therefore an easily identifiable reference point. Like 'public opinion' or 'what the public wants' often get invoked rhetorically as a way of lending legitimacy to particular arguments, so too will politicians, scientists and other key players in environmental debate, often point to the media and – carefully selected – media news stories either to back up their arguments or, perhaps more often, to blame the media for misinforming the public and for stirring up public panics, hysteria and rash political decision-making on important issues or social problems.

The following focuses on two interesting (ab)uses of media coverage by two influential and controversial players in the climate-change debate, namely Al Gore in his film (and book) *An Inconvenient Truth: A Global Warning* (2006) and Danish economist and contrarian Bjørn Lomborg in his most recent book *Cool It: the Skeptical Environmentalist's Guide to Global Warming* (2007) (reference is further made to Lomborg's earlier book, with which he made his debut as environmental contrarian, *The Skeptical Environmentalist* (in English in 2001; originally published in Danish in 1998)).

Case 1: *An Inconvenient Truth: A Global Warning*

With analogies drawn to media reporting on the long-running 'controversy' about the extent of harm caused by and efforts to restrict tobacco/smoking, Al Gore – at a relatively late point in his film, that is, Scene 26 of 32 – makes the argument that the media grossly misrepresent the scientific consensus on climate change, and he goes further to say that the public misconception about the causes of global warming has been 'deliberately created by a relatively small group of people' (note the careful avoidance of any specific identification).

Gore invokes references to advertising and media news coverage, and makes the simple but effective comparison of scientific opinion on climate change as reported by (1) articles/research published in scientific peer-reviewed journals; and (2) newspapers. Speaking to an audience in a subtly lit auditorium, Gore delivers his narrative from a podium against the background of a large central screen and a much smaller screen on the left. The accompanying PowerPoint show is projected onto both screens. With rows of little figures symbolising the scientist/expert authors of the 928 journal articles reviewed rapidly decreasing and numbers rapidly dropping from 928 to 0, Gore makes his point that none of the studies disagreed with the consensus that 'greenhouse gas pollution has caused most of the warming of the last 50 years'. He then goes on to refer to a study of media coverage over 'the last fourteen years' showing that 53 per cent of newspaper articles implied that there was doubt about the cause of global warming. The point of Gore's reference to media coverage is to indicate that arguments about the causes of global warming are deliberately being manipulated and that in view of the nature of media coverage, as illustrated by his example, it is 'no wonder that people are confused'.

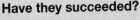

Have they succeeded?

Peer-reviewed, scientific articles:	Articles in the popular press:
928	636
Percentage in doubt as to cause:	Percentage in doubt as to cause:
0%	53%

Figure 7.4 *'Doubt-about-cause-of-climate-change' comparison in* **An Inconvenient Truth.**

Case 2: *Cool It: The Skeptical Environmentalist's Guide to Global Warming*

The highly selective and anecdotal use of media scare stories for the purposes of lining a particular argument perhaps takes on its most unattractive form, when perpetrated in the name of a call for a better informed dialogue. This is the strategy – executed with eloquence and elegance – pursued by Danish economist and controversial climate change contrarian Bjørn Lomborg. Indeed media coverage is the very starting point of his most recent book, *Cool It: The Skeptical Environmentalist's Guide to Global Warming*, which starts with the following sentences:

> Global warming has been portrayed recently as the greatest crisis in the history of civilisation. As of this writing, stories on it occupy the front pages of *Time* and *Newsweek* and are featured prominently in countless media around the world.
>
> (Lomborg, 2007: xi)

The first chapter similarly starts with references to the (in Lomborg's view clearly unduly) 'worried' tone of politicians, writers and, again, the media: 'Likewise, the media pounds us with the messages of ever worsening climate' (Lomborg, 2007: 2) and this is followed by examples of scary headlines conveniently selected from English language newspapers (mostly British) and news magazines (mostly American). A section further on in the book's Chapter 4 is titled 'Instead of smart solutions we get scared witless' with a subsection called 'past bad news', and here some explanations – indeed drawn from the media and communications literature – are offered regarding how the media work:

> Yet, these pervasive, apocalyptic descriptions of global warming persist, strongly aided by the media, as it thrives on bad news. "A good story is usually bad news," writes a textbook for journalists.
> (Lomborg, 2007: 178)
>
> Moreover, journalistic stories tend to focus on conflicts. [. . .]
>
> Closely related to the story of conflict is the question of guilt. It is not uncommon for one of the involved parties to be given the blame for the conflict, which helps to give the news a more human touch.
> (Lomborg, 2007: 179)

Persuasively and eloquently argued though it is, the key problem with Lomborg's use of media examples is that they are just that, and hence do not even live up to Lomborg's own call for reasoned argument based on available evidence, not on eclectic use of partial evidence. Despite the wealth of systematic quantitative studies, including longitudinal studies, of media reporting on climate change and environmental issues generally, and the growing pool of qualitative studies of media reporting, Lomborg makes little or no reference to the evidence that these studies can provide, nor indeed does he make much reference to the growing body of literature on the social and political influences or role of media reporting of climate change and other environmental issues. Where systematic media research *is* referenced, its findings are taken out of context and seamlessly linked to climate change reporting even where studies have little or no bearing on this issue:

> The tabloid papers are forced to focus more on sensation because they depend on their readers finding them exciting enough to buy them every day. A recent study showed how the use of the word 'fear' has increased in American media, actually doubling in headlines. And climate sells particularly well.
>
> (Lomborg, 2007: 179)

The study referred to here is a study by American media and communications professor David Altheide and his colleague Sam Michalowski, published in 1999. Although referred to as a 'recent study' by Lomborg, the media analysis of Altheide and Michalowski's meticulous study in fact focuses on the decade from 1987 to 1996 – perhaps hardly qualifying as 'recent' in relation to the significant changes seen in the public climate-change debate in the last two decades, and most particularly in the last ten years or so. Equally symptomatic of a highly eclectic use of evidence is the point that Altheide and Michalowski's study primarily focuses on crime with little mention of 'environment' and none at all of climate change or global warming. Yet, as the quote above shows, the rhetorically convenient omission of both the dates and the primary focus of Altheide and Michalowski's research makes the deployment of this in support of Lomborg's argument as easy and seamless as simply mentioning 'climate' in the next sentence.

Most tellingly of all perhaps, there is no mention in Lomborg's latest book of Besley and Shanahan's (2004) disciplined empirical test – and consequent criticism – of Lomborg's claims about the media in his first book, *The Skeptical Environmentalist* (2001). Besley and Shanahan argue and, unlike Lomborg, prove their argument with the use of well-recognised and tried methods of media and communications research:

> Statistician Bjorn Lomborg's tacit hypotheses regarding the effect of mass media exposure (what he calls "the Litany") on environmental beliefs are tested using General Social Survey data from 1993, 1994, and 2000. Two core hypotheses and a research question are drawn from Lomborg's The Skeptical Environmentalist for discussion. Lomborg's apparent belief in a strong relationship between stilted media coverage and heightened environmental concern is generally not consistently borne out by the data. Lomborg's failure to distinguish between types of media, particularly television and newspapers, is shown to be problematic.
>
> (Besley and Shanahan, 2004: 861)

Even if Lomborg were right and the overwhelming thrust of media content dealing with environmental issues were alarmist and biased (as some literature described earlier suggests), past research and the data presented here suggest that he goes too far to assume this coverage translates directly into proenvironmental effects, in terms of either concern or action. Even the contention that media content is overwhelmingly proenvironmental seems a significant stretch, given previous narrative and framing research that has shown that the media's messages generally support economic or science interests.

[. . .] Whatever approach Lomborg could have taken, it remains that his approach failed to adequately connect content to effect. Questioning common wisdom—the stated goal of The Skeptical Environmentalist—must remain a key role of scholarly research.

(Besley and Shanahan, 2004: 876–77)

Other (mainly qualitative) approaches

While the study of media and public opinion has been dominated by the key approaches discussed in the previous sections of this chapter, other studies, taking a more micro-sociological approach, have examined some of the complex ways in which different publics, including children (Gauntlett, 1996), negotiate and interpret the science, risk and environmental meanings offered by media coverage (see Corner et al., 1990; Burgess and Harrison, 1993; Corner and Richardson, 1993; Phillips, 2000; Shaw, 2002; Holliman, 2004). Critical of the notion of 'passive' audiences being unilaterally influenced *by* the media,[11] these studies have pointed to the active way in which audiences engage with, interpret and inflect media information and images about environmental matters, particularly within the context of local knowledge (Dunwoody, 2007). Chapman et al. (1997), in a focus-group study of British television audiences, show that audiences draw considerably on media images for discussion of issues of which they have little direct experience. By contrast, 'discussion of environmental problems about which they have direct experience – such as water pollution, vehicle pollution, loss of green space – is less frequently validated by reference to media sources' (Chapman et al., 1997: 183).

Vocabularies, the circulation of claims, forums of meaning creation

Rather than thinking about the relationship between media coverage and public opinion in terms of simple linear agenda-setting processes, one causing the other, we need to think of these as interacting forums of learning and meaning creation (Gamson, 1988; Krimsky and Plough,

1988; Gamson and Modigliani, 1989; see also Lewenstein, 1995). From this perspective, the media, rather than being a single unified factor influencing public opinion and understanding about the environment, are understood as a complex, often contradictory, cultural reservoir of images, meanings, vocabularies, and definitions. The phrases, metaphors and vocabularies used in everyday public talk can, for example, often be traced to the media, while the media themselves, in turn, to varying degrees incorporate the public idiom (Hall et al., 1978) and public turns of phrase (Hansen, 2006) in their coverage and portrayal of environmental issues.

As noted in previous chapters, the media serve as an important reservoir of readily available images, meanings and definitions, and as an important public arena (Hilgartner and Bosk, 1988), where different images and definitions – 'sponsored' by different agents, groups and interested parties – compete and struggle with each other. Environmental meanings, messages, and definitions communicated in any one single medium, format or genre are unlikely to exert any simple linear influence on public beliefs, understanding or behaviour; but the media, in their broad and diverse totality, provide an important cultural context from which various publics draw both vocabularies and frames of understanding for making sense of the environment generally, and of claims about environmental problems more specifically.

Different media constantly interact and 'feed' off each other: quality newspapers set the agenda for other news media; news media deploy images and metaphors 'borrowed' (see also Chapter 5) from film, literature, and popular culture (Weart, 1988, 2003; Macnaghten and Urry, 1998; Turney, 1998); television drama and entertainment pick up and adapt issues and themes that are prominent in news and public debate; advertising media re-work the images and meanings prominent in both media and public debate in consumption terms, conducive to the selling of goods and services. The boom in 'green' advertising around the end of the 1980s, early 1990s – indeed the coining of the term 'green advertising' itself – and the continued centrality of environmental imagery in advertising show, perhaps more blatantly than elsewhere in the media, the significant continuous public reworking and appropriation of environmental meanings and imagery (see the discussion in Chapter 6).

Given the profusion of media images, the diversity of media, and most particularly the diversity of public consumption of media images, the relationship between media images of environmental issues and public perceptions, attitudes or understanding regarding environmental problems is clearly then one that is not best addressed by asking the simple question 'what are the effects of the media?' Nor is the role of the media best addressed in terms of one-directional linear models of communication effects which assume that media reporting *causes* public or political opinion – or vice versa. To begin to understand the role of the media in the communication of environmental issues, we need a different vocabulary and visualisation. We need to think in terms of the public 'circulation of claims' about the environment and we need a vocabulary with terms like dialectic, interaction, reinforcement, engagement, information loops, neural networks, multi-directional, resonance and parallel forums of meaning creation.

Conclusions

Media coverage and representations of environmental issues matter: they play a prominent and significant role in the social construction of environmental issues – not least those that we have little or no direct experiential access to – although pinpointing and quantifying the exact nature and extent of media influence remains a relatively elusive research task. However, more often than not, this is because we are asking the wrong questions. Questions that are themselves stuck in simplistic and outmoded assumptions about direct simple linear media 'effects' are likely to only generate answers that – while statistically often highly robust and sound – tell us little to help explain the truly complex dynamics of public and political opinion formation on environmental and risk issues.

Media coverage (like 'public opinion') is itself an important reference point in the public and political construction of social controversies, and an important ball in the public discursive game-playing characteristic of the rise and fall of major social issues in the public arena.

Media coverage impacts on and interacts with public opinion and political opinion/policy-making in complex ways that are more likely to fit the visual images/metaphors of loops and spirals than those of the one-directional arrows of direct linear effects models of communication.

The media and media coverage of environmental issues are best conceived of as a – continuously changing – cultural reservoir of images, meanings and definitions, on which different publics will draw for the purposes of articulating, making sense of, and understanding environmental problems and the politics of environmental issues.

Environmental issues don't simply present themselves as issues for public and political concern. Environmental issues – and public concern about the environment – are socially constructed. They become issues for public and political concern through complex dialectical processes of claims-making and counter-claims-making. As we have seen, communication and media are core to these processes. The media are at once a public arena where claims-makers compete to have their claims heard and publicised and themselves an active influence on the selection and framing of claims-makers' claims.

It is to the analysis of the dynamic interaction of media, publics, politics, claims-makers and social institutions that we must turn if we wish to begin to understand the processes by which some environmental issues are defined as social problems while others remain socially invisible, why some environmental claims succeed in the public sphere while others wither on the vine or fall by the wayside.

Further reading

Ader, C. R. (1995). A longitudinal-study of agenda-setting for the issue of environmental pollution. *Journalism and Mass Communication Quarterly*, *72*(2), 300–11. A disciplined and succinct application of the agenda-setting framework.

Gamson, W. A., and Modigliani, A. (1989). Media discourse and public opinion on nuclear power: a constructionist approach. *American Journal of Sociology*, *95*(1), 1–37. The 'classic' articulation of a non-linear, dynamic conception of the relationship between media coverage and public opinion.

Priest, S. H. (2009). Reinterpreting the audiences for media messages about science. In R. Holliman, E. Whitelegg, E. Scanlon, S. Smidt, and J. Thomas (Eds.), *Investigating Science Communication in the Information Age: Implications for Public Engagement and Popular Media* (pp. 223–36). Milton Keynes: Oxford University Press and The Open University. Although focusing on science communication, this overview discusses wider media-and-audiences models with relevance to environmental communication.

Shanahan, J., and McComas, K. (1999). *Nature Stories: Depictions of the Environment and Their Effects*. Cresskill, NJ: Hampton Press. See, in particular, Chapter 5: Television's Cultivation of Environmental Concern, pp. 115–45.

Glossary

Cross-references to other glossary terms are in **bold** typeface.

Accuracy in news reporting. A key concern in journalistic professional **ideology** and in objectivist approaches to the sociology of news, sitting alongside concerns about **balance, bias** and **objectivity** in news. The focus on accuracy has been particularly pronounced in studies of science news coverage. For a review of accuracy research, see Singletary (1980). The notion of accuracy assumes the existence of a 'correct' master account or narrative – in relation to science/environment coverage, the correct version is often assumed to be the scientist's account or the scientific paper on which a news report is based. The notion of accuracy has little or no meaning in **constructionist** approaches to news, as the interest here is primarily in mapping the dynamics of various contending accounts/explanations/discourses and the way in which such accounts are promoted, elaborated and cemented in public debate.

Advertising. The promotion or bringing to public notice of goods, information, images through – normally paid for – displays in any medium (e.g. the press, broadcast and other electronic media, billboards, cinema, etc.). Of particular interest in this book are: (1) the use of advertising by government, industry/corporations, NGOs and pressure groups to promote particular definitions/claims regarding environmental matters; and (2) the use of **nature** and natural imagery in the advertising and promotion of a wide variety of consumer goods.

Agenda setting. In communication research, this term refers to the power of the news media to influence public perception of the relative prominence and importance of different events, issues and actors/agencies. Originally formulated as the **power** of the media to influence public perception of the hierarchy of issues – what the public thinks about as opposed to the specific 'for-or-against' direction of **public opinion** – the term has increasingly overlapped with notions of framing to indicate the process by which the boundaries and hierarchy of public discourse are formed and shaped. The classic agenda-setting reference in communication research is McCombs and Shaw, 1972.

Alienation. 'William Kornhauser in the *Politics of Mass Society* (US: Free Press, 1959) argues that the breakdown and decline of community groups and the extended family in modern society produces feelings of isolation and increases the possibility that people will be influenced by the appeals of extremist political groups. Alienation might therefore be a significant variable in determining an individual's receptivity to certain types of communication' (Watson and Hill, 2006: 7).

Alternative media. Can generally be considered as any medium which is not controlled or owned by business corporations or government. The Royal Commission on the Press (1977) delineates the following useful characteristics: alternative media deal with the opinions of minorities; express attitudes 'hostile to widely-held beliefs' and give coverage to subjects and views which do not feature regularly in mainstream media. Watson and Hill's (2006: 168) comment on the internet has particular relevance to questions about how corporations, government and environmental pressure groups all seek to exploit the features of the internet: 'The INTERNET has been seen as potentially the most effective mode of alternative media, by its reach and accessibility and its interactive **power**. However, the risk of being colonized by the "usual suspects", big business and government, through commercialisation and legal restraint, has diminished optimism that struggles for justice and equality can be fought online.'

Attention/legitimacy/action. Solesbury (1976) proposed these as the three key tasks for pressure group campaigning: (1) commanding attention (e.g. in the media); (2) claiming legitimacy (i.e. ensuring that the particular definitions and stance promoted are received and presented in public and/or media debate as legitimate and appropriate within the generally accepted terms of public debate, as opposed to being undermined or rejected as, for example, 'extremist'); and (3) invoking action in the form of political, policy, or legislative changes, or indeed in the form of **public opinion** and behaviour change. The particular usefulness of Solesbury's task list is that it directs critical attention to the need for all three tasks to be met, that is, that getting media coverage alone is of little use to a pressure group if it's the 'wrong' kind of coverage or has no further implications in the form of political/policy change.

Balance/bias/accuracy in reporting. See **accuracy in news reporting** above.

'Blue chip' programmes. A **genre** label used to denote high-cost and expensive-looking nature/wildlife television programmes, often contrasted with 'adventure/presenter-led' programmes. While acknowledging that definitions vary, Bousé (1998: 134) proposes the following core characteristics: the depiction of *mega-fauna*; *visual splendour*; *dramatic narrative*; and the *absence of history, politics*; *people* and *science*.

Carrying capacity. Hilgartner and Bosk (1988) point out that 'all public arenas, operatives, and members of the public have finite resources to allocate to social problems' (p. 60) **Public arenas** such as the press and broadcast media, political institutions, institutions of government, the courts, public institutions, etc. can only entertain or carry a limited number of issues on their agenda at any one point in time. The introduction of new issues on the agenda therefore inevitably has the effect of either reducing the space/time given to other issues already on the agenda or to push them off the agenda altogether. Different arenas can cope with different numbers of issues at any one point in time. The way in which these finite capacities impact on the dynamics between different issues or **social problems** is particularly interesting: do environmental issues, for example, get squeezed off the public agenda during periods when the economy is in trouble?

Circulation of claims. The term is used here principally in contradistinction to traditional linear models of communication (sender > message/medium > audience/recipient), to indicate the interactive and dynamic nature of public debate. A drawback of the 'circulation' metaphor in this context is that it does not adequately express how claims and messages are *changed* as they circulate.

Claims-makers/issue sponsors. Any individual, group, agency or institution involved in making claims about or promoting/sponsoring issues, problem definitions or debate in **public arenas**, such as the media. The term claims-maker originates with Kitsuse and Spector's (1973: 415) definition of social problems as 'the activities of individuals or groups making assertions of grievances and claims with respect to some putative conditions'. In media and communications research, the term 'claims-maker' is often used synonymously with **sources** and actors in news media content. Claims-makers are also frequently referred to as 'issue sponsors' and occasionally as 'issue entrepreneurs'.

Claims-making styles. One of Ibarra and Kitsuse's (1993) four rhetorical dimensions, claims-making styles concern the 'bearing and tone' with which claims are fashioned and presented. Examples include *scientific, comic, theatrical, civic, legalistic and subcultural styles.* While there is overlap with concepts such as discourse, **frame** and **genre**, the focus on style can be useful for understanding why some claims fare much better than others in public, and why some gain popularity and legitimacy more easily than others. (See also **rhetorical idioms, counter-rhetorics, motifs** and **settings**.)

Claims-making tasks. See **Attention/legitimacy/action** above: (1) commanding attention, 2) claiming legitimacy, 3) invoking action.

Commodification. 'The transformation of relationships, formerly untainted by commerce, into commercial relationships, relationships of exchange, of buying and selling' (Encyclopedia of Marxism, 2009). Used here in relation to the use of **nature** symbolism and associated values for selling material products or goods for a profit. Originating in Marxist theory, the term refers to the assignment of economic or profit value to non-material goods such as concepts, ideas, identities or information. Here, the term is used to indicate the process by which advertisers translate the values and identities associated with **nature** or the countryside into purchasable material goods.

Constructionist approach/ constructionism. Originally formulated in relation to the analysis of social problems, the constructionist approach 'breaks with conventional and commonsensical conceptions of **social problems** by analyzing them as a *social process* of definition' (Miller and Holstein, 1993: 6). Spector and Kitsuse (1977/1987: 75–76) define social problems as '*the activities of individuals or groups making assertions of grievances and claims with respect to some putative conditions*', but the most pertinent part of their definition for media and communication research is where they go on to state that the '*central problem for a theory of social problems is to account for the emergence, nature, and maintenance of claims-making and responding activities*'. A constructionist approach to media and communication therefore focuses on the way in which issues, problems, claims and definitions emerge through social processes of communication, enter into and are elaborated in **public arenas** (notably the mass media), provoke and are met with **counter-claims/counter-rhetorics**, etc. The main focus is on accounting for the process of claims-making, not to establish whether claims – or their representation and inflection in media and other public arenas – are **accurate, objective or balanced**.

Content analysis. A systematic and quantitative method for analysing media content, it involves the transparent and systematic coding and counting of specified dimensions or characteristics of content in selected samples of media output. Content analysis is one of the most widely used methods in media and communication research, and has been and continues to be prominently used in analyses of media coverage of environmental issues. Studies examining the longitudinal trends in media coverage of the environment have used content analysis extensively, often – and productively – in combination with qualitative approaches to media content (e.g. discourse analysis) and in combination with **survey** studies of **public opinion**.

Corporate image strategies. Corporate communication strategies designed to improve and promote a positive image of a corporation/business in the public sphere and/or designed to engage with, counter or undermine campaigns or policies perceived as being against or restrictive to the interests of a corporation or business.

Counter-rhetoric/counter-claim. Several scholars have noted the simple **dialectics** of claims-making: for every claim, there is a counter-claim. Counter-rhetorics (Ibarra and Kitsuse, 1993) or counter-claims are discursive strategies for countering or undermining existing claims promoted by adversaries. As such they are less concerned with the construction of thematically coherent claims, and instead focus on ways of chipping away at or undermining the credibility of existing claims. They are not simple 'opposites' in the sense that a claim is countered by claiming the direct opposite, but tend instead to focus on undermining **credibility**, exposing inconsistencies, questioning the robustness of evidence, ridiculing **claims-makers** or questioning their sincerity and credentials, and casting doubt on the validity of claims.

Credibility/trust in news reporting. While journalists, particularly environmental and science correspondents, who tend to stay with their specialist field longer than other types of reporters, may well build up considerable expertise and knowledge relating to their field of reporting, they are not per se 'authorised' or 'accredited' experts. The credibility of their reporting thus has to be actively constructed in news reports, and this is often done through quoting recognisable or recognised expert **sources** (people, institutions or published data). Journalists deploy a range of 'markers' for determining and conveying the standing and credibility of their sources. Fundamentally, the journalistic task of determining, assessing and conveying credibility is made considerably easier through the – over time – cultivation of trustworthy and trusted sources, that is, where evidence and information is supplied by a trusted source, there is little or no need to spend time checking the credentials of sources or the validity of information supplied.

Cultivation analysis. A prominent and influential form of media effects research originally introduced by American communications scholar George Gerbner. Its central proposition is that the long-term repetition of core message patterns in popular media results in a matching world view in media audiences. The more time one spends consuming media news and entertainment, the more one's beliefs and ideas will match those that dominate on television. In the environmental communications field, James Shanahan and colleagues have, since the early 1990s, been at the forefront of testing the relationship between media representations and audience beliefs and opinion regarding the environment and environmental issues.

Cultural packages/media packages. Cultural packages/media packages/**interpretive packages** refer to the notion that claims, arguments, opinions do not exist as mere compilations of atomised words and images, but rather as organised, structured clusters or packages. As Gamson and Modigliani suggest (1989: 3): 'A package has an internal structure. At its core is a central organizing idea, or frame, for making sense of relevant events, suggesting what is at issue. [. . .] This frame typically implies a range of positions, rather than any single one, allowing for a degree of controversy among those who share a common frame. Finally, a package offers a number of different condensing symbols that suggest the core frame and positions in shorthand, making it possible to display the package as a whole with a deft metaphor, catchphrase, or other symbolic device.'

Cultural proximity (as a news value). One of several **news values** described by Galtung and Ruge (1965) in the now classic reference on the structure of news. Geographical, political and cultural proximity thus significantly enhances the likelihood of news coverage: people, events and issues in neighbouring countries of a similar culture are more likely to receive news coverage than their equivalents in countries or regions which are geographically, politically or culturally more distant.

Cultural resonance. The extent to which claims and news accounts are in harmony with, positioned within, activate or 'speak to' generally accepted cultural themes or **narratives**. 'Cultural resonances are used to shape generally recognisable plots (rags to riches, power corrupts). They offer easily recognized social/cultural stereotypes of characters (evil villains, honourable victims, noble heroes and heroines), and they reinforce general social goals, i.e., the underlying or implicit values that shape the way the mainstream media organize their impressions of society' (Ryan, 1991: 79).

Desk journalism (also desk-bound journalism). Journalistic work conducted from the journalist's desk and relying increasingly or principally on information gathering via telephone and the internet. This contrasts with the traditional image of the journalist as 'out and about' attending events, press conferences and tracking down **sources** to be interviewed in face-to-face interviews.

Dialectic. Used here in the sense of spiralling dynamic interaction between claims and counter-claims, and drawing directly on German philosopher Friedrich Hegel's (1770–1831) model of reasoning: a *thesis* is met with an *anti-thesis*, resulting in a new *synthesis* at a higher level, from which the process then repeats.

Direct media effects. A term used in media and communications research to indicate the media's direct influence on audience beliefs, perception, opinion and/or behaviour. The 'direct effects' model of media influence is associated with the early part of the twentieth century and with **mass society** theory, but was severely questioned and criticised as early as the 1940s and 1950s, and is now generally discredited for its overly simplistic and linear view of media influence.

Disaster news. Predominantly used to refer to news about major accidents (chemical spills, oil spills, air crashes, nuclear power-plant accidents, etc.) or natural disasters – earthquakes, tsunamis, volcanic eruptions, floods, droughts, etc. – and their consequences for people, **nature**/wildlife and societies.

Event orientation. The tendency for news to be focused on events rather than issues, and on products/outcomes rather than processes. In media and communications research the key criticism of the observed event orientation of news concerns the way in which the preoccupation with events and actions obscures or ignores the political and historical contextual information necessary for understanding and interpreting the meaning and implications of events/actions.

Excellent public relations function. Term used by Grunig et al. (2002) in their influential introduction to 'excellence' in **PR**: 'An excellent public relations function integrates all public relations programs into a single department or provides a mechanism for coordinating programs managed by different departments' (Grunig et al., 2002: 15).

Forum. The physical **setting**, context or **public arena** (e.g. political institution, the courts, research establishment, the media) for claims-making or debate, or as a focus for media attention. The forum is not simply a neutral or inert stage, but – through its own format requirements and conventions – restricts and sets boundaries for what can be said and how.

Frame(s). Gitlin (1980) defines frames as 'principles of selection, emphasis, and presentation composed of little tacit theories about what exists, what happens, and what matters'. Frames draw attention to particular dimensions or perspectives, and in doing so they also set the boundaries for how what is presented is discussed, interpreted or perceived. 'News frames are almost entirely implicit and taken for granted. [. . .] News frames make the world look natural. They determine what is selected, what is excluded, what is emphasised. In short, news presents a packaged world' (Gamson, 1985: 618).

Framing. 'To frame is to *select some aspects of a perceived reality and make them more salient in a communicating text, in such a way as to promote a particular problem definition, causal interpretation, moral evaluation, and/or treatment recommendation* for the item described' (Entman, 1993: 56). Framing in media coverage involves *selection/accessing* of **sources/claims-makers** and *emphasis* in the presentation/evaluation of arguments/actors. Framing analysis can usefully proceed (see Ryan, 1991) by asking: (1) what is the issue? (2) Who is responsible? (3) What is the solution?

Front-groups/fronting. A group, organisation or coalition of groups created to mask the vested interests of companies, corporations, parties or general stakeholders. Front groups project in the public sphere the appearance of working objectively and for 'the common good'. A prominent example is the Global Climate Coalition, set up with the help of **PR** experts by major oil-producing interests opposed to policies designed to curb CO_2 emissions, by casting doubt on climate change as anthropogenic. Fronting is the communicative process of engaging in/with public debate, without revealing the true interests that lie behind the arguments promoted (see also Norton, 2009: http://info-pollution.com/frontgroups.htm for further examples of fronting and types of front groups).

Gallup. Short for Gallup Poll: 'trademark name for an assessment of public opinion by the questioning of a representative sample, typically as a basis for forecasting votes in an election. It is named after George H. *Gallup* (1901–84), the American statistician who devised the method' (Knowles, 2006).

Genre. A particular type or category of media content, characterised by recognisable conventions of style, form and presentation. Key media genres include: news, documentary, current affairs, chat show, reality show, **advertising**, drama-serial, comedy, editorial, letter to the editor, feature/opinion article, etc. Genre categories are fluid and flexible rather than absolute, and are often deliberately combined (e.g. 'docu-drama') or manipulated for effect.

Globalisation. 'Globalisation theory examines the emergence of a global cultural system. It suggests that global culture is brought about by a variety of social and cultural developments: the existence of a world-satellite information system; the emergence of global patterns of consumption and consumerism; the cultivation of cosmopolitan life-styles; the emergence of global sport such as the Olympic Games, world football competitions, and international tennis matches; the spread of world tourism; the decline of the sovereignty of the nation-state; the growth of a global military system; recognition of a world-wide ecological crisis; the development of world-wide health problems such as AIDS; the emergence of world political systems such as the League of Nations and the United Nations; the creation of global political movements such as Marxism; extension of the concept of human rights; and the complex interchange between world religions. More importantly, globalism involves a new consciousness of the world as a single place' (Scott and Marshall, 2009).

Greenwash[ing]. 'disinformation disseminated by an organisation so as to present an environmentally responsible public image' (Soanes and

Stevenson, 2005). 'A term (combining green and whitewash) that environmentalists use to describe the activity (for example, by corporate lobby groups) of giving a positive public image to practices that are environmentally unsound' (Park, 2007).

Hegemony/hegemonic. 'A term introduced by the early-twentieth-century Italian Marxist theorist Antonio Gramsci to describe a certain kind of **power** that arises from the all-embracing ideological tendencies of mass media to support the established **power** system and exclude opposition and competing values. In brief it is a kind of dominant consensus that works in a concealed way without direct coercion' (McQuail, 2005: 557). Hegemony: 'leadership or dominance, especially by one state or social group over others.' Hegemonic: 'ruling or dominant in a political or social context: *the bourgeoisie constituted the hegemonic class*' (Soanes and Stevenson, 2008).

Hyper-linking. Linking from a website or hypertext document to another website or file. Links embedded in a website or document typically show up as highlighted text or an image and are activated just by clicking on the highlighted text/image. The presence of hyper-links on a **claims-maker's** website should be seen as a deliberate part of claims-making strategy and, at the very least, presents an acknowledgement of the presence of the (possibly opposing or alternative) positions of claims expressed at the sites linked to.

Identity. 'Specific characterisation of person, place, and so on by self and others, according to biographical, social, cultural and other features. Communication is a necessary condition for forming and maintaining identity. By the same token, it can weaken or undermine it. Mass communication is only one amongst several contributory factors' (McQuail, 2005: 557).

Ideology. 'A cohesive set of beliefs, ideas, and symbols through which persons interpret the world and their place within it' (Calhoun, 2002). The underlying world view, value system or perspective which informs, and to some extent, governs the nature and surface manifestation of communication. Ideology, like framing, works effectively by 'naturalising' the view or values that it expresses. The interests served by particular ideologies – that is, who (individuals, institutions, groups, social classes, etc.) benefits from this particular way of 'looking at' or 'defining' the issues, events or actors communicated about – are communicated principally through (1) the particular choice of words/metaphors used in a communicating text;

and (2) the way in which a text is structured both horizontally, that is, the **narrative**, and vertically, that is, the juxtaposition of characters, events and issues within the text.

Image enhancement/image management. The strategic use of **advertising**, **PR** and other planned communication to improve the public image or identity of a corporation, group, political party or public agency. This definition builds on and expands Cox's (2006: 403) definition of environmental image enhancement as 'The use of advertising to improve the image or identity of a corporation, reflecting its environmental concern or performance.'

Information subsidy. The act or process of **sources** providing to journalists or news organisations ready-packaged information that can be easily adapted to the format and other requirements of news. Originating in Oscar Gandy's (1982) influential study *Beyond Agenda Setting: Information Subsidies and Public Policy*, the term is widely used in studies of the relationship between **sources** and journalists in environmental, science and health reporting. Press releases and PR are among the most obvious forms of information subsidy.

Insider/outsider groups. 'Insider groups are regarded as legitimate by government and are consulted on a regular basis. Outsider groups either do not wish to become enmeshed in a consultative relationship with officials, or are unable to gain recognition' (Grant, 2000: 19). The distinction is helpful for appreciating first and foremost that not all pressure groups or NGOs are keen on publicity or see the media as a primary campaigning **forum**. Second, the distinction is helpful for sharpening our understanding of the significance and use of news media to the communication and campaigning strategies of outsider groups, particularly in terms of garnering both financial and political support for their cause.

Intelligence gathering and surveillance as pressure group strategies. While environmental pressure groups often come to public attention through spectacular and newsworthy media stunts and performances, the real key to success is in the meticulous and resource-demanding (i.e. often beyond the resources available to news organisations or individual journalists) surveillance and gathering of intelligence regarding developments in environmental policy **forums**, political negotiations, legislation, etc., followed by carefully targeted dissemination (e.g. to news organisations, through **information subsidies**) of appropriately framed information.

Interpretive packages. 'media discourse can be conceived of as a set of interpretive packages that give meaning to an issue. A package has an internal structure. At its core is a central organizing idea, or frame, for making sense of relevant events, suggesting what is at issue. [. . .] a package offers a number of different condensing symbols that suggest the core frame and positions in shorthand, making it possible to display the package as a whole with a deft metaphor, catchphrase, or other symbolic devices' (Gamson and Modigliani, 1989: 3).

IPCC: Inter-governmental Panel on Climate Change. 'A major international scientific collaboration between hundreds of specialists from around the world, that focuses on the likelihood and probable nature of induced climate change, based largely on forecasts from general circulation models. It was established in 1988 by the World Meteorological Organisation and the United Nations Environment Programme to assess the scientific, technical, and socioeconomic information needed to understand the risk of human-induced climate change' (Park, 2007).

Issue packages. See **interpretive packages** above.

Issue–attention cycle. Downs (1972) proposed the label 'issue–attention cycle' to describe the cyclical manner in which various **social problems** suddenly emerge on the public stage, remain there for a time, and 'then – though still largely unresolved – gradually [fade] from the centre of public attention' (p. 38). Downs identified five distinctive stages in the issue–attention cycle: (1) a pre-problem stage; (2) alarmed discovery and euphoric enthusiasm; (3) realising the cost of significant progress and the sacrifices required to solve the problem; (4) gradual decline of intense public interest; and (5) the post-problem stage, where the issue has been replaced at the centre of public concern and 'moves into a prolonged limbo – a twilight realm of lesser attention or spasmodic recurrences of interest.'

Mass Society. 'A description of modern, industrial society as a mass of undifferentiated and alienated individuals. Mass society became an object of concern in the early nineteenth century and initially reflected a shift in the nature of elitist fears for the body politic. Where the "tyranny of the majority" once expressed fears of disruptive mobs and demagogic rule, the new forces of modernisation implied stronger levelling tendencies that threatened to eliminate the values traditionally identified with social aristocracy – especially excellence and individuality. Fear of the mob gave way to fear of the conformist, degraded mass. [. . .] Marxist and renewed liberal versions of mass-society critique emerged largely in response to Europe's authoritarian turn in the 1930s. In an effort to explain the appeal of Nazism, fascism, and communism, liberal social scientists such as David Riesman (*The Lonely Crowd*, 1950) and William Kornhauser (*The Politics of Mass Society*, 1960) emphasized the decline of traditional religious and moral attachments, and the rise of sophisticated propaganda techniques that could manipulate the mass and achieve consent. The Marxist Frankfurt school contended as early as the 1940s that a mass society of alienated individuals was the inevitable product of a culture industry that served the interests of capitalism' (Calhoun, 2002).

Motifs. One of Ibarra and Kitsuse's (1993: 47) five foci for analysis of claims-making, motifs are defined as recurrent thematic elements, metaphors and figures of speech that encapsulate, highlight or offer a shorthand to some aspect of a **social problem**. Examples: epidemic, menace, scourge, crisis, blight, casualties, tip of the iceberg, the war on (drugs, poverty, crime, gangs, etc.), abuse, hidden costs, scandal, ticking time bomb.

Myth. 'Generally refers to stories that contribute to the elaboration of a cosmological system and to a cohesive social identity – e.g., accounts of origins, explanations of values and taboos, and narrative legitimations of authority. [. . .] Claude Lévi-Strauss is largely responsible for the structuralist approach to myth as a network of interchangeable narrative elements (mythemes) that reveal the basic oppositions that organize a given culture (endogamy and exogamy, animal and vegetable, raw and cooked, and so on). Roland Barthes gave the term a different and highly influential inflection in his book *Mythologies* (1957). For Barthes, myths are the codes that underlie the imagery and practices of much of contemporary culture. Their primary function is to lend the appearance of universality to otherwise contingent cultural beliefs. In this respect, myth occupies much the same place in Barthes's work as ideology in the writing of Antonio Gramsci and Louis Althusser: it naturalizes and secures consent for the status quo' (Calhoun, 2002).

Narrative. 'A telling of some true or fictitious event or connected sequence of events, recounted by a narrator to a narratee (although there may be more than one of each). Narratives are to be distinguished from descriptions of qualities, states, or situations, and also from dramatic enactments of events (although a dramatic work may also include narrative speeches). A narrative will consist of a set of events (the story) recounted in a process of narration (or discourse), in which the events are selected and arranged in a particular order (the plot)' (Baldick, 2008).

Natural history models of issue careers. An analytical frame implying that **social problems** develop or pass through a set of sequentially ordered stages. 'Social problems do not arise full-blown, commanding community attention and evoking adequate policies and machinery for their solution. On the contrary, we believe that social problems exhibit a temporal course of development in which different phases or stages may be distinguished. Each stage anticipates its successor in time and each succeeding stage contains new elements which mark it off from its predecessor. A social problem [. . .] passes through the natural history stages of awareness, policy determination, and reform' (Fuller and Myers, 1941: 321).

Nature documentary/nature programmes. The term 'nature documentary' is widely and broadly used to refer to any (mainly television) non-fiction, informative programme about some aspect of nature. It is distinguished by (generally) adhering to the format and **genre** conventions of 'documentary' and by its content focus on wildlife, plants and other aspects of the natural environment (as opposed to documentaries about social, political or cultural issues). However, as Bousé (1998) indicates by his rhetorically titled article 'Are wildlife films really "nature documentaries"?' there is considerable room for further distinctions within the broad label 'nature documentary', particularly with regard to the differences in story-telling conventions/narrative formats deployed in **wildlife films** and in nature documentaries (see also **blue chip programmes** and **wildlife films**).

Nature/natural. While both 'nature' and 'natural' in common usage inherently suggest an ontological quality, their meaning is of course socially, historically and culturally constructed. Williams (1983: 219) distinguishes three principal meanings of 'nature': '(i) the essential quality and character of something; (ii) the inherent force which directs either the world or human beings or both; (iii) the material world itself, taken as including or not including human beings.'

News cycle. The length of time between each edition of a news outlet: for daily newspapers, twenty-four hours; for traditional radio and television channels, the number of hours between each major news programme. The significance of the news cycle has traditionally related to questions about immediacy, **agenda setting** and competition between news media/organisations. With the advent of twenty-four-hour-news channels and online news, news is potentially updated on a 'rolling' and continuous basis, making the notion of a 'cycle' less immediately relevant, although a certain 'rhythm' can still be apparent. Awareness of 'news cycles' is important to **sources/claims-makers** in relation to timing and targeting claims for optimum effect/impact.

News forum/setting/arena. In principle, any (newsworthy) **setting**, context or **public arena** (e.g. political institution, the courts, research establishment, the media) for claims-making or debate. In practice, the term tends to refer to the particular standard settings or arenas that journalists routinely attend to or monitor for news stories (particularly the institutions of government, international organisations, the courts, research and information/knowledge-producing establishments, etc.).

News values. The set of criteria that journalists and news media use for determining whether to report an event or story. News values vary according to cultural context and target audience. The standard reference is Galtung and Ruge's (1965) classic study *The Structure of Foreign News,* which lists a dozen or so criteria, including *frequency, negativity, unambiguity, meaningfulness* (**cultural proximity** and *relevance*), *continuity, unexpectedness,* etc.

Newsworthiness. The degree to which events/stories meet the **news values** criteria. Frequently used synonymously with news values.

Nostalgia. 'A sentimental longing or wistful affection for a period in the past: [. . .] Something done or presented in order to evoke such feelings: *an evening of TV nostalgia.* [. . .] from Greek *nostos* "return home" + *algos* "pain"' (Soanes and Stevenson, 2005). 'Nostalgia became, in short, the means for holding onto and reaffirming identities which had been badly bruised by the turmoil of the times. In the "collective search for identity" which is the hallmark of this postindustrial epoch – a search that in its constant soul-churning extrudes a thousand different fashions, ecstasies, salvations, and utopias – nostalgia looks backward rather than forward, for the familiar rather than the novel, for certainty rather than discovery' (Davis, 1979: 107–8).

Objectivity. A journalistic professional value that goes together with, and is frequently seen as synonymous with, the professional journalistic news requirements of **accuracy**, fairness, transparency, impartiality, separation of fact from comment, **balance** and lack of **bias**. Critics argue that objectivity in news reporting is impossible and that the journalistic construction of the appearance of objectivity is itself a concealment, whether intended or not, of **bias**.

Paradigmatic and syntagmatic analysis. Syntagmatic analysis is the study of the linear structure of texts, whether at the level of individual sentences and their syntax, or at the level of whole narratives. It is concerned with how meaning arises from the sequential arrangement of words or actions in a text, where a change in sequence may/will result in a different meaning. By contrast, paradigmatic analysis studies the relationship between the words that appear in a text and the reservoir of other words, not chosen, in the underlying language, and it studies the way that meaning is communicated through the structural arrangement and juxtapositions of actors, values and events in a text.

Postmodernism. A 'late 20th-century style and concept in the arts, architecture, and criticism, which represents a departure from modernism and is characterized by the self-conscious use of earlier styles and conventions, a mixing of different artistic styles and media, and a general distrust of theories' (Soanes and Stevenson, 2005). In Berger's (2000: 278) words, 'the old philosophical belief systems that had helped people order their lives and societies are no longer accepted or given credulity. This leads to a period in which, more or less, anything goes'. This characterisation has particular pertinence for environmental, risk and similar science-based communication, where earlier trust and belief in scientific and political authority has eroded. In journalism, news and documentary programming, the postmodernist trend manifests itself as an erosion of traditional journalistic values of factual **accuracy**, impartiality and **objectivity**, but more significantly in a move from 'visual realism' towards a mixing of styles and referencing of other media/texts rather than a 'window-on-the-world' referencing of the 'reality' being portrayed.

Power. A complex concept with many meanings across the various disciplines of the social sciences, but of key interest in the present book is its meaning as the possession of necessary resources (economic, technical or indeed communicative/cultural competence or capital) and associated ability to effect or bring about change – or to prevent change from happening – by influencing and manipulating **claims-making**, media and communications agendas, including the ability to prevent certain claims from making it onto the agendas of the media and other **public arenas**.

PR/public relations. 'Now a reference to all forms of influence carried out by professional paid communicators on behalf of some 'client' and designed primarily to project a favourable image and to counter negative views that might exist. The means are various, ranging from direct communication to providing gifts and hospitality. Public relations is often a source of supply for news media or seeks to influence news in other ways' (McQuail, 2005: 566).

Primary definers. The **claims-makers** or **sources** who influence and shape, through direct quotation or indirect referencing, the media and news agenda. The journalists and media themselves are often referred to as secondary definers. The term 'primary definer' can be and has been used to refer to any source quoted or referred to in media and news content, but in its original definition it was implied or assumed that primary definers were in a position of authority and **power** in society.

Progress package. The progress package (Gamson and Modigliani, 1989) is characterised by beliefs in science, technological innovation, mastery over **nature**, efficiency, economic expansion, adaptability, practicality, expediency, etc. as the solution to problems and the route to a better, safer and more prosperous society. One of its clearest manifestations in public debate about climate change is in the form of proposals to 'manage' and control climate change through technological innovation, that is, to 'invent' ourselves out of trouble.

Public arenas model. A model introduced by Hilgartner and Bosk (1988) for the analysis and understanding of the processes and **forums** of claims-making and social problems construction: 'The collective definition of social problems occurs not in some vague location such as society or **public opinion** but in particular public arenas in which social problems are framed and grow. These arenas include the executive and legislative branches of government, the courts, made-for-TV movies, the cinema, the news media (television news, magazines, newspapers, and radio), political campaign organisations, social action groups, direct mail solicitations, books dealing with social issues, the research community, religious organisations, professional societies, and private foundations. It is in these institutions that social problems are discussed, selected, defined, framed, dramatized, packaged, and presented to the public' (pp. 58–59). The model directs attention to the commonalities (e.g. limited **carrying capacities**) and differences (e.g. time-table/time-cycles) across the major public arenas. It points to the centrality of factors such as competition, selection, format, the routines of operatives, etc. in influencing claims-making processes and it highlights the ways in which effective **claims-makers** tailor and adapt their claims to fit the requirements of **public arenas**.

Public opinion. 'An ill-defined concept, used in many ways, but perhaps most generally it refers to the approval or disapproval of publicly observable positions and behaviour, as expressed by a defined section of a society, and (usually) measured through opinion polls. Consequently, it is often taken to be synonymous with "what the polls report" – about morality, favoured consumer brands, politics, or whatever' (Scott and Marshall, 2009).

Public sphere. 'The conceptual "space" that exists in a society outside the immediate circle of private life and the walls of enclosed institutions and organisations pursuing their own (albeit sometimes public) goals. In this space, the possibility exists for public association and debate leading to the formation of **public opinion** and political movements and parties that can hold private interests accountable. The media are now probably the key institution of the public sphere, and its "quality" will depend on the quality of media. Taken to extremes, certain structural tendencies of media, including concentration, commercialisation and globalisation, are harmful to the public sphere' (McQuail, 2005: 566).

Publicity stunts. A demonstration or performance enacted for the purpose of drawing media and public attention, and for the purpose of getting news media coverage. Publicity stunts are specifically designed to appeal to and exploit core **news values** (unexpectedness, visuality, drama, etc.). On their own, they are of limited use to pressure groups, but as part of a wider campaign strategy they can be a highly effective way of drawing attention to campaign issues.

Realism/realist. In both factual and fictional media content, a mode of representation which is or appears to be accurate, objective, true to life or a 'window on the world'. Conventional news journalism is 'realist' in the sense that it reports the 'objective' facts in an impartial way, as an impartial observer of real events, people and issues without drawing attention to its own constructedness and **genre** conventions. **Nature documentaries** which purport to be simply filming and observing wildlife and natural events 'as they occur' can be described as 'realist' or as adhering to the conventions of realism. Television drama serials or 'soap operas' purporting to portray 'real' people, living in broadly recognisable 'real' environments and dealing with real issues can likewise be characterised as adhering to a realist mode of presentation. The core notion of television merely 'observing life as it happens' is also evident in the **genre** label reality show/reality television.

Rhetoric. 'The art of effective or persuasive speaking or writing, especially the exploitation of figures of speech and other compositional techniques. Language designed to have a persuasive or impressive effect, but which is often regarded as lacking in sincerity or meaningful content: *all we have from the Opposition is empty rhetoric*' (Soanes and Stevenson, 2005).

Rhetorical idioms. Ibarra and Kitsuse (1993: 34) advocate that **constructionist** studies should distinguish 'four overlapping but analytically distinct rhetorical dimensions: rhetorical idioms, **counter-rhetorics**, **motifs**, and **claims-making styles**.' While a dictionary definition of an idiom (literally: peculiar phraseology) is 'a group of words established by usage as having a meaning not deducible from those of the individual words (e.g. *over the moon, see the light*)' or 'a form of expression natural to a language, person, or group of people' (Soanes and Stevenson, 2005), Ibarra and Kitsuse's use of the term 'rhetorical idioms' is wider and refers to the general cluster of words and rhetoric that characterises a particular perspective, moral evaluation or way of 'talking about' a social issue/problem. In this respect their notion of rhetorical idioms is akin to **cultural packages**. '*Rhetorical idioms* are definitional complexes, utilizing language that situates condition-categories in moral universes.[. . .] Each rhetorical idiom calls forth or draws upon a cluster of images. The *rhetoric of loss,* for example, evokes symbols of purity and tends toward nostalgic tonalities. The *rhetoric of unreason* evokes images of manipulation and conspiracy. The *rhetoric of calamity* situates condition-categories amid narratives of widespread devastation, and so on' (Ibarra and Kitsuse, 1993: 34).

Romanticism. 'A movement in the arts and literature which originated in the late 18th century, emphasizing inspiration, subjectivity, and the primacy of the individual' (Soanes and Stevenson, 2008). Characterised by its emphasis on **nature** as pure, good, spiritual, sublime, authentic and pristine, the romantic view contrasted with the earlier Enlightenment period's view of nature as something wild and threatening to be studied, understood, tamed and controlled in the name of civilisation and progress. Both the romantic view and the

utilitarian Enlightenment view continue to inform and influence the constructions of **nature** and the environment in media and public discourse.

Schema. 'Refers to the preconceived frame or script which is typically available to journalists for reporting isolated cases or events. A schema is an aid to communication and understanding, because it provides some wider context and sense-making' (McQuail, 2005: 567).

Science fiction. 'A genre of fiction based on imagined future technological or scientific advances, major environmental or social changes, etc., and frequently portraying space or time travel and life on other planets. Science fiction emerged in the late nineteenth century in the works of writers such as Jules Verne and H.G. Wells, although there are earlier precedents, such as Mary Shelley's *Frankenstein* (1818)' (Deverson, 2004).

Scripts. Akin to **cultural packages**, **narratives**, **schema** and **frames**, scripts can be regarded as the world views or clusters of meaning/ perspective from our cultural reservoir, which help us make sense of our environment and understand how things work, what counts as appropriate or acceptable within our culture. Turney (1998), Huxford (2000) and others have persuasively argued that environment and science correspondents as well as journalists generally rely heavily on readily available cultural scripts and frames, particularly when reporting on new and unfamiliar developments in science and environmental issues.

Settings. Ibarra and Kitsuse (1993) add settings to their four rhetorical dimensions of claims-making (**rhetorical idioms**, **counter-rhetorics**, **motifs** and **claims-making styles**) as an important focus for analysing the construction of **social problems**. Settings – like **forums** and **arenas** – are the physical or abstract (e.g. academia) context in which claims-making is enacted or performed. Settings have important format- , time- and **genre** conventions, which structure what is said, how it is said, and indeed how that which is said, is received, consumed or responded to by the public and by **claims-makers** in other forums. Ibarra and Kitsuse (1993: 54), pointing to the media as an important setting and touching on the format and **genre** conventions which govern different media **genres**, ask: 'What are the explicit or tacit rules for admissible testimony, fairness, objectivity, and so on? How does the visual component of some of these media alter the claim's sense, reception, and structure?' See also **News forum/setting/arena**.

Social constructionism. An approach in sociology and other disciplines which focuses on how our knowledge about the world around us is the result of social processes of definition. It directs attention to the analysis of processes of communication and definition, and to the analysis of the people, media and settings involved in articulating, elaborating, contesting and maintaining claims or definitions (see also **claims-making/claims-makers** and **social problems**). While media and communication processes are important foci in the wider social **constructionist** approach to the analysis of its main focus of concern, **social problems**, the constructionist framework has also become prominent as a framework and analytical approach in the sociology of news. Here, it rejects classic concerns about **bias**, **balance**, **accuracy** and **objectivity** in news journalism, and instead directs attention to the roles of **sources**, journalists and media organisations in the shaping of news content.

Social problems. Kitsuse and Spector (1973: 415) define social problems as 'the activities of individuals or groups making assertions of grievances and claims with respect to some putative conditions'. They reject (structural functionalist) sociological formulations which regard social problems as objective identifiable conditions in society, and argue instead that social problems are the result of social processes of claims-making and definition. Their analytical emphasis is therefore on the rhetorical, discursive and definitional practices of **claims-makers**, on the rhetorical construction of claims (about social problems), and on the processes through which particular problem definitions are elaborated, contested and maintained in **public arenas**.

Source/news source. 'An individual, group or institution that originates a message. In media terms, the source is where information starts, and it is an axiom of good reporting that the material supplied by the source is reliable and true. Best practice suggests that single sources be checked against other sources. It is also a matter of journalistic principle that in some cases the source of information is assured of anonymity' (Watson and Hill, 2006: 273).

Survey. In the general sense: an overview, examination or detailed description of someone or something. In the social sciences, the term mainly, although not exclusively, refers to the systematic collection of data/information, mainly with the use of a questionnaire, about a defined sample of a larger population, for example, a survey of the environmental attitudes of teenagers.

Symbolic annihilation. Term 'used to highlight the erasure of peoples in popular communication. George Gerbner coined the term to describe the "absence" (1972, 44; Gerbner and Gross 1976 [. . .]), "condemnation," or "trivialisation" (Tuchman 1978, 17) of a particular group in the media. Generally applied to women and racial and sexual minorities, symbolic annihilation points to the ways in which poor media treatment can contribute to social disempowerment and in which symbolic absence in the media can erase groups and individuals from public consciousness. [. . .] Language use in the media also contributes to the trivialisation and condemnation of racial groups such as black people in popular communication' (Coleman and Yochim, 2008).

Time/cycle in news. See **News cycle.**

Uncertainty in news reporting. Much attention in studies of science, environment, health and risk communication has focused on the difficulties for journalists, media, politicians, scientists and experts in the handling and management in public communication of the fundamental degree of uncertainty and speculation, characteristic of most emerging scientific, environmental, health, social issues or problems. Where in the past there may have been an unrealistic expectation that expert **sources** and the media could provide clear-cut answers and advice in relation, for example, to major accident, disease or public safety emergencies, there now seems to be a greater recognition – both in the media and in the public – of the complexities of these phenomena and of the difficulty of prediction.

Utilitarian. 'Designed to be useful or practical rather than attractive' (Soanes and Stevenson, 2005). A utilitarian (cf. **romantic** or conservationist) perspective on **nature** is one which sees nature and the environment as something to be mastered, controlled and exploited for the benefit of mankind. The utilitarian view of nature was prominent in the Enlightenment period of eighteenth-century Europe, and continues to be a prominent discourse throughout the twentieth century, particularly in the immediate post-World War II period, and to today.

Utopia/dystopia – and technopia. Utopia and dystopia are what semiologists call 'binary opposites' – one only makes sense/has meaning in relation to the other; when we talk of one, the presence of the other is always implicit or 'understood'. The Oxford English Dictionary (Soanes and Stevenson, 2005) defines utopia as 'an imagined place or state of things in which everything is perfect' and dystopia as 'an imagined place or state in which everything is unpleasant or bad, typically a totalitarian or environmentally degraded one.' Utopian and, perhaps more frequently, dystopian visions of the future are prominent implicit or explicit themes in literature, film, **advertising** and other media content. As such they can often also be seen to inform or influence news reporting on environment, science and technology issues. Rutherford (2000), in his analysis of corporate advertising, introduces the further category *technopia* as 'the corporate version of a technological utopia' (p. 190), corporate advertising projecting the idea that science and more particularly technology are keys to a bright, harmonious and prosperous future free of the environmental, social and other problems of the present.

VNR – video news release. A video recording created by a pressure group, government department, **advertising** agency, **PR** firm, business, corporation or other **source/claims-maker** for distribution to news organisations. While originally referring to video-tape recordings, they are now more likely to be digital recordings. VNRs are the video equivalent of press releases and a visual type of **information subsidy**. VNRs often form an integral and effective part of environmental pressure group campaigning strategies.

Wildlife film. The portrayal or depiction of wildlife (and sometimes domestic animals) through the medium of film. Defining characteristics include the narrative pretence of unmediated observation (a 'window' on wildlife going about its business) and (see Bousé, 1998: 134): the depiction of *mega-fauna*; *visual splendour*; *dramatic narrative*; and the *absence of history, politics*; *people*; and *science*. Bousé argues for a distinction between wildlife films and **nature documentaries**: 'wildlife films are not documentaries; [. . .] they are primarily narrative entertainments that usually steer clear of real social and environmental issues' (p. xiv). See also **'blue chip' programmes** and **nature documentary/nature programmes**.

Notes

1 The term 'vocabulary of public life' is borrowed from Wuthnow (1992).
2 Other semiotic sign-systems, for example, *sound/audio*, may also be significant contributors to the public vocabulary on the environment, but very little work has been done on the role of sound images in communicating the environment and environmental issues.
3 Others, like Craig Trumbo (1996), have on the other hand been acutely conscious of precisely this: 'It must also be emphasized that the issue-attention cycle is a social process model and is not specifically designed to evaluate news media attention to an issue' (1996: 280).
4 Brossard et al. (2004) compare press coverage in the United States with press coverage in France; Mikami et al. (2002) study press coverage in Japan, Europe and the United States; McComas and Shanahan (1999) study press coverage in the United States; Carvalho and Burgess (2005) in the UK; Weingart et al. (2000) in Germany, etc.
5 Overlexicalisation or overwording: a concentration of inter-related terms signalling an intense preoccupation with some aspect of reality (Fairclough 1989) and resulting 'in certain meanings rather than others being repeatedly and routinely foregrounded' (Brookes 1995: 471).
6 'Formulae package concepts simply and memorably; they signify paradigms, model ideas which can be applied to new "instances", however remote from the original referents' (Fowler 1991: 178).
7 Although all the papers drew on military/battle metaphors, these were particularly prominent in the *Mirror* and included such lexical choices as: siege, warriors, battered, fighters, commandos, green army, killing blow, victory.
8 It is important to note, as Widener and Gunter's (2007) analysis makes clear, that these are relative, not exclusive, emphases. As argued previously in this chapter, all discourses are potentially *always available* and receive some degree of hearing across different media, but their relative prominences vary considerably.
9 'Mother Earth' and 'Father Oil' are symbols that themselves of course activate long chains of cultural binaries, for example, pristine, harmonious, unsoiled and unspoilt goodness and fertility versus dirty, aggressive and violent (including sexual violation metaphors – pollution as 'raping Mother Earth') exploitation.
10 In semiotic terms, if the word analysis is concerned with how meaning in texts is derived in the paradigmatic level – our familiarity with how individual words, which appear in a given text, relate to and derive meaning from their relationship with the

underlying language system, then the narrative analysis is concerned with how meaning is derived at the syntagmatic level – the way in which the 'meaning' of a sentence or a whole text only 'falls into place' when we have moved linearly through the text from the beginning through the middle to the end.

11 The notion of a relatively passive audience is implicit at least in the traditional articulation of agenda-setting theory (McCombs and Shaw, 1972), if much less pronounced in the more recent elaborations of agenda-setting theory, for example, through integration with theories of priming and framing (McCombs and Bell, 1996; McCombs, 2004).

Bibliography

Ader, C. R. (1995). A longitudinal study of agenda-setting for the issue of environmental pollution. *Journalism and Mass Communication Quarterly, 72*(2), 300–11.

Adoni, H., and Mane, S. (1984). Media and the social construction of reality: toward an integration of theory and research. *Communication Research, 11*(3), 323–40.

Albaek, E., Christiansen, P. M., and Togeby, L. (2003). Experts in the mass media: Researchers as sources in Danish daily newspapers, 1961–2001. *Journalism and Mass Communication Quarterly, 80*(4), 937–48.

Aldridge, M., and Dingwall, R. (2003). Teleology on television? Implicit models of evolution in broadcast wildlife and nature programmes. *European Journal of Communication, 18*(4), 435–55.

Allan, S. (2006). *Online News: Journalism and the Internet*. London: Open University Press.

Altheide, D. L., and Michalowski, R. S. (1999). Fear in the news: A discourse of control. *Sociological Quarterly, 40*(3), 475–503.

An Inconvenient Truth: A Global Warning [Film/DVD]. Dir. D. Guggenheim. Paramount. 2006.

Anderson, A. (1997). *Media, Culture and the Environment*. London: UCL Press.

Armitage, K. C. (2003). Commercial Indians: Authenticity, nature and industrial capitalism in advertising at the turn of the twentieth century. *Michigan Historical Review, 29*(2), 71–.

Aronson, N. (1984). Science as a claims-making activity: implications for social problems research. In J. Schneider, and J. I. Kitsuse (Eds.), *Studies in the Sociology of Social Problems* (pp. 1–30). Norwood, NJ: Ablex.

Atwater, T., Salwen, M. B., and Anderson, R. B. (1985). Media agenda-setting with environmental issues. *Journalism Quarterly, 62*, 393–97.

Bagust, P. (2008). 'Screen natures': Special effects and edutainment in 'new' hybrid wildlife documentary. *Continuum: Journal of Media and Cultural Studies, 22*(2), 213–26.

Bakir, V. (2006). Policy agenda setting and risk communication – Greenpeace, Shell, and issues of trust. *Harvard International Journal of Press-Politics, 11*(3), 67–88.

Baldick, C. (2008). *The Oxford Dictionary of Literary Terms*. Oxford University Press: Oxford Reference Online. Available: www.oxfordreference.com/views/ENTRY.html?subview = Main&entry = t56.e760 (accessed 27 April 2009).

Banerjee, S., Gulas, C. S., and Iyer, E. (1995). Shades of green – a multidimensional analysis of environmental advertising. *Journal of Advertising, 24*(2), 21–31.

Barthes, R. (1972 [1957]). *Mythologies*. London: Jonathan Cape.

Barthes, R. (1977a). Introduction to the structural analysis of narratives. In R. Barthes (Ed.), *Image, Music, Text: Essays Selected and Translated by Stephen Heath* (pp. 79–129). London: Fontana.

Barthes, R. (1977b). Rhetoric of the image. In R. Barthes (Ed.), *Image, Music, Text: Essays Selected and Translated by Stephen Heath* (pp. 32–51). London: Fontana.

Bauer, M. (1998). The medicalization of science news – from the "rocket-scalpel" to the "gene-meteorite" complex. *Social Science Information Sur Les Sciences Sociales, 37*(4), 731–51.

Bauer, M., Durant, J., and Gaskell, G. (Eds.). (1999). *Biotechnology in the Public Sphere: A European Source-book*. London: The Science Museum.

Bauer, M. W. (2002). Controversial medical and agri-food biotechnology: a cultivation analysis. *Public Understanding of Science, 11*(2), 93–111.

Beck, U. (1992). *Risk Society: Towards a New Modernity* (Mark Ritter, Trans.). London: Sage.

Beckett, K. (1997). *Making Crime Pay: Law and Order in Contemporary American Politics*. New York: Oxford University Press.

Beder, S. (2002 [1997]). *Global Spin: The Corporate Assault on Environmentalism*. (Revised ed.). Totnes, Devon: Green Books.

Bell, A. (1994a). Climate of opinion – public and media discourse on the global environment. *Discourse and Society, 5*(1), 33–64.

Bell, A. (1994b). Media (mis)communication on the science of climate change. *Public Understanding of Science, 3*(3), 259–75.

Bennie, L. G. (1998). Brent Spar, Atlantic oil and Greenpeace. *Parliamentary Affairs, 51*(3), 397–410.

Benoit, W. L. (1995). *Accounts, Excuses, and Apologies: A Theory of Image Restoration Strategies*. Albany, NY: State University of New York Press.

Berger, A. A. (2000). *Media and Communication Research: An Introduction to Qualitative and Quantitative Approaches*. London: Sage.

Besley, J. C., and Shanahan, J. (2004). Skepticism about media effects concerning the environment: Examining Lomborg's hypotheses. *Society and Natural Resources, 17*(10), 861–80.

Best, J. (Ed.). (1995). *Images of Issues: Typifying Contemporary Social Problems* (2nd ed.). New York: Aldine de Gruyter.

Blumer, H. (1971). Social problems as collective behavior. *Social Problems, 18*(3), 298–306.

Borman, S. C. (1978). Communication accuracy in magazine science reporting. *Journalism Quarterly, 55*, 345–46.

Bousé, D. (1998). Are wildlife films really "nature documentaries"? *Critical Studies in Mass Communication, 15*(2), 116–40.

Bousé, D. (2000). *Wildlife Films*. Philadelphia, PA: University of Pennsylvania Press.

Bowman, J. S., and Fuchs, T. (1981). Environmental coverage in the mass media: a longitudinal study. *International Journal of Environmental Studies, 18*(1), 11–22.

Boyce, T. (2006). Journalism and expertise. *Journalism Studies, 8*(6).

Boykoff, M. T. (2007). Climate change and journalistic norms: A case-study of US mass-media coverage. *Geoforum, 38*, 1190–204.

Boykoff, M. T. (2008). Lost in translation? United States television news coverage of anthropogenic climate change, 1995–2004. *Climatic Change, 86*, 1–11.

Boykoff, M. T., and Boykoff, J. M. (2004). Balance as bias: global warming and the US prestige press. *Global Environmental Change-Human and Policy Dimensions, 14*(2), 125–36.

Breed, W. (1955). Social control in the newsroom: a functional analysis. *Social Forces, 33*, 326–35.

Brookes, H. J. (1995). 'Suit, tie and a touch of juju' – the ideological construction of Africa: a critical discourse analysis of news on Africa in the British press. *Discourse and Society, 6*(4), 461–94.

Brookes, S. K., Jordan, A. G., Kimber, R. H. and Richardson, J. J. (1976). The growth of the environment as a political issue in Britain. *British Journal of Political Science, 6*, 245–55.

Brosius, H.-B., and Kepplinger, H. M. (1990). The agenda-setting function of television news. *Communication Research, 17*(2), 183–211.

Brossard, D., Shanahan, J., and McComas, K. (2004). Are issue-cycles culturally constructed? A comparison of French and American coverage of global climate change. *Mass Communication and Society, 7*(3), 359–77.

Buckley, R., and Vogt, S. (1996). Fact and emotion in environmental advertising by government, industry and community groups. *Ambio, 25*(3), 214–15.

Budd, M., Craig, S., and Steinman, C. (1999). *Consuming Environments: Television and Commercial Culture*. New Brunswick, NJ: Rutgers University Press.

Burgess, J., and Harrison, C. M. (1993). The circulation of claims in the cultural politics of environmental change. In A. Hansen (Ed.), *The Mass Media and Environmental Issues* (pp. 198–221). Leicester: Leicester University Press.

Calhoun, C. (2002). *Dictionary of the Social Sciences*. Oxford University Press: Oxford Reference Online. Available: www.oxfordreference.com/views/ENTRY.html?subview = Main&entry = t104.e793 (27 April 2009).

Campbell, F. (1999). *The Construction of Environmental News: A Study of Scottish Journalism*. Abingdon: Ashgate.

Carson, R. (1962). *Silent Spring*. Boston, MA: Houghton Mifflin.

Carvalho, A., and Burgess, J. (2005). Cultural circuits of climate change in UK broadsheet newspapers, 1985–2003. *Risk Analysis, 25*(6), 1457–69.

Castells, M. (2004). *The Power of Identity* (2nd ed.). Malden, MA; Oxford: Blackwell.

Chapman, G., Kumar, K., Fraser, C., and Gaber, I. (1997). *Environmentalism and the Mass Media: The North-South Divide*. London: Routledge.

Cho, B., Kwon, U., Gentry, J. W., Jun, S., and Kropp, F. (1999). Cultural values reflected in theme and execution: A comparative study of US and Korean television commercials. *Journal of Advertising, 28*(4), 59–73.

Cobb, R. W., and Elder, C. D. (1971). The politics of agenda building: an alternative perspective for modern democratic theory. *Journal of Politics, 33*, 892–915.

Cohen, B. C. (1963). *The Press and Foreign Policy*. Princeton, NJ: Princeton University Press.

Coleman, R. R. M., and Yochim, E. C. (2008). Symbolic annihilation. In W. Donsbach (Ed.), *The Blackwell International Encyclopedia of Communication*. Oxford: Blackwell. Available: www.communication encyclopedia.com/public/book?id = g9781405131995_9781405131995 (accessed 29 April 2009).

Collins, H. M. (1987). Certainty and the public understanding of science: science on television. *Social Studies of Science, 17*(4), 689–713.

Condit, C. M., Achter, P. J., Lauer, I., and Sefcovic, E. (2002). The changing meanings of "mutation": A contextualized study of public discourse. *Human Mutation, 19*(1), 69–75.

Conrad, P. (1999). Uses of expertise: sources, quotes, and voice in the reporting of genetics in the news. *Public Understanding of Science, 8*(4), 285–302.

Corbett, J. B. (1998). The environment as theme and package on a local television newscast. *Science Communication, 19*(3), 222–37.

Corbett, J. B. (2002). A faint green sell: advertising and the natural world. In M. Meister and P. M. Japp (Eds.), *Enviropop: Studies in Environmental Rhetoric and Popular Culture* (pp. 141–60). Westport, CT: Praeger/Greenwood Press.

Corbett, J. B. (2006). *Communicating Nature: How We Create and Understand Environmental Messages*. Washington, DC: Island Press.

Corbett, J. B., and Durfee, J. L. (2004). Testing public (un) certainty of science – media representations of global warming. *Science Communication, 26*(2), 129–51.

Corner, J., and Richardson, K. (1993). Environmental communication and the contingency of meaning: a research note. In A. Hansen (Ed.), *The Mass Media and Environmental Issues* (pp. 222–33). Leicester: Leicester University Press.

Corner, J., Richardson, K., and Fenton, N. (1990). *Nuclear Reactions: Form and Response in Public Issue Television*. London: John Libbey.

Cottle, S. (1993). Mediating the environment: modalities of TV news. In A. Hansen (Ed.), *The Mass Media and Environmental Issues* (pp. 107–33). Leicester: Leicester University Press.

Cottle, S. (2000). TV news, lay voices and the visualisation of environmental risks. In S. Allan, B. Adam, and C. Carter (Eds.), *Environmental Risks and the Media* (pp. 29–44). London: Routledge.

Cottle, S. (2004). Producing nature(s): on the changing production ecology of natural history TV. *Media Culture and Society, 26*(1), 81–.

Cottle, S. (2006). *Mediatized Conflict: Developments in Media and Conflict Studies*. Maidenhead: Open University Press.

Cox, R. (2006). *Environmental Communication and the Public Sphere*. London: Sage.

Cracknell, J. (1993). Issue arenas, pressure groups and environmental agendas. In A. Hansen (Ed.), *The Mass Media and Environmental Issues* (pp. 3–21). Leicester: Leicester University Press.

Crawley, C. E. (2007). Localized debates of agricultural biotechnology in community newspapers – a quantitative content analysis of media frames and sources. *Science Communication, 28*(3), 314–46.

Creighton, M. (1997). Consuming rural Japan: The marketing of tradition and nostalgia in the Japanese travel industry. *Ethnology, 36*(3), 239–54.

Cronon, W. (Ed.). (1995). *Uncommon Ground: Toward Reinventing Nature*. New York: Norton.

Daley, P., and O'Neill, D. (1991). Sad is too mild a word – press coverage of the Exxon Valdez oil-spill. *Journal of Communication, 41*(4), 42–57.

Davies, G. (2000a). Narrating the Natural History Unit: institutional orderings and spatial strategies. *Geoforum, 31*(4), 539–51.

Davies, G. (2000b). Science, observation and entertainment: Competing visions of postwar British natural history television, 1946–67. *Ecumene, 7*(4), 432–60.

Davis, A. (2002). *Public Relations Democracy: Public Relations, Politics and the Mass Media in Britain*. Manchester: Manchester University Press.

Davis, A. (2003). Public relations and news sources. In S. Cottle (Ed.), *News, Public Relations and Power* (pp. 27–42). London: Sage.

Davis, F. (1979). *Yearning for Yesterday: a Sociology of Nostalgia*. New York: The Free Press.

de Jong, W. (2005). Limits and possibilities of media-based oppositional politics; Greenpeace versus Shell; The Brent Spar Conflict. In W. de Jong, M. Shaw, and N. Stammers (Eds.), *Global Activism, Global Media* (pp. 110–24). London: Pluto.

Deacon, D., and Golding, P. (1993). Barriers to centralism – local-government, local media and the charge on the community. *Local Government Studies, 19*(2), 176–89.

Dearing, J. W., and Rogers, E. M. (1996). *Agenda-Setting*. (Vol. 6). London: Sage.

Deegan, D. (2001). *Managing Activism*. London: Kogan Page.

DeLuca, K. M. (1999). *Image Politics: The New Rhetoric of Environmental Activism (Revisioning Rhetoric)*. London: Guilford Publications.

DeLuca, K. M. (2000). Imaging nature: Watkins, Yosemite, and the birth of environmentalism. *Critical Studies in Media Communication, 17*(3), 241–60.

DeLuca, K. M., and Peeples, J. (2002). From public sphere to public screen: Democracy, activism, and the "violence" of Seattle. *Critical Studies in Media Communication, 19*(2), 125–51.

Deverson, T. (2004). *The New Zealand Oxford Dictionary*. Oxford University Press: Oxford Reference Online. Available: www.oxfordreference.com/ views/ENTRY.html?subview = Main&entry = t186.e47660 (accessed 30 April 2009).

Diani, M. (2001). Social movement networks: virtual and real. In F. Webster (Ed.), *Culture and Politics in the Information Age: A New Politics?* (pp. 117–28). London: Routledge.

Dingwall, R., and Aldridge, M. (2006). Television wildlife programming as a source of popular scientific information: a case study of evolution. *Public Understanding of Science, 15*(2), 131–52.

Donohue, G. A., Olien, C. N., and Tichenor, P. J. (1989). Structure and constraints on community newspaper gatekeepers. *Journalism Quarterly, 66*, 807–12.

Donohue, G. A., Tichenor, P. J., and Olien, C. N. (1995). A guard dog perspective on the role of media. *Journal of Communication, 45*(2), 115–32.

Downs, A. (1972). Up and down with ecology – the issue-attention cycle. *The Public Interest, 28*, 38–50.

Doyle, J. (2007). Picturing the clima(c)tic: Greenpeace and the representational politics of climate change communication. *Science as Culture, 16*(2), 129–50.

Dunlap, R. E. (1991). Trends in public opinion toward environmental issues – 1965–90. *Society and Natural Resources, 4*(3), 285–312.

Dunlap, R. E. (2006). Show us the data – The questionable empirical foundations of "The Death of Environmentalism" thesis. *Organization and Environment, 19*(1), 88–102.

Dunwoody, S. (1979). News-gathering behaviors of specialty reporters: a two-level comparison of mass media decision-making. *Newspaper Research Journal, 1*(1), 29–41.

Dunwoody, S. (1980). The science writing inner club: a communication link between science and the lay public. *Science, Technology, and Human Values, 5*, 14–22.

Dunwoody, S. (2007). The challenge of trying to make a difference using media messages. In S. C. Moser and L. Dilling (Eds.), *Creating a Climate for Change: Communicating Climate Change and Facilitating Social Change* (pp. 89–104). Cambridge: Cambridge University Press.

Dunwoody, S., and Griffin, R. J. (1993). Journalistic strategies for reporting long-term environmental issues: a case study of three Superfund sites. In A. Hansen (Ed.), *The Mass Media and Environmental Issues* (pp. 22–50). Leicester: Leicester University Press.

Durant, J., Hansen, A., and Bauer, M. (1996). Public understanding of the new genetics. In M. Marteau and J. Richards (Eds.), *The Troubled Helix* (pp. 235–48). Cambridge: Cambridge University Press.

Edelman, M. (1988). *Constructing the Political Spectacle*. Chicago, IL: University of Chicago Press.

Einsiedel, E. (1988). *The Canadian Press and the Environment*. Paper presented at the The XVIth Conference of The International Association for Mass Communication Research, Barcelona, Spain.

Einsiedel, E., and Coughlan, E. (1993). The Canadian press and the environment: reconstructing a social reality. In A. Hansen (Ed.), *The Mass Media and Environmental Issues* (pp. 134–49). Leicester: Leicester University Press.

Elbro, C. (1983). *Det overtalende landskab: ideer om menneske og samfund i digternes og annonceindustriens naturskildringer i 1970'erne*. København: C.A. Reitzel.

Encyclopedia of Marxism. (2009). *Commodification*. Marxists Internet Archive. Available: www.marxists.org/glossary/terms/c/o.htm#commodification (available 26 April 2009).

Entman, R. M. (1993). Framing: toward clarification of a fractured paradigm. *Journal of Communication, 43*(4), 51–58.

Entman, R. M. (2003). Cascading activation: Contesting the White House's frame after 9/11. *Political Communication, 20*(4), 415–32.

Ericson, R. V., Baranek, P. M., and Chan, J. B. L. (1987). *Visualizing Deviance: a Study of News Organization*. Milton Keynes: Open University Press.

Ericson, R. V., Baranek, P. M., and Chan, J. B. L. (1989). *Negotiating Control: a Study of News Sources*. Milton Keynes: Open University Press.

Eurobarometer. (2008, March). *Attitudes of European Citizens Towards the Environment*. European Commission. Available: http://ec.europa.eu/public_opinion/archives/ebs/ebs_295_sum_en.pdf (accessed 3 March 2009).

Evernden, N. (1989). Nature in industrial society. In I. Angus, and S. Jhally (Eds.), *Cultural Politics in Contemporary America* (pp. 151–64). New York: Routledge.

Eyerman, R., and Jamison, A. (1989). Environmental knowledge as an organizational weapon: the case of Greenpeace. *Social Science Information, 28*(1), 99–119.

Fairclough, N. (1989). *Language and Power*. London: Longman.

Fan, D. P., Brosius, H. B., and Kepplinger, H. M. (1994). Predictions of the public agenda from television coverage. *Journal of Broadcasting and Electronic Media, 38*(2), 163–77.

Fowler, R. (1991). *Language in the News: Discourse and Ideology in the Press*. London: Routledge.

Frewer, L. J. (2002). The media and genetically modified foods: Evidence in support of social amplification of risk. *Risk Analysis, 22*(4), 701–11.

Friedman, S. (2004). And the beat goes on: the third decade of environmental journalism. In S. Senecah, S. Depoe, M. Neuzil, and G. Walker (Eds.), *The Environmental Communication Yearbook, vol 1* (Vol. 1, pp. 175–87). London: Lawrence Erlbaum Associates.

Friedman, S. M. (1986). The journalist's world. In S. M. Friedman, S. Dunwoody, and C. L. Rogers (Eds.), *Scientists and Journalists: Reporting Science as News* (pp. 17–41). New York: The Free Press.

Friedman, S. M., Dunwoody, S., and Rogers, C. L. (Eds.). (1986). *Scientists and Journalists: Reporting Science as News*. New York: The Free Press.

Friedman, S. M., Gorney, C. M., and Egolf, B. P. (1992). Chernobyl coverage:

how the US media treated the nuclear industry. *Public Understanding of Science, 1*(3), 305–23.

Fuller, R., and Myers, R. (1941). The natural history of a social problem. *American Sociological Review, 6*(June), 320–28.

Funkhouser, G. R. (1973). The issues of the sixties: an exploratory study in the dynamics of public opinion. *Public Opinion Quarterly, 37*(1), 62–75.

Gaber, I. (2000). The greening of the public, politics and the press, 1985–99. In J. Smith (Ed.), *The Daily Globe: Environmental Change, the Public and the Media* (pp. 115–26). London: Earthscan Publications.

Galtung, J., and Ruge, M. H. (1965). The structure of foreign news. *Journal of International Peace Research, 1*, 64–90.

Gamson, W. (1985). Goffman's legacy to political sociology. *Theory and Society, 14*(5), 605–22.

Gamson, W. A. (1988). A constructionist approach to mass media and public opinion. *Symbolic Interaction, 11*(2), 161–74.

Gamson, W. A., and Modigliani, A. (1989). Media discourse and public opinion on nuclear power: a constructionist approach. *American Journal of Sociology, 95*(1), 1–37.

Gandy, O. H. (1982). *Beyond Agenda Setting: Information Subsidies and Public Policy*. Norwood, NJ: Ablex Publishing.

Gans, H. J. (1979). *Deciding What's News*. New York: Vintage.

Gans, H. J. (2004). *Deciding What's News*. New York: Northwestern University Press.

Gaskell, G., Bauer, M. W., Durant, J., and Allum, N. C. (1999). Worlds apart? The reception of genetically modified foods in Europe and the US. *Science, 285*(5426), 384–87.

Gauntlett, D. (1996). *Video Critical: Children, the Environment and Media Power*. Luton: University of Luton Press.

Geller, G., Bernhardt, B. A., Gardner, M., Rodgers, J., and Holtzman, N. A. (2005). Scientists' and science writers' experiences reporting genetic discoveries: Toward an ethic of trust in science journalism. *Genetics in Medicine, 7*(3), 198–205.

Gerbner, G. (1972). Violence in television drama: trends and symbolic functions. In G. A. Comstock and E. A. Rubinstein (Eds.), *Media Content and Control: Television and Social Behavior* (Vol. 1, pp. 28–187). Washington, DC: U.S. Government Printing Office.

Gerbner, G., and Gross, L. (1976). Living with television: the violence profile. *Journal of Communication, 26*(2), 173–99.

Gerbner, G., Gross, L., and Morgan, M. (1986). Living with television: the dynamics of the cultivation process. In J. Bryant and D. Zillmann (Eds.), *Perspectives on Media Effects* (pp. 17–40). Hillsdale, NJ: Lawrence Erlbaum Associates.

Gerbner, G., Gross, L., Morgan, M., and Signorielli, N. (1994). Growing up with television: the cultivation perspective. In J. Bryant and D. Zimmerman (Eds.),

Media Effects: Advances in Theory and Research (pp. 17–41). Hillsdale, NJ: Lawrence Erlbaum Associates.

Gibson, R., and Ward, S. (1999). Party democracy on-line: UK parties and ICTs. *Information, Communication and Society, 2*(3), 340–67.

Gillan, K., and Pickerill, J. (2008). Transnational anti-war activism: Solidarity, diversity and the internet in Australia, Britain and the United States after 9/11. *Australian Journal of Political Science, 43*(1), 59–78.

Gitlin, T. (1980). *The Whole World is Watching: Mass Media in the Making and Unmaking of the New Left.* Berkeley, CA: University of California Press.

Glasgow University Media Group. (1976). *Bad News.* London: Routledge & Kegan Paul.

Goldenberg, E. N. (1975). *Making the Papers: Access of Resource Poor Groups to the Metropolitan Press.* Lexington, MA: D.C. Heath.

Goldman, R., and Papson, S. (1996). *Sign Wars: the Cluttered Landscape of Advertising.* New York: Guilford Press.

Gooch, G. D. (1996). Environmental Concern and the Swedish Press – a case-study of the effects of newspaper reporting, personal experience and social interaction on the public's perception of environmental risks. *European Journal of Communication, 11*(1), 107–27.

Goodell, R. (1987). The role of the mass media in scientific controversy. In H. T. Engelhardt, and A. L. Caplan (Eds.), *Scientific Controversies* (pp. 585–97). Cambridge: Cambridge University Press.

Gore, A. (2006). *An Inconvenient Truth: The Planetary Emergency of Global Warming and What We Can Do About It.* London: Bloomsbury.

Grant, W. (2000). *Pressure Groups and British Politics* (2nd edn.). Basingstoke: Palgrave.

Greenberg, M. R., Sachsman, D. B., Sandman, P. M., and Salomone, K. L. (1989). Risk, drama and geography in coverage of environmental risk by network TV. *Journalism Quarterly, 66*(2), 267–76.

Greenberg, M. R., Sandman, P. M., Sachsman, D. B., and Salomone, K. L. (1989). Network television news coverage of environmental risk. *Environment, 31*(2), 16–20, 40–44.

Grunig, L. A., Grunig, J. E., and Dozier, D. M. (2002). *Excellent Public Relations and Effective Organizations: A Study of Communication Management in Three Countries.* Mahwah, NJ: Lawrence Erlbaum.

Gutteling, J. M. (2005). Mazur's hypothesis on technology controversy and media. *International Journal of Public Opinion Research, 17*(1), 23–41.

Habermas, J. (1989). *The Structural Transformation of the Public Sphere : an Inquiry into a Category of Bourgeois Society.* Cambridge, MA: MIT Press.

Hall, S. (1975). The 'structured communication' of events. In UNESCO (Ed.), *Getting the Message Across* (pp. 115–45). Paris: The UNESCO Press.

Hall, S. (1981). The determinations of news photographs. In S. Cohen and J. Young (Eds.), *The Manufacture of News* (Revised ed., pp. 226–43). London: Constable.

Hall, S. (1982). The rediscovery of 'ideology': return of the repressed in media studies. In M. Gurevitch, T. Bennett, J. Curran, and J. Woollacott (Eds.), *Culture, Society and the Media* (pp. 56–90). London: Methuen.

Hall, S., Critcher, C., Jefferson, T., Clarke, J., and Roberts, B. (1978). *Policing the Crisis*. London: Macmillan.

Halloran, J. D., Elliott, P., and Murdock, G. (1970). *Demonstrations and Communication*. Harmondsworth: Penguin.

Hansen, A. (1990). *The News Construction of the Environment: a Comparison of British and Danish Television News*. Leicester: Centre for Mass Communication Research, University of Leicester.

Hansen, A. (1993). Greenpeace and press coverage of environmental issues. In A. Hansen (Ed.), *The Mass Media and Environmental Issues* (pp. 150–78). Leicester: Leicester University Press.

Hansen, A. (1994a). Journalistic practices and science reporting in the British press. *Public Understanding of Science, 3*(2), 111–34.

Hansen, A. (1994b). *Trends in Environmental Issues Coverage in the British National Press*. London: Centre for Mass Communication Research, University of Leicester, and WBMG (Environmental Communications).

Hansen, A. (2000). Claimsmaking and framing in British newspaper coverage of the Brent Spar Controversy. In S. Allan, B. Adam, and C. Carter (Eds.), *Environmental Risks and the Media* (pp. 55–72). London: Routledge.

Hansen, A. (2002). Discourses of nature in advertising. *Communications, 27*(4), 499–511.

Hansen, A. (2006). Tampering with nature: 'nature' and the 'natural' in media coverage of genetics and biotechnology. *Media, Culture and Society, 28*(6), 811–34.

Hansen, A. (2007). Producing education coverage – a study of education correspondents and editors in the national and regional press. In L. Hargreaves, M. Cunningham, T. Everton, A. Hansen, B. Hopper, D. McIntyre, C. Oliver, T. Pell, M. Rouse, and P. Turner (Eds.), *The Status of Teachers and the Teaching Profession in England: Views from Inside and Outside the Profession: Evidence Base for the Final Report of the Teacher Status Project* (pp. 67–83). London: Department for Education and Skills.

Hansen, A., and Linné, O. (1994). Journalistic practices and television coverage of the environment: an international comparison. In C. Hamelink, and O. Linné (Eds.), *Mass Communication Research: On Problems and Policies* (pp. 369–83). Norwood, NJ: Ablex.

Hansen, A., and Machin, D. (2008). Visually branding the environment: climate change as a marketing opportunity. *Discourse Studies, 10*(6), 777–94.

Hargreaves, I., and Ferguson, G. (2000). *Who's Misunderstanding Whom? Bridging the Gulf of Understanding between the Public, the Media and Science*. Swindon: ESRC.

Hargreaves, I., Lewis, J., and Speers, T. (2004). *Towards a Better Map: Science, the Public and the Media*. Swindon: ESRC.

Hartmann, P. (1976). Industrial relations and the news media. *Industrial Relations Journal, 6*(4).

Herman, G., and Holly, J. (2001). Trade unions and the internet. In S. Lax (Ed.), *Access Denied in the Information Age* (pp. 33–44). Basingstoke: Palgrave.

Hilgartner, S. (1990). The dominant view of popularization – conceptual problems, political uses. *Social Studies of Science, 20*(3), 519–39.

Hilgartner, S., and Bosk, C. L. (1988). The rise and fall of social problems: a public arenas model. *American Journal of Sociology, 94*(1), 53–78.

Holbert, R. L., Kwak, N., and Shah, D. V. (2003). Environmental concern, patterns of television viewing, and pro-environmental behaviors: Integrating models of media consumption and effects. *Journal of Broadcasting and Electronic Media, 47*(2), 177–96.

Holliman, R. (2004). Media coverage of cloning: a study of media content, production and reception. *Public Understanding of Science, 13*(2), 107–30.

Hornig, S. (1990). Television's NOVA and the construction of scientific truth. *Critical Studies in Mass Communication, 7*(1), 11–23.

Hornig, S., Walter, L., and Templin, J. (1991). Voices in the news: Newspaper coverage of Hurricane Hugo and the Loma Prieta earthquake. *Newspaper Research Journal, 12*(3), 32–45.

Howlett, M., and Raglon, R. (1992). Constructing the environmental spectacle: green advertisements and the greening of the corporate image. *Environmental History Review, 16*(4), 53–68.

Huxford, J. (2000). Framing the future: science fiction frames and the press coverage of cloning. *Continuum: Journal of Media and Cultural Studies, 14*(2), 187–99.

Ibarra, P. R., and Kitsuse, J. I. (1993). Vernacular constituents of moral discourse: an interactionist proposal for the study of social problems. In J. A. Holstein and G. Miller (Eds.), *Reconsidering Social Constructionism: Debates in Social Problems Theory* (pp. 25–58). Hawthorne, NY: Aldine de Gruyter.

Iyengar, S., and Kinder, D. R. (1987). *News That Matters*. Chicago, IL: University of Chicago Press.

Iyer, E., and Banerjee, B. (1993). Anatomy of green advertising. *Advances in Consumer Research, 20*, 494–501.

Jordan, G. (1998a). Indirect causes and effects in policy change: The Brent Spar case. *Public Administration, 76*(4), 713–40.

Jordan, G. (1998b). Politics without parties: a growing trend? *Parliamentary Affairs, 51*, 314–28.

Kavada, A. (2005). Civic society organisations and the internet: the case of Amnesty International, Oxfam and the World Development Movement. In W. D. Jong, M. Shaw, and N. Stammers (Eds.), *Global Activism, Global Media* (pp. 208–22). London: Pluto.

Kellert, S. R. (1995). Concepts of nature east and west. In M. E. Soule, and G. Lease (Eds.), *Reinventing Nature: Responses to Postmodern Deconstruction* (pp. 103–22). Washington, DC: Island Press.

Kielbowicz, R. B., and Scherer, C. (1986). The role of the press in the dynamics of social movements. In G. Lang, and K. Lang (Eds.), *Research in Social Movements, Conflicts and Change* (pp. 71–96). Greenwich, CT: JAI Press Inc.

Kilbourne, W. E. (1995). Green advertising – salvation or oxymoron. *Journal of Advertising, 24*(2), 7–19.

Kitsuse, J. I., and Spector, M. (1973). Toward a sociology of social problems: social conditions, value judgments and social problems. *Social Problems, 20*(4), 407–19.

Klapper, J. (1960). *The Effects of Mass Communication.* New York: Free Press.

Knowles, E. (Ed.). (2006). *A Dictionary of Phrase and Fable.* Oxford: Oxford University Press.

Kornhauser, W. (1959). *The Politics of Mass Society.* New York: The Free Press.

Kress, G. (1997). Language in the Media. In O. Boyd-Barrett (Ed.), *M.A. Mass Communications, Distance Learning* (Vol. Module 9, Unit 49, pp. 13–43). Leicester: University of Leicester.

Krieghbaum, H. (1967). *Science and the Mass Media.* New York: New York University Press.

Krimsky, S., and Plough, A. (1988). *Environmental Hazards: Communicating Risks as a Social Process.* Dover, MA: Auburn House.

Lacey, C., and Longman, D. (1993). The press and public access to the environment and development debate. *Sociological Review, 41*(2), 207–43.

LaFollette, M. C. (1990). *Making Science our Own: Public Images of Science 1910–1955.* Chicago, IL: The University of Chicago Press.

Lahtinen, R., and Vuorisalo, T. (2005). In search for the roots of environmental concern – Water management and animal welfare issues in the Finnish local press in 1890–1950. *Scandinavian Journal of History, 30*(2), 177–97.

Lax, S. (2004). The internet and democracy. In D. Gauntlett, and R. Horsley (Eds.), *Web Studies* (2nd edn, pp. 217–29). London: Arnold.

Lee, J. A. (1989). Waging the seal war in the media: Toward a content analysis of moral communication. *Canadian Journal of Communication, 14*(1), 37–56.

Leiss, W., Kline, S., and Jhally, S. (1997). *Social Communication in Advertising: Persons, Products and Images of Well-being* (2nd edn). London: Routledge.

Lewenstein, B. V. (1995). From fax to facts – communication in the cold-fusion saga. *Social Studies of Science, 25*(3), 403–36.

Lewenstein, B. V. (2001). Expertise in the media. *Social Studies of Science, 31*(3), 441–44.

Lewis, J., Williams, A., and Franklin, B. (2008). A compromised fourth estate? UK news journalism, public relations and news sources. *Journalism Studies, 9*(1), 1–20.

Limoges, C. (1993). Expert knowledge and decision-making in controversy contexts. *Public Understanding of Science, 2,* 417–26.

Lin, C. A. (2001). Cultural values reflected in Chinese and American television advertising. *Journal of Advertising, 30*(4), 83–94.

Lindahl, R. (1983). Media concentration on local political campaigns. *Gazette, 31*(2), 99–115.

Linder, S. H. (2006). Cashing-in on risk claims: on the for-profit inversion of signifiers for "global warming". *Social Semiotics, 16*(1), 103–32.

Linné, O., and Hansen, A. (1990). *News Coverage of the Environment: a Comparative Study of Journalistic Practices and Television Presentation in Danmarks Radio and the BBC.* Copenhagen: Danmarks Radio Forlaget.

Lippmann, W. (1922). *Public Opinion.* New York: Harcourt Brace.

Lomborg, B. (2001). *The Skeptical Environmentalist : Measuring the Real State of the World.* Cambridge: Cambridge University Press.

Lomborg, B. (2007). *Cool it: the Skeptical Environmentalist's Guide to Global Warming.* London: Marshall Cavendish: Cyan Communications Ltd.

Lowe, P., and Morrison, D. (1984). Bad news or good news: environmental politics and the mass media. *The Sociological Review, 32*(1), 75–90.

Lowe, P. D., and Rüdig, W. (1986). Review article: political ecology and the social sciences – the state of the art. *British Journal of Political Science, 16*, 513–50.

Lukes, S. (1974). *Power: A Radical View.* London and Basingstoke: Macmillan.

Macnaghten, P., and Urry, J. (1998). *Contested Natures.* London: Sage.

Manning, P. (2001). *News and News Sources: a Critical Introduction.* London: Sage.

Marchand, R. (1985). *Advertising the American Dream : Making Way for Modernity, 1920–1940.* Berkeley, CA: University of California Press.

Martin, D. C. (2004). Apartheid in the great outdoors: American advertising and the reproduction of a racialized outdoor leisure identity. *Journal of Leisure Research, 36*(4), 513–35.

Mazur, A. (1981). Media coverage and public opinion on scientific controversies. *Journal of Communication, 31*(2), 106–15.

Mazur, A. (1984). The journalists and technology: reporting about Love Canal and Three Mile Island. *Minerva, 22*(Spring), 45–66.

Mazur, A. (1990). Nuclear power, chemical hazards, and the quantity of reporting. *Minerva, 28*, 294–323.

Mazur, A. (1998). Global environmental change in the news – 1987–90 vs 1992–96. *International Sociology, 13*(4), 457–72.

Mazur, A., and Lee, J. (1993). Sounding the global alarm: environmental-issues in the united-states national news. *Social Studies of Science, 23*(4), 681–720.

McComas, K., and Shanahan, J. (1999). Telling stories about global climate change – Measuring the impact of narratives on issue cycles. *Communication Research, 26*(1), 30–57.

McComas, K. A., Shanahan, J., and Butler, J. S. (2001). Environmental content in prime-time network TV's non-news entertainment and fictional programs. *Society and Natural Resources, 14*(6), 533–42.

McCombs, M. (2004). *Setting the Agenda: The Mass Media and Public Opinion.* Cambridge: Polity.

McCombs, M., and Bell, T. (1996). The agenda-setting role of mass communication. In M. B. Salwen and D. W. Stacks (Eds.), *An Integrated*

Approach to Communication Theory and Research (pp. 93–110). Mahwah, NJ: Lawrence Erlbaum Associates.

McCombs, M. E., and Shaw, D. L. (1972). The agenda-setting function of mass media. *Public Opinion Quarterly, 36*, 176–87.

McGeachy, L. (1989). Trends in magazine coverage of environmental issues. *Journal of Environmental Education, 20*, 6–13.

McQuail, D. (2005). *McQuail's Mass Communication Theory* (5th edn). London: Sage.

Menashe, C. L., and Siegel, M. (1998). The power of a frame: An analysis of newspaper coverage of tobacco issues – United States, 1985–96. *Journal of Health Communication, 3*(4), 307–25.

Mikami, S., Takeshita, T., and Kawabata, M. (1995). The media coverage and public awareness of environmental issues in Japan. *Gazette, 3*, 209–26.

Mikami, S., Takeshita, T., Kawabata, M., Sekiya, N., Nakada, M., Otani, N., and Takahashi, N. (2002). *Unsolved Conflict among Europe, Japan and USA on the Global Warming Issue: Analysis of the Longitudinal Trends in News Frame.* Paper presented at the IAMCR Conference, Barcelona, Spain.

Miller, D. (1999). Risk, science and policy: definitional struggles, information management, the media and BSE. *Social Science and Medicine, 49*(9), 1239–55.

Miller, G., and Holstein, J. A. (1993). Reconsidering social constructionism. In J. A. Holstein and G. Miller (Eds.), *Reconsidering Social Constructionism: Debates in Social Problems Theory* (pp. 5–23). Hawthorne, NY: Aldine deGruyter.

Miller, M. M., and Riechert, B. P. (2000). Interest group strategies and journalistic norms: News media framing of environmental issues. In S. Allan, B. Adam, and C. Carter (Eds.), *Environmental Risks and the Media* (pp. 45–54). London: Routledge.

Mills, C. W. (1940). Situated actions and vocabularies of motives. *American Sociological Review, 6*, 904–13.

Mitman, G. (1999). *Reel Nature: America's Romance with Wildlife on Film.* Cambridge, MA: Harvard University Press.

Molotch, H., and Lester, M. (1974). News as purposive behaviour. *American Sociological Review, 39*, 101–12.

Molotch, H., and Lester, M. (1975). Accidental news: the great oil spill. *American Journal of Sociology, 81*(2), 235–60.

Moon, Y. S., and Chan, K. (2005). Advertising appeals and cultural values in television commercials – A comparison of Hong Kong and Korea. *International Marketing Review, 22*(1), 48–66.

Moore, B., and Singletary, M. (1985). Scientific sources' perceptions of network news accuracy. *Journalism Quarterly, 62*(4), 816–23.

MORI. (2005). *Information about Science and Technology,* [World Wide Web]. MORI. Available: www.ipsos-mori.com/polls/2005/nesta.shtml (28 October 2007).

Mueller, B. (1987). Reflections of culture – an analysis of Japanese and American advertising appeals. *Journal of Advertising Research, 27*(3), 51–59.

Murrell, R. K. (1987). Telling it like it isn't: representations of science in Tomorrow's World. *Theory, Culture and Society, 4*, 89–106.

Negra, D. (2001). Consuming Ireland: Lucky Charms cereal, Irish Spring soap and 1-800-SHAMROCK. *Cultural Studies, 15*(1), 76–97.

Nelkin, D. (1995). *Selling Science: How the Press Covers Science and Technology* (2nd revised edn). New York: W.H. Freeman.

Nelson, V. (2005). Representation and images of people, place and nature in Grenada's tourism. *Geografiska Annaler Series B-Human Geography, 87B*(2), 131–43.

Nisbet, M. (2009). Communicating climate change: why frames matter for public engagement. *Environment: Science and Policy for Sustainable Development, March-April*, 1–15. Available: www.environmentmagazine.org/March-April%202009/Nisbet-full.html (3 February 2009).

Nisbet, M. C., and Huge, M. (2006). Attention cycles and frames in the plant biotechnology debate – Managing power and participation through the press/policy connection. *Harvard International Journal of Press-Politics, 11*(2), 3–40.

Nisbet, M. C., and Lewenstein, B. V. (2002). Biotechnology and the American media – The policy process and the elite press, 1970 to 1999. *Science Communication, 23*(4), 359–91.

Norton, J. (2009). *Front Groups*. Jim Norton. Available: http://info-pollution.com/frontgroups.htm (27 April 2009).

O'Meara, D. J. (1978). *Coverage of Environmental Issues in Two Newspapers, 1962–1977*. Unpublished unpublished master's thesis, Ohio State University, Columbus, Ohio.

Oreskes, N. (2004). The scientific consensus on climate change. *Science, 306*(5720), 1686.

Park, A., Curtice, J., Thomson, K., Jarvis, L., and Bromley, C. (Eds.). (2001). *British Social Attitudes – The 18th Report*. London: Sage.

Park, C. (2007). *A Dictionary of Environment and Conservation*. Oxford Reference Online: Oxford University Press. Available: www.oxfordreference.com/views/ENTRY.html?subview = Main&entry = t244.e3501 (27 April 2009).

Patterson, P. (1989). Reporting Chernobyl: cutting the government fog to cover the nuclear cloud. In L. M. Walters, L. Wilkins, and T. Walters (Eds.), *Bad Tidings: Communication and Catastrophe* (pp. 131–47). Hillsdale, NJ: Lawrence Erlbaum Associates.

Petersen, A. (2001). Biofantasies: genetics and medicine in the print news media. *Social Science and Medicine, 52*(8), 1255–68.

Peterson, R. T. (1991). Physical-environment television advertisement themes – 1979 and 1989. *Journal of Business Ethics, 10*(3), 221–28.

Phillips, L. (2000). Mediated communication and the privatization of public problems – Discourse on ecological risks and political action. *European Journal of Communication, 15*(2), 171–207.

Phillips, L., Bridgeman, J., and Ferguson-Smith, M. (2000). *The BSE Inquiry: Report, Evidence and Supporting Papers of the Inquiry into the Emergence and Identification of Bovine Spongiform Encephalopathy (BSE) and Variant Creutzfeldt–Jakob Disease (vCJD) and the Action Taken in Response to it up to 20 March 1996*. London: The Stationery Office.

Phillips, M., Fish, R., and Agg, J. (2001). Putting together ruralities: towards a symbolic analysis of rurality in the British mass media. *Journal of Rural Studies, 17*(1), 1–27.

Pickerill, J. (2003). *Cyberprotest: Environmental Activism Online*. Manchester: Manchester University Press.

Podeschi, C. (2002). The nature of future myths: Environmental discourse in science fiction film, 1950–99. *Sociological Spectrum, 22*(3), 251–97.

Porritt, J., and Winner, D. (1988). *The Coming of the Greens*. London: Fontana.

Priest, S. H. (2009). Reinterpreting the audiences for media messages about science. In R. Holliman, E. Whitelegg, E. Scanlon, S. Smidt, and J. Thomas (Eds.), *Investigating Science Communication in the Information Age: Implications for Public Engagement and Popular Media* (pp. 223–36). Milton Keynes: Oxford University Press and The Open University.

Propp, V. (1968). *Morphology of the Folktale*. London: University of Texas Press.

Protess, D. L., Cook, F. L., Curtin, T. R., Gordon, M. T., Leff, D. R., McCombs, M. E., and Miller, P. (1987). The impact of investigative reporting on public opinion and policy-making: targeting toxic waste. *Public Opinion Quarterly, 51*(2), 166–85.

Reese, S. D. (2001). Prologue – framing public life: a bridging model for media research. In S. D. Reese, O. H. Gandy, and A. E. Grant (Eds.), *Framing Public Life: Perspectives on Media and Our Understanding of the Social World* (pp. 7–31). Mahwah, NJ: Lawrence Erlbaum Associates.

Reisner, A., and Soult, G. (2007, 2 August). *Covering Biotech Opponents: News Sources in the GMO Debate*. Paper presented at the annual meeting of the Rural Sociological Society, Marriott Santa Clara, Santa Clara, California.

Riesman, D. (1950). *The Lonely Crowd: a Study of the Changing American Character*. New Haven, CT: Yale University Press.

Rogers, R., and Marres, N. (2000). Landscaping climate change: a mapping technique for understanding science and technology debates on the World Wide Web. *Public Understanding of Science, 9*(2), 141–63.

Rose, C. (1998). *The Turning of the Spar*. London: Greenpeace.

Rose, C. (2005). *How to Win Campaigns: 100 Steps to Success*. London: Earthscan.

Rothman, S. (1990). Journalists, broadcasters, scientific experts and public opinion. *Minerva, 28*(2), 117–33.

Rothman, S., and Lichter, S. R. (1987). Elite ideology and risk perception in nuclear energy policy. *American Political Science Review, 81*(2), 383–404.

Royal Commission on the Press. (1977). *Final Report: Royal Commission on the Press*. London: H.M.S.O.

Rutherford, P. (1994). *The New Icons? The Art of Television Advertising*. Toronto, London: Toronto University Press.

Rutherford, P. (2000). *Endless Propaganda: the Advertising of Public Goods*. Toronto: University of Toronto Press.

Ryan, C. (1991). *Prime Time Activism: Media Strategies for Grassroots Organizing*. Boston, MA: South End Press.

Sachsman, D. B. (1973). *Public Relations Influence on Environmental Coverage (in the San Francisco Bay Area)*. Unpublished Doctoral dissertation, Stanford University.

Sachsman, D. B. (1976). Public relations influence on coverage of environment in San Francisco Area. *Journalism Quarterly, 53*, 54–60.

Sachsman, D. B., Simon, J., and Valenti, J. M. (2006). Regional issues, national norms: a four-region analysis of U.S. environment reporters. *Science Communication, 28*(1), 93–121.

Sahlins, M. (1977). *The Use and Abuse of Biology*. London: Tavistock Publishers.

Schama, S. (1995). *Landscape and Memory*. London: HarperCollins.

Schlesinger, P. (1990). Rethinking the sociology of journalism: source strategies and the limits of media centrism. In M. Ferguson (Ed.), *Public Communication: the New Imperatives* (pp. 61–83). London: Sage.

Schlesinger, P., and Tumber, H. (1994). *Reporting Crime: the Media Politics of Criminal Justice*. Oxford: Clarendon Press.

Schneider, J. W. (1985). Social problems theory: the constructionist view. *Annual Review of Sociology, 11*, 209–29.

Schoenfeld, A. C. (1980). Newspersons and the environment today. *Journalism Quarterly, 57*, 456–62.

Schoenfeld, A. C., Meier, R. F., and Griffin, R. J. (1979). Constructing a social problem – the press and the environment. *Social Problems, 27*(1), 38–61.

Schudson, M. (1989). The sociology of news production. *Media, Culture and Society, 11*(3), 263–82.

Schudson, M. (2005). Four approaches to the sociology of news. In J. Curran, and M. Gurevitch (Eds.), *Mass Media and Society* (4th edn, pp. 172–97). London: Hodder Arnold.

Scott, J., and Marshall, G. (2009). *A Dictionary of Sociology*, [World Wide Web]. Oxford University Press: Oxford Reference Online. Available: www.oxford reference.com/views/ENTRY.html?subview = Main&entry = t88.e937 (27 April 2009).

Scott, K. D. (2003). Popularizing science and nature programming – The role of "Spectacle" in contemporary wildlife documentary. *Journal of Popular Film and Television, 31*(1), 29–35.

Scutt, R., and Bonnet, A. (1996). *In Search of England: Popular Representations of Englishness and the English Countryside* (Working papers 22). Newcastle upon Tyne: University of Newcastle upon Tyne, Department of Agricultural Economics and Food Marketing; Centre for Rural Economy.

Shanahan, J. (1993). Television and the cultivation of environmental concern: 1988–92. In A. Hansen (Ed.), *The Mass Media and Environmental Issues* (pp. 181–97). Leicester: Leicester University Press.

Shanahan, J. (1996). Green but unseen: marginalizing the environment on television. In M. Morgan, and S. Leggett (Eds.), *Mainstream(s) and Margins: Cultural Politics in the 90s*. Westport, CT: Greenwood.

Shanahan, J., and McComas, K. (1997). Television's portrayal of the environment: 1991–95. *Journalism and Mass Communication Quarterly, 74*(1), 147–59.

Shanahan, J., and McComas, K. (1999). *Nature Stories: Depictions of the Environment and Their Effects*. Cresskill, NJ: Hampton Press.

Shanahan, J., Morgan, M., and Stenbjerre, M. (1997). Green or brown? Television and the cultivation of environmental concern. *Journal of Broadcasting and Electronic Media, 41*(3), 305–23.

Shaw, A. (2002). "It just goes against the grain". Public understandings of genetically modified (GM) food in the UK. *Public Understanding of Science, 11*(3), 273–91.

Shoemaker, P. J. (1991). *Gatekeeping*. London: Sage.

Signitzer, B., and Prexl, A. (2007, 23–25 July). *Communication Strategies of 'Greenwash Trackers' – How Activist Groups Attempt to Hold Companies Accountable and to Promote Sustainable Development*. Paper presented at the IAMCR Conference, Paris, France.

Silverstone, R. (1984). Narrative strategies in television science. *Media, Culture and Society, 6*(4), 377–410.

Singer, E. (1990). A question of accuracy: How journalists and scientists report research on hazards. *Journal of Communication, 40*(4), 102–16.

Singletary, M. (1980). *Accuracy in News Reporting: A Review of the Research* (ED181456 ERIC). Washington, DC: American Newspaper Publishers Association.

Smith, C. (1992). *Media and Apocalypse: News Coverage of the Yellowstone Forest Fires, Exxon Valdez Oil Spill, and Loma Prieta Earthquake*. Westport, CT: Greenwood Press.

Smith, C. (1996). Reporters, news sources, and scientific intervention: the New Madrid earthquake prediction. *Public Understanding of Science, 5*(3), 205–16.

Smith, J. (2005). Dangerous news: media decision making about climate change risk. *Risk Analysis, 25*(6).

Smith, M., and Ferguson, D. (2001). Activism. In R. Heath (Ed.), *Handbook of Public Relations* (pp. 191–300). London: Sage.

Snow, D. A., and Benford, R. D. (1988). Ideology, frame resonance, and participant mobilization. In B. E. A. Klandermans (Ed.), *From Structure to Action: Social Movement Participation across Cultures* (pp. 197–217). Greenwich, CT: JAI.

Soanes, C., and Stevenson, A. (2005). *The Oxford Dictionary of English (revised edition)*. Oxford University Press: Oxford Reference Online. Available: www.oxfordreference.com/views/ENTRY.html?subview = Main&entry = t140.e32745 (27 April 2009).

Soanes, C., and Stevenson, A. (2008). *The Concise Oxford English Dictionary*. Oxford University Press: Oxford Reference Online. Available: www.oxford reference.com/views/ENTRY.html?subview = Main&entry = t23.e25653 (27 April 2009).

Social Trends 29. (1998). London: The Stationery Office Agencies.

Social Trends 32. (2002). London: The Stationery Office Agencies.

Social Trends 33. (2003). London: The Stationery Office Agencies. Available: www.statistics.gov.uk/StatBase/ssdataset.asp?vlnk = 6230&Pos = &ColRank = 1&Rank = 272 (accessed 11 March 2008).

Solesbury, W. (1976). The environmental agenda: An illustration of how situations may become political issues and issues may demand responses from government; or how they may not. *Public Administration, 54*, 379–97.

Soper, K. (1995). *What is Nature?* Oxford: Blackwell.

Soroka, S. N. (2002). Issue attributes and agenda-setting by media, the public, and policymakers in Canada. *International Journal of Public Opinion Research, 14*(3), 264–85.

Spector, M., and Kitsuse, J. I. (1973). Social problems: a reformulation. *Social Problems, 21*(2), 145–59.

Spector, M., and Kitsuse, J. I. (1977). *Constructing Social Problems*. Menlo Park, CA: Cummings.

Spector, M., and Kitsuse, J. I. (1987). *Constructing Social Problems*. New York: Aldine de Gruyter.

Spector, M., and Kitsuse, J. I. (2000). *Constructing Social Problems* (new edn). New Brunswick, NJ: Transaction Publishers.

Speers, T. (2005). A picnic in March: media coverage of climate change and public opinion in the United Kingdom. In G. Humphrys and M. Williams (Eds.), *Presenting and Representing Environments (Geojournal Library)* (pp. 121–35). Dordrecht/Boston/London: Kluwer Academic Publishers.

Stallings, R. A. (1990). Media discourse and the social construction of risk. *Social Problems, 37*(1), 80–95.

Stallings, R. A. (1995). *Promoting Risk: Constructing the Earthquake Threat*. New York: Aldine De Gruyter.

Stocking, S. H. (1999). How journalists deal with scientific uncertainty. In S. M. Friedman, S. Dunwoody, and C. L. Rogers (Eds.), *Communicating Uncertainty: Media Coverage of New and Controversial Science* (pp. 23–42). Mahwah, NJ: Lawrence Erlbaum Associates.

Strodthoff, G. G., Hawkins, R. P., and Schoenfeld, A. C. (1985). Media roles in a social-movement – a model of ideology diffusion. *Journal of Communication, 35*(2), 134–53.

Surette, R. (2007). *Media, Crime, and Criminal Justice: Images and Realities* (3rd edn). Belmont, CA: Thomson/Wadsworth.

Swidler, A. (1986). Culture in action: symbols and strategies. *American Sociological Review, 51*(2), 273–86.

Swingewood, A. (1977). *The Myth of Mass Culture*. London: Macmillan.

Tankard, J. W., and Ryan, M. (1974). News source perceptions of accuracy of science coverage. *Journalism Quarterly, 51*, 219–25.

Tarrow, S. (2005). *The New Transnational Activism*. Cambridge: Cambridge University Press.

Taylor, C. E., Lee, J. S., and Davie, W. R. (2000). Local press coverage of environmental conflict. *Journalism and Mass Communication Quarterly, 77*(1), 175–92.

Ten Eyck, T. A., and Williment, M. (2003). The national media and things genetic – coverage in the New York Times (1971–2001) and the Washington Post (1977–2001). *Science Communication, 25*(2), 129–52.

The Pew Global Attitudes Project. (2007, 27 June 2007). *Global Unease with Major World Powers: Rising Environmental Concern in 47-Nation Survey*. Available: http://pewglobal.org/reports/display.php?ReportID = 256 (accessed 27 April 2009).

The Pew Global Attitudes Project. (2008, 18 December 2008). *Global Public Opinion in the Bush Years (2001–2008)*. The Pew Research Center. Available: http://pewglobal.org/reports/display.php?ReportID = 263 (accessed 27 April 2009).

The Pew Research Center for the People and the Press. (2009, 22 January 2009). *Economy, Jobs Trump All Other Policy Priorities in 2009: Environment, Immigration, Health Care Slip Down the List*. The Pew Research Center. Available: http://people-press.org/report/485/economy-top-policy-priority (accessed 22 April 2009).

Thomas, L. (1995). In Love With Inspector-Morse – feminist subculture and quality television. *Feminist Review, (51)*, 1–25.

Thomas, L. (2002). *Fans, Feminisms and 'Quality' Media*. London: Routledge.

Thompson, J. B. (1990). *Ideology and Modern Culture: Critical Social Theory in the Era of Mass Communication*. Oxford: Polity Press.

Tichenor, P. J., Donohue, G. A., and Olien, C. N. (1980). *Community Conflict and the Press*. Beverly Hills, CA: Sage.

Tichenor, P. J., Olien, C. N., Harrison, A., and Donohue, G. A. (1970). Mass communication systems and communication accuracy in science news reporting. *Journalism Quarterly, 47*(4), 673–83.

Trench, B. (2009). Science reporting in the electronic embrace of the internet. In R. Holliman, E. Whitelegg, E. Scanlon, S. Smidt, and J. Thomas (Eds.), *Investigating Science Communication in the Information Age: Implications for Public Engagement and Popular Media* (pp. 166–80). Milton Keynes: Oxford University Press and The Open University.

Trumbo, C. (1995). Longitudinal modelling of public issues: an application of the agenda-setting process to the issue of global warming. *Journalism and Mass Communication Monographs, 152*.

Trumbo, C. (1996). Constructing climate change: claims and frames in US news coverage of an environmental issue. *Public Understanding of Science, 5*(3), 269–83.

Tuchman, G. (1978). The symbolic annihilation of women by the mass media. In G. Tuchman, A. Kaplan Daniels, and J. Benet (Eds.), *Hearth and Home: Images of Women in the Mass Media* (pp. 3–17). New York: Oxford University Press.

Tumber, H. (Ed.). (1999). *News*. Oxford: Oxford University Press.

Turney, J. (1998). *Frankenstein's Footsteps: Science, Genetics and Popular Culture*. London: Yale University Press.

Ungar, S. (1992). The rise and (relative) decline of global warming as a social-problem. *Sociological Quarterly, 33*(4), 483–501.

Ungar, S. (2003). Global warming versus ozone depletion: failure and success in North America. *Climate Research, 23*(3), 263–74.

Urry, J. (1995). *Consuming Places*. London: Sage.

Urry, J. (2001). *The Tourist Gaze: Leisure and Travel in Contemporary Societies* (2nd edn). London: Sage.

Wade, S., and Schramm, W. (1969). The mass media as sources of public affairs, science, and health knowledge. *Public Opinion Quarterly, 33*, 197–209.

Wakefield, S. E. L., and Elliott, S. J. (2003). Constructing the news: The role of local newspapers in environmental risk communication. *Professional Geographer, 55*(2), 216–26.

Wall, G. (1999). Science, nature, and The Nature of Things: An instance of Canadian environmental discourse, 1960–94. *Canadian Journal of Sociology-Cahiers Canadiens De Sociologie, 24*(1), 53–85.

Wall, M. (2002). The Battle in Seattle – how nongovernmental organizations used websites in their challenge to the WTO. In E. Gilboa (Ed.), *Media and Conflict: Framing Issues, Making Policy, Shaping Opinions* (pp. 25–43). Ardsley, NY: Transnational Publishers.

Wallack, L., Woodruff, K., Dorfman, L., and Diaz, I. (1999). *News for a Change: An Advocate's Guide to Working with the Media*. London: Sage.

Watson, J., and Hill, A. (2006). *Dictionary of Media and Communication Studies* (7th edn). London: Arnold.

Weart, S. (2003). *The Discovery of Global Warming*. Cambridge, MA: Harvard University Press.

Weart, S. R. (1988). *Nuclear Fear: a History of Images*. Cambridge, MA: Harvard University Press.

Weber, M. (1930). *The Protestant Ethic and the Spirit of Capitalism*. London: Unwin University Books.

Weingart, P., Engels, A., and Pansegrau, P. (2000). Risks of communication: discourses on climate change in science, politics, and the mass media. *Public Understanding of Science, 9*(3), 261–83.

Wernick, A. (1997). Resort to nostalgia: mountains, memories and myths of time. In M. Nava (Ed.), *Buy This Book: Studies in Advertising and Consumption*. London: Routledge.

Westerstaahl, J., and Johansson, F. (1987). *Tjernobylnedfallet och myndighetsbeskeden (The Chernobyl Fall-out and the Advice from Public Authorities)*. Stockholm: SPF.

White, D. M. (1950). The gatekeeper: a case study in the selection of news. *Journalism Quarterly, 27*, 383–90.

Widener, P., and Gunter, V. J. (2007). Oil spill recovery in the media: Missing an Alaska native perspective. *Society and Natural Resources, 20*, 767–83.

Wiegman, O., Gutteling, J. M., Boer, H., and Houwen, R. J. (1989). Newspaper coverage of hazards and the reactions of readers. *Journalism Quarterly, 66*(4), 846–52.

Wiener, C. (1981). *The Politics of Alcoholism: Building an Arena around a Social Problem*. New Brunswick, NJ: Transaction.

Wikipedia. (2009). *Planet Earth*. Wikipedia. Available: http://en.wikipedia.org/wiki/Planet_Earth_(TV_series) (accessed 7 May 2009).

Wilkins, L. (1987). *Shared Vulnerability*. New York: Greenwood.

Wilkinson, C., Allan, S., Anderson, A., and Petersen, A. (2007). From uncertainty to risk?: Scientific and news media portrayals of nanoparticle safety. *Health Risk and Society, 9*(2), 145–57.

Williams, R. (1973). *The Country and the City*. London: Chatto & Windus.

Williams, R. (1983 [1976]). *Keywords: a Vocabulary of Culture and Society*. London: Flamingo/Fontana.

Williamson, J. (1978). *Decoding Advertisements: Ideology and Meaning in Advertising*. London: Marion Boyars.

Wilson, A. (1992). *The Culture of Nature: North American Landscape from Disney to the Exxon Valdez*. Cambridge, MA: Blackwell.

Wilson, K. M. (2000). Drought, debate, and uncertainty: measuring reporters' knowledge and ignorance about climate change. *Public Understanding of Science, 9*(1), 1–13.

Worcester, R. M. (1994). *Sustainable Development: Who Cares?* (Conference paper): MORI and WBMG, London, UK.

Wuthnow, R. (Ed.). (1992). *Vocabularies of Public Life: Empirical Essays in Symbolic Structure*. London: Routledge.

Yin, J. (1999). Elite opinion and media diffusion – Exploring environmental attitudes. *Harvard International Journal of Press-Politics, 4*(3), 62–86.

Zehr, S. C. (2000). Public representations of scientific uncertainty about global climate change. *Public Understanding of Science, 9*(2), 85–103.

Zucker, H. G. (1978). The variable nature of news media influence. In B. D. Ruben (Ed.), *Communication Yearbook* (Vol. 2, pp. 225–40). New Brunswick, NJ: Transaction.

Subject index

Name index